First Edition

THIRTY-FIRST STAR

OTHER BOOKS BY THE SAME AUTHOR

JAPAN TODAY

YOUNG JAPAN

THE TREE OF LIGHT

THE NATION AT WAR

THE ROMANCE OF JAPAN

COTTON AS A WORLD POWER

THE FIRST FORTY-NINER

JAPAN DEFIES THE WORLD

THE LION OF THE VIGILANTES

AMERICA: PAGEANTS AND PERSONALITIES

JESSIE BENTON FRÉMONT
(*Portrait by T. Buchanan Read,*
in the Southwest Museum, Los Angeles)

THIRTY-FIRST STAR

STAR

by James A. B. Scherer

G. P. PUTNAM'S SONS, NEW YORK

To "OLD ROANOKE"

In Her Centennial Year

CONTENTS

ILLUSTRATIONS

INTRODUCTION

BEFORE the gringo came, California seems to have been visited only by Asiatics and Spaniards.

The Asiatics arrived in prehistoric times, by way of Bering Strait and in disconnected driblets; moving slowly southward along lines of least resistance, to build so-called cliff dwellings here in North America east of the great mountain chain linking the two American continents, but many of them continuing on down into Mexico, Central America, and Peru, where they developed in the course of ages a civilization based on maize, or Indian corn, instead of rice as in Eastern Asia, or wheat as in the Near East and Europe. Primordial man has not been found in the Americas, all of the thousands of exhumed skulls being classed by anthropologists as mongolian or mongoloid, an origin corroborated by some of the so-called Indian languages or dialects.[1]

Only a few of these Asiatic infiltrations of untutored humanity trickled down the westward slope of the long mountainous backbone into what is now California, and remained there, to be patronized by Drake in 1579 and evangelized by Spanish missionaries two centuries later.

The first European to discover Alta or Upper California was the Portuguese explorer Juan Rodríguez Cabrillo, who in

[1] Readers interested in the first Americans could not do better than consult Dr. A. L. Kroeber's article, "Ethnology," under "North America" in the 14th edition of the Encyclopaedia Britannica, and the same author's book, "Anthropology" (New York, 1923), sections 25 and 177 ff.

the service of Cortes sailed up from New Spain—the Mexico and South America of today—in 1542 as far as Cape Mendocino, which he named. Dying during the voyage, he intrusted his command to his chief pilot, Bartolomé Ferrelo, who in 1543 reached the southern tip of Oregon, and then made his way back to New Spain.

Although Spanish enterprise discovered California in 1542 as it had discovered America fifty years earlier, no attempt at settlement occurred until after arrival of the first Franciscan missionaries, led by the heroic Junípero Serra in 1769. As Josiah Royce puts it, the chief significance of the missions is simply that they first began the colonization of California. Even so, colonization proceeded very slowly, the first *pueblo* being San José, founded in 1777, and the second Los Angeles, in 1781, two centuries after Drake had claimed the entire province of California for Elizabeth of England and renamed it New Albion.

During those two centuries, except for the thrust of Russia down the coast from Alaska, California was a sort of No Man's Land, inhabited by a few Indians and a handful of Spanish officials, its vast resources unsuspected. To Washington and the Atlantic seaboard it seemed another world; six months away around the Horn, and overland almost unreachable because of vast stretches of bad lands and then the Cyclopean walls of the Sierra Nevada blocking the end of the trail. Only a few venturesome Yankees ever got there, and fewer returned.

Eighteen forty-one seems a good year from which to date the American effort at occupation, for it was then that John A. Sutter began to build a fort in the Sacramento wilderness and John C. Frémont married Jessie Benton in Washington. With these two men the active struggle for California began, but it did not end until the Civil War was nearly over.

Few Americans realize how the question of admitting California into the Union in 1850 became entangled in a critical phase of our national history, by occasioning in the United States Senate its greatest debate, which fanned sectional passions and perhaps hastened the Civil War. Fewer still realize that California, largely because of its unexampled production of gold, became during the war an apple of contention between North and South, or how its final fixture in the national flag as thirty-first star came about.

In revealing the drama of the thirty-first star there will be a lot of scene-shifting, especially between Washington and San Francisco, while a good many actors will cross the stage, for that is the way the play evolved. But Jessie Benton Frémont, as charming as she was talented and as patriotic as she was brave, stood in the wings throughout the most critical years (1846-1864), and we could not wish a better stage director, for she could say literally of the variegated scenes, "All of which I saw, and a part of which I was." During those years California was not merely California, but the microcosm of a confused nation; a fact which adds to its complications without subtracting from its interest.

The Author.

DRAKE'S PLATE OF BRASS (REDUCED). *Copyright 1937, by the California Historical Society*

THOMAS HART BENTON

port, the worrying of Spaniards had been the chief aim of his career. Now, twelve years after that onslaught, he braved the passage of Cape Horn, sailed up the South American coast, captured many Spanish vessels little and big, weighted his *Golden Hind* with many bullion bars "the bigness of a brick-bat eche," not to mention emeralds "half a finger long" for his queen, and was rounding the world on his way home to her. After coasting up to Oregon, "from whose high and snow-couered mountaines the North and North west winds send abroad their frozen nimphes, to the infecting of the whole aire with this insufferable sharpnesse," he failed to find the long-sought Northwest Passage, retreating down the coast to his Californian anchorage. Although so near the great Bay of St. Francis, he seems never to have seen it; due, perhaps, to "thicke mists and most stinking fogges." He called California *New Albion* for two reasons: "the one in respect of the white banks and cliffes, which lie toward the sea; the other, that it might haue some affinitie, euen in name also, with our owne country, which was sometime so called."

As for the inhabitants, "nothing could perswade them, nor remoue the opinion, which they had conceiued of vs, that wee should be Gods." On July 6, 1579, their king, or *Hyóh*, visited Drake and his men in the "bulwarke" they had constructed, accompanied by "about 100. tall and warlike men" and a great multitude of ordinary subjects, all of them singing and dancing:

. . . saving only the women, who danced but kept silence. As they danced they still came on: and our General perceiving their plain and simple meaning, gave order that they might freely enter without interruption within our bulwark: unto whom both the king and divers others made several orations, or rather indeed supplications, that he would take the province and kingdom into his hand, and become their king and patron: making signs that they would resign unto him their right and title in the

whole land and become his vassals in themselves and their pos-
terities: which that they might make us indeed believe that it
was their true meaning and intent, the king himself with all the
rest with one consent, and with great reverence, joyfully singing
a song, set the crown upon his head, enriched his neck with all
their chains, and, offering unto him many other things, honored
him by the name of *Hyóh*—adding thereunto (as it might seem)
a song and dance of triumph; because they were not only visited
of the gods (for so they still judged us to be) but the great and
chief god was now become their god, their king and patron, and
themselves were become the only happy and blessed people in
all the world.

So when the *Golden Hind* was repaired, the prince of
Protestant pirates (on August 2) sailed away in her as the
confirmed king of California; crossed the Pacific to the Spice
Islands, and sailing thence, by a roundabout route to beef-
eating England, sharpset for spices, arrived at Deptford in
the autumn of 1580. Ultimately, he fully realized his goal,
which was, to quote the British historian H. A. L. Fisher, "by
incessant and ubiquitous plunderings, to drive Spain into
war. Nothing was safe from him, neither the towns on the
Spanish Main, nor the route taken by the Peruvian treasure-
bearers across the Isthmus of Panama, nor the Pacific Coast,
nor the Spice Islands. In the year before the Armada sailed,
he burned the shipping in Cadiz harbor. Before that, on his
return from encompassing the globe, his compatriots called
him 'The Master Thief of the Unknown World,' and his
Queen, who had gone shares in the loot, went down expressly
to Deptford to knight the great discoverer and the head of
the pirates' profession."

Spain never recovered from the Armada disaster. The
British divide credit for that turning-point in history between
Sir Francis Drake and his God, to judge from the immense
bronze statue of the former on Plymouth Hoe, bearing on

its pedestal the scriptural text, "He blew with His winds and they were scattered." Spain's reach had always exceeded her grasp, and now, as she began to decline, her grasp relaxed on her far-flung colonies.

3

MEANWHILE, "the Colossus of the North," as Tsarist Russia was called, moved east across Siberia toward the north Pacific Coast like an inexorable glacier. In 1706 the glacier reached Kamchatka. Twenty-two years later Vitus Bering sailed through the strait that bears his name, where, as Drake surmised, "the Asian and American continent come very neere one to the other." As large bodies move slowly, it was not until 1784 that the Russians staked their first claim in North America; on the island of Kodiak, which abounded in otters. In 1799 they were to discover Alaska, and found Sitka.

Sea otters wielded an almost incredible influence in the development of our own interest in the Northwest coast in competition with the Russians. Senator Thomas Hart Benton (1782-1858) recounts in his *Thirty Years' View* the strange manner in which "the Oregon country" was brought to the attention of the leading American expansionist of all time, Thomas Jefferson. "The Connecticut Marco Polo," young John Ledyard, while a corporal of marines under Captain James Cook on his famous third voyage, was one of the first two white men of American birth—the other being a Virginian also serving under Cook, Lieutenant John Gore—to see our Northwest coast and marvel at the fur trade plied by Russians between that coast and China. On meeting Minister Jefferson in Paris, Ledyard so impressed that genius with the importance of the Oregon country that Jefferson induced him to accept a Russian passport and undertake a journey through Siberia back to Nootka Sound (Vancouver Island), examine

the Northwest, and thence cross the continent to Virginia.
Those familiar with the Ledyard saga believe that his daring
pedestrian enterprise might have succeeded had not Catherine the Great become suspicious of American designs on Russian enterprise, and had him arrested as a spy while he was
still struggling through Siberia. Although thwarted in his
immediate undertaking, his persuasive eloquence, besides
inspiring Jefferson with an unquenchable interest in the
Northwest, incited Atlantic Coast capitalists such as Robert
Morris and Samuel Shaw to build ships and with them wres-
tle for the Chinese fur trade with the Russians of Nootka
Sound and the Aleutians. Washington Irving found that as
early as the summer of 1792 twenty-one American ships,
mostly from Boston, visited the Northwest coast, loading
themselves down with sea otter furs for the adornment of
luxury-loving Chinese mandarins. "Doubtless God might
have made more beautiful furs, but doubtless He never did."
The mandarins so admired them that in seven years they
bought from Yankee traders 100,000 pelts, their demand continuing so long as the supply lasted. Return cargoes in silk
and tea piled up wealth on the Atlantic seaboard; a new era
opened in American commerce.

The new Pacific trade routes developed ports in Hawaii
and "the Oregon country," and paved the way for American
settlement of the latter. When, about 1820, the fur trade
began to decline, whaling took its place. By that time an independent trade in silk and tea had become so important
that, to save insurance on these treasure cargoes, fleet clipper
ships were evolved for them with such success that by 1855
the foreign tonnage in Chinese waters was 24,000 tons American, only 18,000 British, and the balance of 16,000 tons
"miscellaneous."

So the Russian fur trade, first reported by a Connecticut

Yankee, not only acquainted us with our Northwest coast, but made us supreme in maritime commerce.

4

MEANWHILE, the Russians pushed on down the Pacific Coast to California. By 1804 their intentions had become so plain that a Yankee skipper, William Shaler of the *Lelia Byrd,* sounded an alarm in the *American Register,* adding a hint clearly intended for Washington, that "the conquest of this country would be absolutely nothing; it would fall without an effort to the most inconsiderable force." Washington remained deaf, but in 1805 the Tsar's temperamental chamberlain, Nikolai Rezánov, made his master's imperial ambitions unmistakable. Going to Sitka and finding its Russian settlers almost famished, he bought the Yankee ship *Juno* with all its food-stuffs, distributed these among his compatriots, and then boldly piloted his fast-sailing copper-bottomed American vessel down the Pacific Coast to challenge Yankee trade with the Californian Spaniards. "What was sold to the Spaniards by the Bostonians," he bluntly claimed—cloth, linen, iron-ware—"ought to be supplied by the Russians from factories in Siberia, in exchange for breadstuffs" with which to feed the Sitka settlers.

Rezánov swept through the Golden Gate, defying the presidio's challenge, on the morning of April 5, 1806, coolly chose an anchorage out of range of the guns, and sent two of his officers ashore. In the absence of the Commandant at Monterey—the old Pacific capital 130 miles farther down the coast—young Luis Argüello received the Russians with that hospitality which few Californians could withhold, even from potential enemies.

Here begins that romance of which Bret Harte was to tell

in his narrative poem, "Concepcion de Arguello, Presidio de San Francisco." Rezánov, a dashing young widower, wrote to his minister of commerce that while awaiting the Commandant and Governor Arrillaga from Monterey, "we visited every day at the house of the hospitable Argüello, and soon became intimate there. Among the beautiful sisters of Luis Argüello, Doña Concepcíon has the name of being the beauty of California, and your Excellency will agree with me when I say that we were sufficiently rewarded for our sufferings, and passed the time very pleasantly."

Doña Concepción, who was only fourteen, fell in love with a man willing to harness courtship in the service of diplomacy. When Father Argüello and Governor Arrillaga arrived, "I frankly tell you," he said to them, "that we [the Russians in Sitka] need bread, which we can get from Canton; but, as California is nearer to us, and has produce which it cannot sell, I have come here to negotiate with you a preliminary agreement, to be sent to our respective courts." To his own court he later wrote, "Seeing that my situation was not improving, expecting every day that some misunderstanding would arise, and having but little confidence in my own people, I resolved to change my politeness for a serious tone. Finally, I imperceptibly created in Doña Concepción an impatience to hear something serious from me . . . which caused me to ask for her hand, to which she consented. My proposal created consternation in her parents, who had been reared in fanaticism. The difference in religion and the prospective separation from their daughter made it a terrible blow for them. They ran to the missionaries, who did not know what to do; they hustled poor Concepción to church, confessed her, and urged her to refuse me, but her resolution finally overcame them all. The holy fathers appealed to the decision of the throne of Rome, and if I could not accomplish my nuptials, I had at least the preliminary act performed, the marriage contract drawn up, and forced them to betroth us."

Once betrothed, Rezánov became virtual master in the Argüello home. "From this time," he boasted, "I managed this port [of San Francisco] as my interests required."

The chief interest engaging him was the laying of foundations for Fort Ross, or Russ, on a cliff some fifty miles up the coast. When fully developed and settled, "broad bands of rolling meadows and gently sloping wheat fields extended up and down the rocky, cragged coast above the cliffs. Behind them rose dark wooded hills of enthralling beauty. On a level stage formed by the projecting cliffs the fort was erected. A square palisade flanked by two log bastions enclosed the principal buildings, among which there was a pretty wooden chapel." [1] The colony at length became so vigorous that Senator Benton, Washington watch-dog of the Pacific coast, had his country warned in the *St. Louis Enquirer,* which he controlled, that the Russian Emperor was "occupied with a scheme worthy of his vast ambition—the acquisition of the gulf and peninsula of California and the Spanish claim to North America. We learn this not from diplomatic correspondence, but from American fur traders, who learn it from the Russian traders now protected by the Emperor in carrying off our furs."

Rezánov's romance occupied him only six weeks, but its aftermath lasted thirty-six years. He departed northward with his ship *Juno* laden to the water line, and fed the Sitka settlers; but on his long journey overland back to his master the Tsar, he died: March 1, 1807. Doña Concepción, faithfully awaiting his return, did not learn of his death until 1842, when she was fifty years old. Her informant was Sir George Simpson, of the Hudson's Bay Company.

Washington at last listened to Senator Benton's warnings, when in 1822 an imperial *ukase* sought to close the North

[1] Zollinger (see Acknowledgments), p. 58.

Pacific to all "foreign" vessels. This *ukase* was generally in-
terpreted as Alexander's notice of intention to seize the
Oregon country and California. Next year the promulgation
of our Monroe Doctrine warned off all encroachments in the
North Pacific as well as in Spanish America, with the com-
prehensive announcement that the American continents were
no longer open to colonization by any European power. The
Tsar Alexander had no stomach for fighting, so Fort Ross
began to languish. By 1841, when Sutter's Fort got under
construction in the Sacramento wilderness, it was ready to
sell out to the ambitious builder.

5

SIR GEORGE SIMPSON, quite as devoted to British interests as Rezánov was to the Russian-American Fur Company
and its master the Tsar, indiscreetly wrote a book that fell into
Senator Benton's hands and made him even more suspicious
of Britain's designs on California than he had been of the
Tsar's. Designed to reawaken London's interest in Drake's
"New Albion," this book emphasized Mexico's indifference
to its undefended colony in the north, much as Skipper
Shaler had said to Washington: "Come and take it." "Mexico
has more intercourse with China than with California," wrote
Sir George. "Advices are not received in Mexico from Monterey above once or twice a year. The last deputy elected by
California to the Mexican Congress informed me that during the two years he served, he only received two letters
from California." And in his diary Sir George took note of
Sutter's Fort. "The Americans, as soon as they become masters of the interior through Sutter's establishment, will soon
discover that they have a natural right to a maritime outlet;
so that whatever may be the fate of Monterey and the more
southerly ports, San Francisco will, to a moral certainty,

sooner or later fall in the possession of the Americans," should not the British take it first!

Sir George Simpson's book reminded Senator Benton that in the case of Texas, also, English officials had hobnobbed with deputies to the Mexican Congress, and that the English appetite had been officially reported at that time as sharp-set not only for the Lone Star Republic, but for its neglected sister in the north. Benton recalled the frantic warnings sent by our minister in Mexico to Daniel Webster, Tyler's first Secretary of State: "I *know* that England has designs on California, and has actually made a treaty with Mexico securing to British creditors the rights to lands there in payment of their debts, and that England will interpose this treaty in the way of a cession of California, and that in ten years she will own the country.—She has already control of the Sandwich Islands, of the Society Islands, New Zealand, etc., etc., and through the agency of that embryo East India Monopoly [the Hudson's Bay Company], she will ere long have a monopoly of the commerce of the Pacific, and not an American flag will fly on its coasts."

6

SENATOR BENTON'S suspicions of Sir George Simpson as governor of the Hudson's Bay Company were equaled only by his efforts to stir up Washington on behalf of the Pacific Coast; yet it was not until another ardent expansionist, John C. Calhoun of South Carolina, became Tyler's Secretary of State, that we even had a consul in California. In 1844 Calhoun told a friend, Congressman William M. Gwin of Mississippi, that he intended offering Mexico $10,000,000 to move her border-line southward from the Oregon country so that its western end would start midway between the bays of San Francisco and Monterey, running thence eastward to the Rio Grande, and thus giving us undisputed mastery of the enormous bay of San Francisco, which Calhoun coveted. Calhoun predicted to Gwin that a city would grow up upon that bay rivaling or even outdoing New York, as "it would have no such competitors as Boston, Philadelphia, and Baltimore," and must inevitably become the terminus of a grand oceanic highway between Asia and the Western world. Among Calhoun's first acts as Secretary of State was the appointment of Thomas Oliver Larkin as United States consul at Monterey, where he had lived as a successful and honored merchant since his arrival in 1832. No background of the story here to be told could be complete without touching in his figure and that of his charming wife, the first American bride in California.

During his long voyage from Boston to Hawaii in the bark *Newcastle,* the personable young bachelor spent many pleasant hours in the company of a Mrs. Rachel Holmes, another New Englander, going out to join her husband in the Islands. On their arrival there, Larkin learned of the recent death of Mr. Holmes; learned with tempered distress, as his New England conscience had "crept too near" the lady. Hawaii was in those days the only way to California, being a waystation between Boston and Canton, while Monterey and Yerba Buena (later San Francisco) were on the road to nowhere, even the ships bound to the Oregon country giving them the go-by. When Larkin finally found himself in Monterey, the memory of the lovely widow so possessed him that he opened a correspondence, necessarily long drawn out because of infrequent communications between the mainland and the Islands, but at length successful.

Between his engagement and the arrival of his bride, Larkin busied himself in the erection of a house so well built that it is still a good one, lived in by his descendants after more than a century: two-storied, spacious, its thick walls of sun-dried adobe supporting a flattish roof of perdurable redwood "shakes" projecting over generous balconies, and some of its many windows still paned with the glass especially imported by *Don Tomás* in honor of his bride.

With that assiduous attention to details that was to make him such a good consul, Larkin had corresponded not only with his ladylove, but with the Honolulu consul. Consul Jones seems to have owned a ship which sometimes sailed between Honolulu and Santa Barbara. When she next came over her consul owner was aboard her, as well as Mrs. Rachel Holmes. Consuls have authority to perform the wedding ceremony on the high seas, so Larkin had himself conveyed through Santa Barbara Bay out to the bark, and climbed aboard laden with many mysterious bundles, for he was ever a good provider; and Consul Jones read the rites.[2]

In the old mission town of Santa Barbara the Vallejo clan of Monterey, into which Larkin's half-brother had married, had passed the word along that *Don Tomás* deserved and must receive the grand fiesta reserved for nuptials, so when the newly-weds came ashore from Consul Jones's bark one of the great Californian families outdid itself to honor them. The spirit of Old Spain still survived among the aristocrats of this former Spanish colony, its irresistible culture and charm having been imported by way of Mexico.

Larkin seems to have been the sole American resident of Monterey who had not foresworn his Protestant faith so as to become a naturalized Mexican and thus improve his business chances, but in spite of such stubbornness the native sons and daughters had come to like him, and when they

---

[2] According to Reuben L. Underhill in his biography *From Cowhides to Golden Fleece*, although Rayner W. Kelsey gives a different version in Volume I of *Publications of the Academy of Pacific Coast History*.

saw his delicate blonde bride their warm hearts melted and ran over.

From the heavily stocked Hawaiian warehouses he had ordered foreign luxuries to be sent across—wines from Paris, conserves from London—but these were the merest trivial trimmings for the Gulliverian feast provided by the lavish Santa Barbarans: choicest cuts of antelope, deer, and grizzly broiling in savory pits where juicy young oxen slowly roasted; fresh game brought in from the mountains by the *caballeros;* vegetables and fruits grown in the Mission gardens; and everything served to gay groups clustered under the live-oaks, not by hired servants, but by the great ladies themselves, assisted by their sparkling daughters, as a special mark of consideration for their *Yanqui* guests.

For three days and three nights a colorful scene unrolled in the brilliant sunshine or under the rounding moon, for never has man devised more decorative costumes than those of Old Spain. *Señoras* and *señoritas* whirled untiringly in rhythmic dances, with lace mantillas or silken shawls draped over white arms and shoulders, with long tresses of jet wound high about tortoise-shell combs iridescent with pearls, vivid sashes encircling their slender waists, skirts of the most costly satin billowing as they whirled; the *caballeros,* old and young, gay with long multi-colored shawls called *serapes* draped over short silk jackets and flowery waistcoats—all to the incessant music of guitars and viols, varied now and again with spontaneous bursts of song in which everybody joined.

At long last *Don Tomás,* who had become a passable linguist, said *Adios* to his opulent hosts, bowing low over the hand of the dignified Governor of the province, General José Figueroa; and then, rowing his bride out to the bark in waiting, sailed with her up to Monterey.

7

IN VIEW of what John C. Calhoun told Dr. William M. Gwin in the very year of Larkin's appointment as Consul, one cannot escape the surmise that this appointment was the preliminary step toward that acquisition of the province which Tyler's successor, President James K. Polk, boldly announced as one of the main objectives of the party in power. Calhoun's offer of $10,000,000 for a shifting of the boundary line seems actually to have reached the President of Mexico through the American secret agent Col. G. L. Thompson, only to be scornfully rejected—which served but to harden Polk's determination.

The Hon. Joel R. Poinsett of Charleston, who will figure in this story, had discovered England's intention when serving as our first minister to Mexico away back in 1825.[3] Henry Clay, then the Secretary of State, pointedly directed his attention to the Monroe Doctrine, promulgated, as already noted, in 1823. Clay called Poinsett's attention especially to two passages in President Monroe's congressional message, as follows: "We could not view an interposition for oppressing them [the Spanish-American republics] or controlling in any other manner their destiny, by any European power, in any other light than as a manifestation of an unfriendly disposition toward the United States," and, "The American continents should no longer be subjects for any new European colonial settlement." Clay assumed, in his instructions to Poinsett, that the Mexican government would be grateful for those declarations, as well as for our prompt recognition of its independence. But Poinsett found the Mexican officials as cool toward him and the United States as they were per-

[3] The poinsettia plant bears his name, as he introduced it from Mexico.

fervid toward Commissioner Mackie of London, who had been in Mexico continuously since the promulgation of the Monroe Doctrine, opposing it by every means within his power as instructed by the British minister of foreign affairs, George Canning.

Canning's policy had so far prevailed that Poinsett soon classified all Mexicans as "those friendly to the American system championed by the United States, and those friendly to the European system championed by England," the latter group seeming to him overwhelmingly preponderant. But, despite the maze of difficulties in which he became entangled, Poinsett managed himself so well that under President Victoria he had the satisfaction of seeing conditions exactly reversed. Even his critics now concede that his entanglement in the domestic Masonic strife "was practically forced upon him," while such an authority as Justin Smith wonders whether a better man for his post "could have been chosen or even created."

Naturally, Poinsett never forgot his Mexican experiences, nor that England, during his entire official career, seemed avid for colonies on the western hemisphere, no matter where. Although Lord Aberdeen, Canning's successor, appeared less keen for Western possessions than Canning had been, the appetite of British overseas officials in general continued insatiable. And Aberdeen himself instructed his vice-consul at Monterey, James A. Forbes, on the last day of 1844, that while Her Majesty's government could not interfere as between Mexico and its northern colony, they would on the other hand "view with much dissatisfaction the establishment of a protectoral power over California by any other foreign State," meaning of course the United States.

This final attitude of Aberdeen's must have been occasioned by the looming annexation of Texas, achieved in 1845. He would have "viewed with satisfaction" a Texas and a

California independent of both Mexico and the United States, and, perhaps, would have left it at that. But such was not the attitude of such overseas English officials as Vice-Consul Forbes, the ubiquitous Sir George Simpson of the Hudson's Bay Company, and Admiral Seymour of H. M. S. *Collingwood,* which will sail into this story in due time.

8

UP in the north, England's westward push across the continent toward "the Oregon country" and "New Albion" had got as far as the Mississippi when the Declaration of Independence was signed. But not until Thomas Jefferson had become President and bought the vast tract known as "Louisiana" (in 1803), thus transforming a seaboard string of colonies into a continental power—not until then did England begin to view us not only with much dissatisfaction, but with alarm. After Jefferson followed up his Louisiana purchase by remembering John Ledyard and dispatching Lewis and Clark to the Oregon country (in 1804), the "Oregon question" began to take the spotlight in our relations with England; and held it until its settlement in 1846, meanwhile exerting distinct influences on the Californian situation.

George Vancouver, who had been a British shipmate of Ledyard's on Captain Cook's third voyage, had been commissioned in 1791 to go to the Northwest and take over from Spain certain territory she had seized there and been too weak to hold. Vancouver, after visiting Australia and New Zealand on the way and then Tahiti and Hawaii, sighted "New Albion" in latitude 39° 27′ on April 18, 1792, and from that point northward minutely examined the coast. After discovering the Strait of Georgia he circumnavigated the large island that bears his name. Fort Vancouver, which now lies within the State of Washington, was not named after him until 1825, when Dr. John McLoughlin had become the Pacific Coast factor of the Hudson's Bay Company. Although McLoughlin himself scrupulously abstained from any interference with the natural rights or claims of the United States, and ultimately became an American citizen, some of his associates, such as Sir George Simpson, were—as already intimated—not so considerate. Sir George, who made it a point to visit California often, and get acquainted with the masses of its people, wrote flatly that "the feeling of the different classes of the natives is favorable to Great Britain, while they look on the United States, and her citizens, with much jealousy and alarm.—I have reason to believe they would require very little encouragement to declare their independence of Mexico, and place themselves under the protection of Great Britain."

9

THE masses of the "Californians"—a term confined throughout this book to the native sons and daughters—of course fell far below the standards of the wealthy aristocrats by whom *Don Tomás* Larkin and his bride were feasted at Santa Barbara. Luckily for us, an able seaman who was also a gifted writer looked in on Monterey soon after the Larkins had established their home there, and left us a picture of the masses.

Besides their love of finery and their showy manners, what most impressed Richard Henry Dana of the bark *Pilgrim* was their gentle speech. Even roughish fellows wrapped in horse-blankets and topped by torn *sombreros* spoke elegant Spanish in cultivated voices. Dana, becoming sententious, characterized the average lazy Californian as a man blighted by a curse, which had deprived him of all good qualities but pride, a fine manner, and a cultivated voice.

Monterey struck him as the pleasantest place in California. Its center was a square surrounded by one-story adobe buildings, but showing off half a dozen cannon, only three being mounted. This was the presidio, or fort.

The Monterey presidio lay open and defenseless. Several officers with sonorous titles lorded it over eighty soldiers. All were ill paid, ill fed, ill clothed, and not disciplined at all. Nevertheless the presence of the governor-general of the province made Monterey the capital. As "the General" was the direct appointee of Mexico City, all other officers deferred to him, including the *alcalde,* or mayor. Courts simply did not exist, but Protestants were debarred by unwritten law from holding property, or even from local residence except for a week or two, unless attached to some ship lying in harbor. All *Yanquis* and Englishmen except Larkin had become naturalized Catholics, for "a man leaves his conscience at Cape Horn." Both groups speaking English, they were lumped together as *Ingles.* As all the *Ingles* except Larkin had Californian wives, and practiced economy and thrift, they rapidly acquired property, and controlled nearly all trade. Immense quantities of silver circulated, the only other medium of exchange being cowhides, dubbed "California bank-notes." There was no bank, no credit system, no field for investment except the pasture. Goods bought at shipside were paid for in cowhides, trundled in from the ranches in rough ox carts with huge creaking wheels sawn off from tree trunks; or perhaps packed in on mules.

Most of the Monterey houses were plastered, with red tile roofs. Rooms intercommunicated across a patio or court. Furniture comprised a bed or two, a few chairs and tables, a cracked mirror, a crucifix, and a painted under-glass model of a miracle. The mild climate made fireplaces and chimneys unnecessary. Kitchens were outhouses. Indians did all chores, even the poorest Californian family hiring at least one, his wage being only his feed and a breechclout or so.

All Californians seemed centaurs. Stables, however, were nonexistent, the horses running loose and grazing, but dragging long lassos behind them, by which they could be caught when needed. A man caught his mount of a morning, saddled it and leaped on, used it for that day only, and caught another next morning. Walking was a lost art. On a long or rapid journey the traveler would ride one horse down, catch another, transfer his bridle and saddle, and so on to journey's end. No better horsemen ever existed. Training began at the age of four or five, when stirrups had to be looped up to accommodate the short baby legs.

Heavy saddles were strapped on with all one's might. They had big "loggerheads" or pommels about which the lasso was tightly coiled when not in use. Stirrups were all boxed, to avoid catching on twigs when galloping through a forest or thicket.

The spurs were cruel: as big as saucers, rimmed with four or five rowels an inch in length, and usually dull and rusty. Scarred flanks proved their cruelty, and sometimes the whole barrel was red and clotted after a bullock chase. Exhibitions of horsemanship included bull baiting.

Other Monterey sports were cockfighting, gambling of infinite variety, "fandangoes," and "every kind of amusement and knavery." Trappers and hunters, occasionally dropping in from Oregon or across the Sierra, were frequently "entertained" down to their last fur, or even stitch.

Despite all this, nothing but their flabby character held the Montereyans back. The climate was ideal, the soil as fertile as any heart could wish, the situation extremely beautiful, water pure and plentiful. The harbor won the approval even of the grouchy Yankee skippers, its only bad wind blowing from the north. Despite its indifferent holding-ground, Dana heard of only one vessel being driven ashore there.

10

WHAT the Larkin home was to the *Ingles* of Monterey and
to new arrivals by sea, Sutter's Fort, two hundred miles or
so northeastward in the Sacramento valley, became to nearly
all tenderfeet arriving overland. The fort's construction,
begun in 1841 by a remarkable adventurer with a flair for
empire-building, took four years. Like Larkin's house, it was
built so solidly that today it remains as sound as ever, the
main show-place of Sacramento, which grew up about it.

"New Helvetia," as its German-Swiss builder liked to call
his fort, was, as in due time described by Frémont and others,
a quadrangle of 300 by 160 feet, hemmed in by adobe walls
three feet thick and eighteen high; a garrison that could accommodate a thousand men. Two corners were reinforced
by bastions, beneath which lay dungeons. "By and by a second thinner wall was built within the outer one, leaving an
even distance of seventeen feet between the two. This inter-
mural space was then roofed over and divided into numerous compartments serving as work-shops, store-rooms, and
sleeping quarters for the garrison and laborers"[4]—most of
these were Indians, whom Sutter knew how to handle. Near
the center of the great enclosure stood his dwelling, with a
large distillery and other buildings, such as the smithy. The
site was a semi-stagnant stream which at times became lively,
and at all times communicated with the *Rio de los Americanos,* or American River, whose confluence with the mighty
Sacramento was only two miles off. "The latter is here a
noble river," said Frémont, "about three hundred yards
broad, deep and tranquil, with several fathoms of water in
the channel, and its banks continuously timbered."

[4] Zollinger, p. 90.

An enormous iron-bound gate in the south wall of the fort, constantly guarded, was under orders to be opened to all white men, rich or poor; so that New Helvetia became and long remained the Mecca of overland immigrants.

Sutter's acquisitive instincts rivaled his talents as a spender. He stocked his spacious stronghold with everything he could lay his hands on, including the entire portable equipment of Fort Ross, when Russia at length retired from the approaching struggle. This left the field to the adventurous Americans, the watchful British, an ambitious Frenchman, and the shiftless Californians themselves, to say nothing of Mexico. What flag should fly there? What hand would pluck the golden pomegranate from its withered Spanish stem?

II

THEODORE ROOSEVELT thought so much of Thomas Hart Benton, despite a repellent but innocuous pomposity in the man, that he wrote a biography of Benton thirty years after his death. Benton interested "T. R." for various reasons. Born in North Carolina of proud stock, but "land-poor," his father's death left him while young as the eldest of a brood of children. He helped his stalwart mother with these while schooling himself with the excellent library left by his father, a lawyer, and as a student at Chapel Hill. His university course was never completed, for the widow Benton migrated westward to the Tennessee wilderness, where her husband had acquired an immense land grant.

So it was that the Bentons joined that "gradual and continual progress of the European race toward the Rocky Mountains" that impressed Alexis de Tocqueville as having "the solemnity of a providential event—like a deluge of men rising unabatedly and daily driven onward by the hand of God."

Young Tom Benton in his wilderness home antedated Lincoln in combining rail-splitting with pine-knot study of the law, followed by a speedy election to the legislature after admission to the Tennessee bar under the patronage of Andrew Jackson. At the opening of the War of 1812 he joined Jackson's volunteers, and at its close resumed his law practice, but this time in the Territory of Missouri. When Missouri became a State in 1821 he went to Washington as its first senator, and remained continuously until 1851, which explains his *Thirty Years' View.*

While all these circumstances interested his biographer, Roosevelt's admiration was elicited chiefly by Benton's "sensitive purity of character," his unswerving loyalty to the Union despite his Southern birth, and his congressional leadership in the winning of the farthest West.

A vivid glimpse of Benton's personality is afforded by the autobiographical sketch he prepared—in the third person—as a preface to his famous book:

He detested office seeking, and all changes in politics followed by demand for office. He refused many offices which were pressed upon him—the mission to Russia, by President Jackson; war minister, by Mr. Van Buren; minister to France, by Mr. Polk. Politically, Col. Benton always classed democratically, but with very little regard for modern democracy, founded on the platforms which the little political carpenters reconstruct about every four years, generally out of office timber, sometimes green and sometimes rotten. He admitted no platform of political principles but the Constitution, and viewed as impertinent and mischievous the attempt to expound the Constitution periodically in a set of hurrah resolutions juggled through the fag-end of a packed convention.

Col. Benton was married, after becoming Senator, to Elizabeth, daughter of Col. James McDowell, of Rockbridge County, Virginia, and of Sarah his wife, born Sarah Preston. Mrs. Benton died in 1854, having been struck with paralysis in 1844, and from the time of that calamity her husband was never known to go to any place of festivity or amusement.

Such was "one of Plutarch's men," whose Washington mansion, a century ago, became by remarkable coincidences the power-house to generate and distribute some of the principal forces that revealed California to the American people and ultimately fixed the lone star of its Bear Flag in our national banner.

PART TWO

FRÉMONT AND THE
BEAR FLAG

THE BENTONS' WASHINGTON
HOME IN 1841

1

"OLD BULLION," the friendly nickname affixed to Senator Benton because of his devotion to sound money, expresses him as well as "Old Hickory" expressed his leader, Andrew Jackson. Benton was sterling in the rough.

Jackson's nickname arose from the Southern quagmires. While as a border captain he led his Tennessee troops on foot through the swamps to fight the British, one Tennesseean yelled, "He's tough!" and another yelled back, "Yes, as tough as hickory," hickory being the toughest thing he knew.[1]

Benton became a lieutenant colonel during the Natchez expedition, and one of Jackson's aides. Nevertheless, after the two returned to Tennessee, the junior lodged a bullet in the senior's arm, where it rankled many years. For the border captain served as second to a duelist in an affair of honor with Benton's younger brother, provoking Thomas to the caustic comment that this seemed a mighty poor business for one of Jackson's standing—mixing up in a duel between youths. Busybodies tattled, and Jackson threatened to horsewhip Tom Benton on sight. The occasion came in Nashville, when Jackson, from the Nashville Inn, spied the Benton boys in the City Hotel across the way, and strode over. Tom's pistol was quicker than his horsewhip.

[1] From *The Life of Andrew Jackson*, by Marquis James, copyright 1933, 1937, 1938. Used by special permission of the Publishers, The Bobbs-Merrill Company.

Nineteen years later, when Old Hickory was president and Senator Benton his devoted follower, the tough old man decided suddenly to get rid of the rankling bullet; he sent for his physician, scorned an anesthetic, and attended a dinner party the same evening. A wag of a cabinet officer having offered to restore Benton's property, Benton as waggishly declined it, saying that the president had acquired clear title to it in common law by twenty years' peaceable possession. "Only nineteen," corrected the joker. "Oh, that's all right," retorted Benton. "In consideration of the special care taken of it—keeping it about his person, and all that—we'll waive the odd year!" [2]

Another bullet fired from one of the Benton pistols during that fracas pierced the thin wall of the old hotel into a room where the infant John Charles Frémont, eight months old, lay asleep while his vagabond parents saw the town.[3] In 1841 he became Senator Benton's son-in-law.

Having been in the Senate twenty years, Old Bullion had now become one of its "big four," the others being Clay, Calhoun, and Webster. Roosevelt rates him as a little less able,

---

[2] *Ibid.*, pp. 152, 591.

[3] "Vagabond" is here used in its original sense, "having no fixed habitation, wandering." That describes the condition of M. Charles Frémon, formerly teacher of French in Richmond, Virginia, after he eloped thence with Mrs. Anne Beverley Whiting, an "F. F. V." who at seventeen had married a 65-year-old livery-stable proprietor nearly old enough to be her grandfather. His shameless newspaper advertisement of her runaway with "an execrable monster of baseness and depravity" is preserved in Cardinal Goodwin's *Frémont. Wanderlust* seems to have been inborn in the French *émigré*, and while he and his runaway wife were trying to exorcise it, John Charles was born,—probably in a Savannah inn, January 21, 1813. His father died five years later, when his impoverished mother took her three children to live in Charleston, a rare old city that in those days never consulted Dun & Bradstreet in making up its social register. John Charles and his younger brother—a sister had died in infancy—were duly confirmed in St. Philip's Church with a class of young aristocrats, John Charles becoming a protégé of Joel R. Poinsett, with results of major importance, as told in the text.

intellectually, than the other three, but morally their superior.
Gerald W. Johnson humorously depicts him standing in the
Senate "like a bull in the ring, while the incomparable pic-
adors Webster, Clay, and Calhoun circled around and
around, prodding him."

Clay and Webster belonged to the Whig party, whose
watchword was compromise. Calhoun and Benton, both
Democrats, stood at opposite poles regarding the Union.
Benton, like Jackson, abhorred the other Carolinian, Calhoun, at least politically, as his credo was at first nullification
and later secession. Clay of Kentucky, whose wife was Benton's cousin, was the senior statesman of this quartet, being
five years older than the other three, who were all born in
1782. Never, before or since, has any such brilliant galaxy
appeared in the Senate.

In 1841 the Benton family had long occupied a spacious
C Street mansion famed for its hospitality. Five young
people enlivened it, Randolph and four sisters: Sarah the
eldest, and Jessie Ann, aged seventeen, coming next. The
family had two other homes, one in St. Louis, much more
inaccessible from Washington than in these days of rapid
travel, and the other in the Shenandoah Valley of Virginia.
This was the one that Jessie liked the best of all: her birth-
place, the McDowell manor house, where her mother had
grown up, and near Lexington, whose Virginia Military Institute—the West Point of the South—was later to give
Stonewall Jackson to assist Robert E. Lee in the Civil War.

2

JESSIE BENTON'S earliest exploit, which occurred when
she was only three,[4] illustrates not only her precocity, but her

---

[4] Born May 31, 1824, at Cherry Grove, Virginia; died at Los Angeles,
California, December 27, 1902.

extraordinary relationship with her father from the very beginning. He surprised her and Sarah in the library of their Washington home in the act of defacing, with colored crayons, the manuscript of an important speech. Sarah burst out crying, but Jessie used strategy. "Who did this?" thundered Old Bullion, although he knew too well. Jessie smiled up into his angry face and asked, "Is you funnin'?"

When he repeated his ominous question still more vehemently, she scrambled up and planted her feet wide apart as she shouted with confident laughter,

"A little girl who says HURRAH FOR JACKSON!"

Catching her up in his arms he held her close, only saying, "Don't you see, Darling, you have given Father a great deal of trouble?"

When she recalls this incident after reaching maturity she wonders by what flash of instinct she went straight to the hidden spot in her father's armor. "Did he feel even then the germ of that instinctive sympathy which made us one?"

As she is to play the leading lady in the California drama, it seems important to know her well, from childhood up.

As a little girl she went often to the White House, with Old Bullion, "a healthy little girl with the red-brown curls, brown eyes, and delicately tinted oval features which already foretold her beauty." Old Hickory, a childless widower with a pathetic love of children, seemed to her not at all the implacable despot his enemies called him, but a lovable old gentleman smoking a long reed pipe, whose only fault was that as she leaned against his knee he would at times get so lost in discussion with her father that the bony fingers playing among her curls would forget themselves and tighten and pull and hurt, so that she must catch her father's understanding eye to obtain relief, for squawk she would not!

Her preference for Old Bullion's companionship to that of her mother and the other children was so marked that a corner of the library gradually became hers; visitors often repressing their amusement at seeing a solemn-eyed child stretched out upon the carpet, slowly turning the pages of large illustrated tomes as she spelled out certain words, while concealing her impatience for the visitors to leave, so that her father might resume his proper duty, namely, her private education.

She absorbed many a lesson in politics and diplomacy as she grew older. Dr. Benjamin Franklin, she deduced, had in the early days the only good diplomatic post, the one in Paris, where the political trend made him welcome, like Jefferson after him. London was the worst, at least when James Monroe had to put up with it. She remembered hearing how that gentleman, at the first state dinner to which he was invited, had been rescued from ignominy by the Russian ambassador at the Court of St. James. "James Monroe doesn't care where he eats his dinner," Monroe said to Jessie's father, "but to find the American Minister placed at the bottom of the table between two German legates from principalities no bigger than my farm in Albemarle county, made me mad!"—so mad, in fact, that as he sat down from drinking the health of the English sovereign he plumped his wineglass down into his finger-bowl, splashing water on the table and causing the two Prussians to exchange sarcastic smiles. The Russian Ambassador, taking it all in, jumped quickly to his feet, proposing the toast, "The President of the United States, General Washington!"

"Then I saw clear again," said Mr. Monroe, "and when my country had been honored I arose and thanked the courteous Ambassador, offering as my own toast, 'The Emperor of Russia!'"

So influential was Russia in England at that time that this thoughtful act distinctly raised our standing there, besides making Russia more popular here; especially in the showy person of Count Bodisco, whose marriage to a Washington girl became the social sensation of Jessie Benton's girlhood.

When fourteen she entered Miss English's fashionable school for girls, at Georgetown, across the Potomac. Anything but a tractable pupil, she chose as her chum one of the day scholars who was likewise a daredevil, and the two of them frequently escaped recitations by hiding in the leafy top of a big mulberry tree—until a lynx-eyed teacher in an upper story of the school building broke up the rendezvous by peering down from her window to see what made so much color and sound in the big tree-top.

Miss English, a stickler for order, never forgot this, and when Jessie Benton at the next spring festival carried the election of a beautiful friend for May Queen, the principal voided the election in favor of a girl "who had the entire approbation of all the teachers."

Jessie organized a mutiny by swearing in a majority of the girls to pretend to headaches on May Day, but Miss English retaliated by marching them all off to the infirmary and enforcing hot senna tea, the prescribed remedy for megrims.

Imagine, then, Jessie's triumph when it was suddenly announced that Bodisco the Magnificent was to marry the deposed May Queen! That he was past sixty, and Harriet only sixteen, was a mere detail. What counted was the fact that Harriet was now endorsed by a higher authority, even, than the principal and all the teachers.

Despite a short and stout body, surmounted by a broad Kalmuck face, furred across by shaggy whiskers that failed to hide a wide mouth with projecting teeth, Bodisco's heart was as big as his fortune, and that was very big indeed. He was also a protocol man, and overlooked no detail in making his wedding An Event. He was so finical about all ceremonies that whenever one went wrong he could be seen wringing his hands and murmuring dismally, "What a bad-manage ceremony!" The preparations for his own wedding naturally engrossed him.

Jessie was even younger than the bride, but Bodisco wanted her as chief bridesmaid for that very reason. In his judgment, she "de-emphasized" his bride's youth. James Buchanan, a bachelor senator who had been minister to Russia and was not too much younger than the groom, balanced Jessie off as her partner, while the British Minister —"a withered, cynical, silent, gray little old man"—stood next the groom, with the bride's younger sister on his arm. President Van Buren was there, with all the officials that could be collected, including the Diplomatic Corps in full regalia, not to mention a swarm of ladies elegantly dressed.

An imposing "milliner and mantua-maker from London" created Jessie's gown, a rich and stately one, the first grown-up dress she had ever worn. It was a perfect day in spring, and despite the amplitude of the festal house on the heights of Georgetown, the invited and uninvited guests overflowed into hall and piazzas and the grounds, while out in the street the serried carriages were surrounded and even covered by hordes of sight-seers.

Jessie, in an upper room with the bride, impatiently awaited the signal to descend, which must come from the Great Bodisco himself. The bride, peeking between the blinds at the crowds outside, seemed completely mistress of the occasion. "Girls, here comes the carriage," she cried. "See the satin rosettes on the horses, the big bouquets on the servants! Bodisco says I *must* wear this cloak when we drive off—hot thing! Oh, here are your camellias, and a pearl ring for each of you from Bodisco! But I'm hungry, and Bodisco says it would be bad form to eat anything until the state breakfast is served!"

At last the anxious Master of Ceremonies appeared, Bodisco himself, first reading out all the names in order, and then marshaling the wedding party down a narrow back stairway so as to enter the big room where Bishop Johns would perform the ceremony. There, behind folding doors, waited the over-ripe groomsmen, together with Cousin Henry Clay, who would give away the bride, her father being only an insignificant clerk. Then Bodisco, his memorandum still in his hand, directed each couple into position; he and his bride facing the doors, the other couples spreading out from them fan-wise. At the correct moment he gave his signal, the doors were flung open, and Bishop Johns in full canonicals did his duty.

After this excursion into high society, Jessie entered another "female seminary" somewhat reluctantly. Less studious than ever, she spent the remainder of her time there stirred by a vague expectancy.

3

"THE handsomest young man that ever walked the streets of Washington" returned from exploration and buffalo hunting in the far West just at the click of opportunity.

It was her father who introduced him to Jessie. Old Bullion's admiration was won not only by the young man's charm, but because the elegant statesman, Mr. Poinsett of Charleston, now Van Buren's Secretary of War, praised him so highly. Mr. Poinsett had befriended the fatherless and somewhat erratic lad in Charleston, and on coming to Washington had got him a berth in the Topographical Survey. This meant that he had joined a professional explorer, Monsieur J. N. Nicollet, in an expedition to the head waters of the Mississippi and Missouri rivers in 1838-39. During their long and adventurous months together, Frémont, the son of a Frenchman, had become as a son to the Parisian academician, associate of Arago and Laplace, who introduced him to the best society of Baltimore and St. Louis. Nicollet reported his young assistant as "fearless in the face of heat, cold, and Indians, quick at learning the scientific procedure of exploration, accurate in astronomical observation and the detailed study of geology and botany." His course in the old College of Charleston served him well.

Such facts Mr. Poinsett now repeated to Senator Benton, who was further impressed by the fact that the crotchety but competent Chief of the Coast Survey, the Swiss scientist Hassler, had invited so young a man to share bachelor quarters with him and M. Nicollet on Capitol Hill.

So when the dignified statesman and the youthful explorer met in the Poinsetts' drawing-room, each took stock of the other intently. Frémont, at first somewhat awed by Benton's immense fund of information on the Northwest, although he had never seen it, soon forgot himself in answering rapid-fire questions, while his questioner, in turn, felt so surprised and pleased by the youngster's ability not only to answer, but to warm up to the battle-cry of "Westward Ho" that he went home to C Street and told Mrs. Benton that they must certainly ask him to dinner.

Jessie's Grandmother McDowell, a dainty diminutive lady who was spending the winter in Washington, took the dark young stranger to her heart at once, to say nothing of Mrs. Benton and the two younger girls. He was told that their sisters were away at school, but would he not call again the next evening, and go with the family to a concert there?

He would! The next evening the family party, arriving early, were shown into the reception room, where Jessie, rushing in all radiant and eager to greet her home folk, stopped short before reaching her father's arms, for, standing beside him, an Adonis in army uniform had fixed his deep-set blue eyes on her in open admiration.

On returning to bachelor hall that night, Frémont confided to his father confessor, M. Nicollet, that he had fallen in love, and that at first sight, with a brown-eyed beauty ten years his junior. Jessie, meanwhile, was confiding to her sister Sarah how glad she was that she had worn a dress that made her look older, for she had sat throughout the concert beside an eloquent army officer ten years her senior, who had not only sailed South American waters and lived in the tents of the Cherokees—during his salad-days, while residing in Charleston—but whose words fairly dripped color as he told of prairie fires and buffalo hunts in the far Northwest.[5]

Months passed before the long vacation, but Frémont's ardor did not cool. He then came so often to the hospitable home that his intentions could not be doubted, just as the shining eyes and glowing cheeks of Jessie told their story to the watchful eye of Old Bullion. Forthright as ever, he growled to the young man that Jessie was too young for matrimony, and that when she did marry he devoutly hoped she would not subject herself to the unsettled existence of an army officer's wife. He is even reported to have objected to Frémont's way of parting his hair, to which Jessie retorted that he never parted it at all! The old tyrant limited their meetings to an occasional week end, when Grandmother McDowell would preside over a Virginia dinner, peanut-fed ham and all.

When President Harrison died, Frémont had an inspiration. Hassler's home on Capitol Hill happened to be the perfect spot from which to view the state parade. So he got the exclusive loan of the large room overlooking the Avenue, filled it with flowers, and invited a bevy of ladies, including Jessie and her dainty grandmother. It was a snowy day, but a wood fire crackled merrily in the fireplace. "As the plumed hearse with its six white horses bore the body of the Presi-

[5] George Creel, *Sons of the Eagle:* Indianapolis, 1927, p. 187.

dent down the long slope of Capitol Hill, the older guests stood at the windows, struck to silence by the wailing of the funeral march and the solemn tramping of the crowds that followed the hearse. Over by the fire sat Frémont and Jessie, lost to everything but their own happiness." [6]

Frémont proposed, and Jessie accepted on conditions of the strictest secrecy, for she knew her father.

As the strains of music faded, the elders returned from the windows, Frémont replenished the fire, served a substantial tea, and in due time bade his guests a soldierly and sedate good afternoon.

Next morning the potted plants that had embowered Hassler's front room reached the C Street house with Mr. Frémont's compliments to Jessie's mother. When, by discreet inquiries, the Bentons learned from Nicollet that this young man, whom they had thought on duty with his corps, had "suffered from a cold and been granted sick leave," they became alarmed to the point of counterplot. Mrs. Benton paid a secret call on Mrs. Poinsett and frankly revealed her discomfiture; Benton called on Poinsett. A few days later, Frémont was dismayed to receive orders to drop the topographic maps he was at work on, and get ready at once to lead a surveying party to the faraway Des Moines River country. It was a promotion, but at what a cost! Nicollet tried to help him by protesting the loss of such an efficient aide, but it was "government orders, no recourse." The promoted lieutenant wrote an impassioned farewell letter to Jessie, and got ready for a six months' absence.

Now that Old Bullion had his way, the father in him triumphed sufficiently over the autocrat to allow Jessie and her lover to meet and say goodby. They were given a scant half-hour of privacy, but when at last they had said farewell the sight of Jessie's stricken face so moved her father that

[6] Mrs. C. C. Phillips (See Acknowledgments).

he promised that if at the end of a year they still loved each other, they might marry. Frémont, bowing low, gravely thanked him, and then bade the family, one by one, goodby.

Near the close of his six months' banishment, he got a letter from Nicollet—"Everyone here and in Baltimore inquires after you, even the Benton household. The young girls returned home ten days later than they expected on account of the grandmother who died at the moment when they were about to set out on their journey to Washington. *She* is quite happy and impatient to see you."

Immediately on Frémont's return to the capital he called on the Benton household "to pay his respects." Old Bullion watched. As the young man entered the drawing-room the demeanor of both the young people removed the last vestige of doubt of their deep attachment. But he still remained stubborn, although his position became more difficult. The experiment of separation proved a boomerang. Frémont's return from strange faraway places on which he discoursed eloquently made him a lion of lions.

Jessie hoped for a while that this astounding popularity might induce her parents to remit the remaining half-year of probation, but when they continued unmoved she feared another "promotion." Infrequent meetings at her home were now pieced out with clandestine trysts under the wing of kind Mrs. Crittenden, wife of Cousin Henry Clay's Kentucky colleague. At last on an exciting day Mrs. Crittenden waited anxiously with Jessie while Frémont and his foster-father, Nicollet, called on three Protestant clergymen in succession in behalf of a secret wedding. But Old Bullion's fame as a fighter was too well known; the clergymen were men of peace. Mrs. Crittenden was a Catholic, and one of grim determination. She called on Father Van Horseigh, and on October 19, 1841, he performed the sacrament of matrimony secretly. Immediately the couple separated, Jessie promising to let John Charles know the very first propitious moment for braving her father's wrath.

Early in November, when the covert bridegroom went down to Baltimore to see Nicollet, critically ill, he found him worrying over his complicity in the secret wedding. "Disclose the truth without further delay," he begged. Frémont replied, "The sooner the better, but Mrs. Frémont must say when." He reported the incident to Jessie at their next meeting, urging her to consent to his interview with her father at once. "No, we'll explain together," Jessie said. "Come again tomorrow; I'll arrange the interview."

The old lion roared. The explorer had faced stampeding buffaloes and Indians in their wildest war-paint without quailing, but turned livid as he told his enraged father-in-law of an ended honeymoon.

Jessie had thought herself ready for anything, but instead of the bitter upbraiding she expected, he violated hospitality by shouting to her husband, "Get out of my house! Jessie shall stay here!"

Stepping closer to her husband and slipping her arm through his, she looked with her beautiful brown eyes deep into his blue ones, and repeated the words of Ruth, "Whither thou goest I will go, where thou lodgest I will lodge, thy people shall be my people, thy God my God."

After what seemed a long silence, Old Bullion acknowledged himself beaten. Gruffly he said to Frémont, "Go get your belongings and come back here! I will prepare Mrs. Benton."

After the Senator broke the terrible news, his wife joyfully hurried the preparation of a sunny suite large enough for Frémont's study, and he became a son of the household, like Randolph.

Old Bullion really rejoiced in his daughter. His training had firmed her character, as it had directed her eager mind in its quest of knowledge, and developed her ardent emotions. Was she not his favorite daughter? She was deeply in love, and was loved in return. It was a godsend to have her stay under his roof.

THE FIRST AND SECOND
FRÉMONT EXPEDITIONS

1

IN 1839 Old Hickory had written to his White House successor, Van Buren, in connection with the Oregon question, "Britain is a proud & domineering nation, and the spirit breathed by Wellington & other lords in parliament, shew a hostile spirit lurking in their bosoms." He added that if the United States were forced to fight, "My feeble arm if providence permits it, shall be once more raised in defense of our government & glorious union, sustained by fifty thousand volunteers to chastise the temerity of British insolence." At the same time he wrote to another friend, "I have been taking one bottle of the Matchless Sanative [a patent medicine], which has improved my health very much, & I feel in strength & appetite, that another will cure me—& if a British war should ensue, which god forbid, I will be able to foill their army in the field."

Benton, as one of the Boanerges of the Senate, thundered away at the British in the manner of his aged leader, but his rigid sense of justice kept him from joining the popular jingoistic cry, "Fifty-four forty or fight," as he knew well enough that the forty-ninth parallel represented a just boundary line. For this he doggedly contended, and was as willing as Jackson to go to the battle-field for it. But he was always a practical statesman, and had frequently proclaimed in his Senate speeches that the way to establish our hold on Oregon was to inhabit it. This axiom of Benton's was what led to Frémont's first independent expedition; for Old Bullion no sooner had an explorer in the family than he set about using him to improve the road to Oregon.

Benton's debates on Oregon—which in those days denoted all of the Northwest between the California of the Mexicans and the Alaska of the Russians—brought to light an almost incredible ignorance of the whole vast West. Dickerson of New Jersey, for instance, avowed that it would never be more than an Indian hunting-ground; that the whole area between Council Bluffs and the Rockies could not be cultivated; and that "all the sea-otters we shall ever take upon the coast of Oregon Territory would not pay the expense of marching a single company across the Rocky Mountains." Even the map later used by President Polk in his study of the Oregon question showed the Great Salt Lake emptying into the Pacific through three tremendous rivers, ending respectively with the mouth of the Columbia, San Francisco Bay, and the Gulf of California.

At the time of Jessie's marriage her father was deeply concerned, together with his colleague Senator Linn and Secretary Poinsett, in plans for a survey of the Rocky Mountain section of the road to Oregon that would not only determine the character of the famous South Pass and in other ways make the trek more attractive to settlers, but also attract them in greater numbers through the wide publicity an expedition would secure. Nicollet was to conduct it, but when he fell fatally ill Frémont's young figure loomed up. Called into discussion with the expansionists, "I felt I was being drawn into the current of important political events," he said later. "The object of this expedition was not merely a survey; beyond that was its bearing on the holding of our territory on the Pacific; and the contingencies it involved were large."

President Tyler's New Year reception of 1842 was to cast the Frémont die. The day was perfect, and when Hassler's huge London-built "ark" drew up before the White House with Lieutenant and Mrs. Frémont in it, such a crowd was gathered as the capital had not seen since the Bodisco wedding. This was the public's first chance to see the principals of a still more sensational wedding, and as Frémont in uniform, with Jessie in a dark blue velvet gown, descended and the Marine Band struck up, a lusty cheer rang out, while the crowds pressed closer to the portals. Once inside, the young couple were hailed by Senators Linn and King and escorted to the President, afterward shaking hands with such dignitaries as Daniel Webster and John C. Calhoun and the resplendent General Winfield Scott. The plans of the expansionists had now matured, including their support of Frémont. That night at the Benton home Linn conferred with his elder colleague on ways and means for obtaining a $30,000 appropriation for the "Frémont Expedition," and in due time the funds were turned over to the Topographical Bureau with instructions to the young leader "to explore the country between the Missouri River and the Rocky Mountains."

2

FRÉMONT'S first expedition, which began on May 2, 1842, and ended with his return to Washington on October 17 of the same year, was outfitted with the meticulous care that always characterized its conductor when dealing with such matters. For articles unobtainable in Washington he went to New York, and bought only the best. He also ordered, while there, the flag still to be seen in the Southwest Museum at Los Angeles: with an eagle in one corner surrounded by stars to represent the States, but clutching, besides the usual arrows, a pipe of peace, designed to tell the Indians that they might have peace or war, as they chose.

Most of the twenty-three men in the party were French Creoles graduated from the fur trade, Basil Lajeunesse their leader. But young Randolph Benton went along, and in the steamboat journey up the Missouri River from St. Louis Frémont met and engaged Kit Carson, already a famous scout, who became his chief assistant and always remained his true friend. John Bigelow's *Memoir of Frémont*, composed in large part by Jessie, contains Kit's own story. A Kentuckian of North Carolina stock, two years older than Frémont, he was carried in infancy to Missouri, and when only fifteen joined a trading party to Santa Fé, New Mexico. In a year or so he became an expert trapper, a dead shot, an unerring guide. Slight and blond, he played on his deceptive appearance to deflate some of the bullies of the plains, who abounded. He told Bigelow of an occasion when he made an end of a big Frenchman who boasted of his exploits in thrashing Canadians, but who sneered at Americans, saying that "they could all be whipped with little switches." Kit mildly suggested that as he himself seemed to be the smallest American then present, the bully might begin with him. Preferring a rifle to a little switch, while Kit hauled out a pistol, the Frenchman mounted a mustang and Kit jumped on another, whereupon, galloping apart for about a hundred paces, the two wheeled and charged. Their two shots rang out as one, but Kit's was a split second quicker. It spoiled his adversary's aim before knocking him dead; Kit escaped with a grazed left eye. "This affair," he told Bigelow, "was the only serious personal quarrel I ever had." He later told a Senate committee that he felt under more obligations to Frémont than to any other man alive, while Frémont wrote of him, "Carson and Truth mean the same thing."

Followed by Kit and the twenty trappers, Frémont, in due time, hoisted his novel flag on a jagged peak near the South Pass, believing it to be the highest in the Rockies. But Frémont's Peak has an elevation of only 13,730 feet, while the State of Colorado alone boasts thirty peaks of 14,000 feet or over. What really counted was Frémont's scientific data on the Pass, through which Oregon-bound settlers might cross the Continental Divide, which he fixed precisely. More important even than this was his demonstration that Senator Dickerson's "great American desert" had no existence, but that the immense stretch of country between the Missouri and the foothills of the Rockies was fertile, with excellent pasturage. He exploded the fallacy that "a Sahara occupied the regions that are now the very granary of the United States."

Benton did not have to wait long for results from this expedition in the form of settlers. Before the year was over, according to Roosevelt, "a caravan of over a thousand Americans made the journey from the frontiers of Missouri, taking with them their wives and their children, their flocks and herds; carrying their long rifles on their shoulders, and their axes and spades in the great canvas-topped wagons. The next year two thousand more settlers of the same sort in their turn crossed the vast plains, wound their way among the Rocky Mountains through the pass explored by Benton's son-in-law, and, after suffering every kind of hardship and danger, descended the western slope of the watershed to join their fellows by the banks of the Columbia." When American settlers were once in possession of the disputed territory, it became evident that the period of Great Britain's sway was over.

3

ON RETURNING to Washington from this his first expedition, Frémont found Jessie in childbirth, and laid his novel flag reverently across the bed, in dedication of all his work to her. As soon as she could leave their baby girl Lily, she became her husband's highly efficient partner in preparing his report. This, when published, was praised for the literary finish she had imparted to it as well as for its scientific data, amply deserving the special honors it received from the Senate and the War Department, to say nothing of the almost universal laudation of the press, which spread it throughout the country. Benton was so pleased that he arranged for a second and larger expedition, which left Washington in the spring of 1843, not to return until August of the following year.

Jessie deserves as much credit as her father for this second expedition, which was to introduce California to America, for it was her quick perception and bold initiative that prevented its recall before fairly begun. She herself has told the story better than any one else.

In the month of March, 1843, I accompanied Mr. Frémont to St. Louis, where the second expedition was fitted out. That through, he left for the frontier, where men and animals were gathered. Following out my duty of secretary, I was to open the mail and forward to the camp at Kaw Landing, now Kansas City, all that in my judgment required Mr. Frémont's attention. One day there came for him an official letter from his colonel,[7] the chief of the Topographical Bureau: it was an order recalling him to Washington, whither he was directed to return and explain why he had armed his party with a howitzer; saying that it was a scientific, not a military expedition, and should not have been

[7] Col. J. J. Abert.

so armed. I saw at once that this would make delays which would involve the overthrow of great plans, and I felt there was a hidden hand at work. Fortunately my father was absent from St. Louis, and I could act on my own instinct. Without telling any one of the order I put it away and hurried off a messenger to Mr. Frémont—one of his men, Basil Lajeunesse, who was to join him with the last things. I feared a duplicate letter might have been sent on to the frontier; but the river mail was very irregular and slow, and I charged Basil to make all haste, for much depended on that letter. I wrote Mr. Frémont that he *must not ask why*, but must start at once, ready or not ready. The animals could rest and fatten at Bent's Fort. "Only GO." There was a reason, but he could not know it; my father would take care of everything. And as we acted together unquestioningly, he did go immediately.

We were in that older time when there was no telegraph to paralyze individuality. Else the grand plan with its gathered strength and fullness, ripening and expanding from Jefferson's time to now, almost its culminating hour, would have fallen before petty official routine. I suspected some obscure intrigue, such as had recalled the young traveler Ledyard when he had already crossed Russia into Siberia in carrying out the design of Mr. Jefferson, then minister to France, for opening up the Columbia River—an intrigue that had thus balked and overthrown the foresight of Jefferson, . . . and the energetic ambition of Ledyard. It was now my happy privilege to be of use in counteracting a like evil interference. With the distance and the slow mails between the frontier and Washington I could count on gaining time enough for a good start for the party. . . .

When my father returned he entirely approved of my wrongdoing, and wrote to the Secretary of War that he would be responsible for my act, and that he would call for a court martial on the point charged against Mr. Frémont. But there was never any further question of the wisdom of his arming the party sufficiently. In fact it had been but a pretext, for which the colonel, a quiet man, had been used. I had so grown into my father's purpose that now, when my husband could be of such large aid to its accomplishment, I had no hesitation in risking for him all consequences. Upon this second expedition hinged great results. *It made California known in a way which roused and enlisted our people and led directly to its being acquired.*[8]

While Jessie's narrative charms us with its warm human interest and its naïveté, its frank revelation of her irresistible audacity, yet, on the other hand, to the military mind it must have seemed highly reprehensible. It struck a blow at that discipline, that unquestioning obedience to orders, which is the very core of military efficiency. Frémont, it is true, went on his way with his second expedition—Basil Lajeunesse reached him in time—and took with him the brass twelve-pounder, issued at his request from the St. Louis Arsenal by Colonel Stephen Watts Kearny, commanding the Third Military Division. But, leaving Jessie's reasoning aside, and even conceding its validity, it might in the long run have been better for his reputation had her message never reached him, for his obedience to his eighteen-year-old wife was held against him.

4

WHAT was "the grand plan, ripening and expanding from Jefferson's time to now, almost its culminating hour"—a plan which, Jessie knew, so warmed her father's heart that she "had no hesitation in risking all consequences" in preventing it from being impeded? It was the acquisition not only of Oregon, but of California; so that, in Benton's own swelling phrase, we might "own the country from sea to sea, upon a breadth equal to the Mississippi, and embracing the whole temperate zone." Through conversations between her father

[8] "The Origin of the Frémont Explorations," *Century Magazine*, March, 1891. Author's italics.

and his friends, she knew that California now hung like
some ripe fruit ready to drop at a touch; that Englishmen,
and even Frenchmen, were reaching out to pluck the golden
pomegranate; and that time was of the essence of our inter-
ception.

As for the howitzer, it might almost have been a millstone
hung about Frémont's neck, considering the trouble it was
to cost him. It not only served no useful purpose, but slowed
down the party when the going got rough, and finally had
to be dumped in the wilds of the Sierra Nevada mountains
without ever being fired except to make a noise. And Frémont's failure to return it rankled like a stubborn burr in the
rough breast of Colonel Kearny, who, with all his faults, was
essentially a soldier. He felt responsible for having issued
the cannon, and seems never to have forgiven its custodian
for involving him all the more deeply by packing army property away off to No Man's Land and finally dumping it there
amid the snows.[9]

Why all this trouble about a northern route to San Francisco Bay, when it might have been reached via the ancient
Santa Fé trail to Los Angeles, and then up the Coast? To
ask this question discloses an entirely pardonable unfamili-
arity with the magnificent distances of the West, to say
nothing of its difficult terrain. The maps look simple enough,
and the distances thereon short, but in reality, to cut a
hypotenuse southwestwardly from St. Louis to Los Angeles
and thence traverse the base of a tremendous triangle up

[9] The howitzer was patterned after a French type developed for mountain warfare in Algiers. Information furnished by Colonel Truman Martin of
the Presidio of San Francisco would seem to indicate that the brass gun
proper weighed 220 pounds plus 295 more for carriage and implements, 238
for two ammunition chests, and 31 for the shafts, footing up to 784 pounds,
to say nothing of a quantity of twelve-pound shot that had to be taken along
as ammunition; approximately, half a ton altogether!

to "the Bay" meant adding a thousand miles or so to a hypothetical beeline from St. Louis westward. Besides, travel over the old Santa Fé-Los Angeles trail was attended not only by great privations but by constant dangers. The New Mexicans and Californians themselves limited their use of it to an annual caravan, heavily guarded.

Never was an American exploring party better equipped than Frémont's second. The instruments were Frémont's pride, including an excellent refracting telescope, two pocket chronometers, two sextants, a reflecting circle, both a syphon and a cistern barometer, and a variety of compasses. Packed into the light spring wagon specially provided for these instruments was a collapsible rubber boat. There were a dozen large carts, each drawn by a pair of Missouri mules. Stowed among the tents were many gifts for the Indians. If the outfit could be criticized at all it was on the score of food. There was plenty of flour, rice, coffee and sugar, but one authority drily observes that the howitzer's weight in dried beans would have proved highly serviceable. The armament comprised Hall's breech-loading rifled carbines, fired by flintlock, but using ready-fixed ball-and-powder cartridges, which could be rapidly reloaded.

Kit Carson did not join the party until they came in sight of Pike's Peak, but for guide Frémont had chosen Kit's famous runner-up, Thomas Fitzpatrick, a man of exceptional mind and character, sometimes called by the Indians "White-Head" because of the legendary whitening of his hair during three days of peril, but more commonly "Broken Hand," from the mutilation of his left hand by a rifle explosion. Jacob Dodson, a six-foot Negro youth devoted to the Bentons, and two Delaware Indian hunters proved invaluable. Charles Preuss, an expert topographer who had assisted on the first expedition, rejoined this one, and Frémont enjoyed the companionship of two gentlemen-adventurers, Messrs. Talbot and Dwight. Altogether he had thirty-nine followers, not counting supernumeraries.

Although the Great Salt Lake had already been discovered by the scout Jim Bridger, very few white men had seen it, and nothing authentic was known about it. Frémont tingled with excitement when, on September 6, 1843, he reached the summit of a butte and suddenly beheld far below him the waters of the inland sea stretching in still and solitary grandeur beyond the limit of his vision. "To travelers so long shut up among mountain ranges," he wrote to Jessie, "a sudden view over the expanse of silent waters had in it something sublime. Several large islands raised their high rocky heads out of the waves; but whether or not they were timbered was still left to our imagination, as the distance was too great to determine if the dark lines upon them were woodland or naked rock. . . . It was one of the great points of the exploration; and as we looked eagerly over the lake in the first emotions of excited pleasure, I am doubtful if the followers of Balboa felt more enthusiasm when, from the heights of the Andes, they saw for the first time the great Western Ocean."

This entirely natural comparison of his party's enthusiasm with that felt by the followers of Balboa was later distorted by critics into a doubly false claim on his part: a claim to the discovery of the lake, and then the presumptuous placing of his misclaimed feat on a par with the discovery of the Pacific! It reminds one of the Oregon demagogue's denunciation of him for claiming the discovery of the South Pass through the Rockies; the hillbilly being apparently incapable of distinguishing between the discovery of the Pass and the scientific data about it that Frémont so expertly reckoned and reported.

The rubber boat overproved its collapsibility during Fré-

mont's use of it, with Kit Carson, in an exploration of the
Great Salt Lake, wrecking them near the middle of it. But
they landed on an island, where they spent a windy night,
listening to the waves breaking heavily on the shore "like
the roar of an ocean surf." "The strangeness of our situation,"
says Frémont, "made this one of the most interesting nights
I remember during our long expedition. . . . We felt pleasure also in remembering that we were the first who, in the
traditionary annals of the country, had visited the islands,
and broken, with the cheerful sound of human voices, the
long solitude of the place." When, in their patched-up boat,
they hove again in sight of their worried companions, the
brass howitzer bellowed out a welcome.

Two days after this adventure, Frémont boiled down five
gallons of the water, obtaining fourteen pints of "very fine-
grained and very white salt," of which he records the analysis. He also took observations on the botany and biology of
the lake, and it was his subsequent report on it and its valley
that induced Brigham Young to lead his Mormon hosts
thither and set up their State of Deseret. "Thence I continued
the line of the first expedition down the line of the Columbia
to Fort Vancouver," he wrote,[10] "where my expedition connected, as ordered, with Wilkes's survey of the coast. I returned to the Dalles of the Columbia, and took up the examination of the coast mountains and worked my way southward along the flanges of the Pacific coast, searching the
approaches into the Sierra Nevada for a railway passage to
the ocean. A river, the 'Buenaventura,' indicated upon a map
furnished me by the Hudson's Bay Company as breaking
through the mountains, was found not to exist; and at length,
by a rough winter passage, we forced our way across the
great Sierra into what was then the shadowy land of California, soon to become a familiar name to the civilized world.

[10] *Century Magazine*, April, 1891.

By this passage the Central Pacific Railway now enters. Descending the American Fork of the Sacramento River, we reached Sutter's Fort, in the 'Great California Valley,' early in March."

<h2 style="text-align:center">5</h2>

FRÉMONT could thus coldly summarize in a single paragraph his first march into California, in a magazine article written many years after the event. But his vivid day-by-day reports so impressed John Bigelow when Jessie communicated them to him that he thought "the powers of human endurance had never been so fully tested before." A few high lights may be borrowed from these reports to illuminate the obscure and hazardous journey.

From Fort Vancouver—just across the river from the present city of Portland—Frémont boated up the Columbia seventy-odd miles to The Dalles, a town named for a cataract; from here he sent his flotilla back to the fort in charge of Judge Peter H. Burnett, of Tennessee and Missouri, who will figure in this book later as California's first Governor.[11]

Having provisioned his twenty-five men and 104 mules and horses for three months, Frémont left The Dalles on November 25, 1843, driving before him a small herd of cattle to be butchered if fish and game failed. He had disposed of all vehicles except the stout howitzer carriage, which always

[11] Burnett in his *Recollections* (p. 134) recorded his impressions of Frémont: "He was then about thirty years old, modest in appearance, and calm and gentle in manner. His men all loved him intensely. He gave his orders with great mildness and simplicity, but they had to be obeyed. There was no shrinking from duty. He was like a father to those under his command. At that time I thought I could endure as much hardship as most men, especially a small, slender man like Frémont; but I was wholly mistaken. He had a small foot, and wore a thin calf-skin boot; and yet he could endure more cold than I could with heavy boots on. I never traveled with a more pleasant companion. His bearing toward me was as kind as that of a brother."

COLONEL FRÉMONT

GENERAL FRÉMONT

demanded the full services of a mule and a driver, and sometimes more. As guide to his first objective, Klamath Lake, he
hired two Klamath Indians and a Siwash.

At first his hardships were not too severe to dull his eye
to the grandeur of sights along the way. On breaking his
first camp, Mt. Rainier and Mt. St. Helens raised their white
foreheads high into the sunny morning, the snow that capped
them "being entirely covered with a hue of rosy gold."
Within a few days he reached a plateau from which six
giant peaks were visible, and where the songs of cataracts
shook the air. On December 5 he enjoyed the rare sight of
a lunar rainbow. Five days later his guides falsely announced
Klamath Lake, and he did not know that it was only Klamath
Marsh, some thirty miles away. From the middle of the marsh
he saw smoke ascending, and ordered the howitzer fired,
whereon the smoke died down, the marsh-dwelling Indians
never having heard such a noise. Their dwellings he found
to be large round huts, about twenty feet in diameter, with
rounded tops from which through a door they descended
into the interior. Being an inveterate animal fancier, he
bought from an Indian a roly-poly puppy, which he named
after the tribe and their marsh, "Klamath."

Tarrying for a day amid the luxuriant grasses, he was
forced on leaving to bid farewell to his false guides, as they
insisted they had kept their bargain. Thereafter he was left
to the misguidance of an erratic map Dr. John McLoughlin
had given him, or of others just as bad. As he headed east,
snow began to fall, and next morning his thermometer regis-
tered zero. Presently the trail became so steep and rocky
that several mules had to be hitched to the howitzer, which
the men regarded as a "jinx." Day by day their hardships
mounted, the snow not only attaining a depth of three feet,
but being incrusted with such a hard and sharp coating of
ice that the feet of both men and beasts were cut as by

knives. Nevertheless much toilsome climbing brought them to a crest from which a sudden view of summer gave them fresh courage. A thousand feet straight below them they saw a smiling valley centered with a sky-blue sunlit lake. A storm raged round them, and "a nipping and an eager air" bit them, so that they could hardly credit their eyesight. The contrast so impressed their leader that he coined the still current names, "Winter Ridge" and "Summer Lake"—midway across southern Oregon. Southeast of the lake, he was to name another one Lake Abert after his chief; but its water disappointed him, and water had become a sharp problem. In making the descent from winter to summer a mule bearing a precious kit slipped from a precipice and executed a series of somersaults from which the mule was rescued without injury, but not the kit. But the howitzer survived!

On Christmas Eve camp was pitched on a little lake of wholesome water, which so refreshed the men that as Christmas morn broke they got some fun out of their jinx by bellowing a greeting to its sleeping defender. He took it in good part, and doled out in honor of the day minute rations of brandy, and even coffee with real sugar in it. But they had now been a month on the road, and were still in Oregon!

New Year's Eve found the party encamped in a desolate desert basin, where water could be had only by breaking thick blocks of ice. To add to their troubles, Indians had begun to steal their horses, a persecution that continued. On the first day of 1844 they trudged through a sunless gorge deep beneath beetling crags, their feet weighted with a shining salty sand. The roar of hot springs almost deafened them, and if they lifted their eyes to the hills they saw them burnt a charcoal black. A choking fog descended on them, veiling the trail so effectively that they had to walk more by faith than by sight. Frémont later confessed to Jessie that the aspect so frightened him that he determined to bear away to the southward, "keeping close along the mountains in the full expectation of reaching 'the Buenaventura River,'" which the McLoughlin map assured him flowed through the mountains to the ocean. He was marching through a fabulous Inferno in search of a fabled stream.

To cap all his troubles, feed now ran so low that he had to send Broken Hand out scouting for grass. He returned to report a little on the heights, near an enormous geyser, and when this was harvested the remaining animals were saved, fifteen having been lost. Two or three days later Frémont broke away from the march, with Kit Carson and Alexis Godey, to reconnoiter. Climbing a peak, they marveled at the sudden vision of a vast expanse of sea-green water some two thousand feet below them, with waves curling in the breeze "like the surf of an ocean." Again encouraged, the whole party clambered down to the beach of this "inland sea," where they celebrated the night with a barbecue of the last of their cattle. Frémont gave the name "Pyramid Lake" to this discovery, as an apparent replica of the Tomb of Cheops rises up from the lake to a height of six hundred feet. Steep ranges hem the lake in on east and west, and in skirting the base of one of them the surf rose so high that the howitzer had to be abandoned until the storm subsided, when it was once more rescued. The river that enters Pyramid Lake supplied the party with such a plenitude of food that Frémont called it Salmon Trout River, but it is now called the Truckee. He was still searching for the Buenaventura, and pressed ever southward. He felt mightily encouraged whenever Carson or Broken Hand or Godey thought they had found beaver-cuttings, which are discoverable nowhere, so they said, except on ocean-bound streams.

But these "beaver-cuttings" always turned out to be something else, even on the stream now called the Carson River —after Kit—along which they trailed for some distance.

Frémont, always merciful to his beasts, got a shock about this time, on learning that every one of them was either lame or foot-sore. This discovery possibly accounts for his sudden renunciation of his plan to drive homeward from the Sierras across the Rockies, which were notoriously painful for animals. But a more likely cause was the insolent challenge of the "Snowy Sawtooth Range," which no white man had ever crossed in winter. Frémont never took a dare, and nothing could be more challenging, more forbidding, more seemingly impossible of attack than this sky-soaring, ice-coated, perpendicular wall, rising in more than one spot to a height of 14,000 feet, and tipped all along its awful summit with gigantic gleaming spikes. Sierra passes, now thoroughly known, were then quite unknown; now well paved, they were paved then only with the most formidable obstacles. But Frémont, beholding danger, must have felt strongly attracted. Once attracted, his mentality was such that he would almost inevitably begin to search his mind for excuses to yield to temptation. Was he not probing for "a railway passage to the ocean"? Might he not, perhaps, find it somewhere up there, amid those seemingly unattainable heights, if only he boldly seized his opportunity? Nor was that all! Up at Fort Vancouver he had connected his reconnaissance, as ordered, with Lieutenant Charles Wilkes's naval surveys of the North Pacific coast.[12] But Wilkes, as he must have known, had sent two separate detachments of his command overland, all the way down the coast to Sutter's Fort. *Sutter's Fort!* The name electrified everybody that penetrated into the far western wilderness; they felt its tingle, longed to see the fort. It would certainly electrify Frémont. And he had

[12] P. 53.

his justification, he must have believed, for giving up all thought of home and setting out for the romantic and mysterious fort, midwinter though it was, trusting to luck and his indomitable pluck to come across it! For, when he found it, he would have connected his reconnaissance with the Wilkes surveys at their southern as well as their northern end, thus exceeding his instructions in the very best sense of the phrase!

But this is mere speculation. Frémont's cogitations as he camped at the foot of the terrible bastions of the Cyclops Wall cannot be surely known. But it does seem likely that he reflected, *"Beyond the Alps lies Italy!* Somewhere beyond those challenging barriers lies the Italy of America, smiling in sunshine and flowers! Why not break a path to it, so that there may be not only an Oregon Trail, but a clear-cut California Trail too?"

At any rate, the Cæsar of our western wilderness here made his decision. His Rubicon was not a river, but a range of mountains "as bleak, empty and bitter as the Himalayas themselves, with no life or movement save the terrific storms which sweep across the peaks and valleys—a silent, frozen waste of snow and rock."

6

JANUARY 19, 1844, Frémont cast his die. Breaking camp on the Carson River, he trailed upstream, camping the first night 4,319 feet above sea-level, and the next night near the undiscovered Comstock Lode. Had he now ascended Carson Valley and crossed the range that flanks it, he would have struck at once the famous "California Trail" of the forty-niners; but he pushed farther southward, penetrating Mason Valley, and on January 23 camped on the East Walker River, due east from Walker Lake.

He surmised correctly that ever since leaving Summer Lake in southern Oregon he had been flanking the outlying eastern buttresses of the Sierra Nevada Range, hence crossing rivers that drained eastward into the thirsty desert basins. What he wanted was a gap or pass to transfer him to the westward drainage. In probing for one, he finally crossed what is now the Nevada-California boundary, as he climbed steadily upward. Among the heights he met a wrinkled, toothless Washoe Indian, who offered to sell him pine-nuts and said he could show him the pass he was seeking. Hopeful, he recorded, on January 28, near Bridgeport, due north of Mono Lake, "Today we went through the pass with all the camp," but "did not succeed in getting the howitzer in!" It was rescued next day, however, a day he recorded as the most laborious so far, "the steep ascents and deep snow exhausting both men and animals." The old Indian had lied. Several other Indians came into camp to see him, and in a camp-fire chat succeeded in convincing him that the streams he was fording still drained eastward, and that he must still conquer "the Great Ridge." Nevertheless, much as they professed to commiserate with him, they could not be induced to guide him, so he was left to pilot his own path through the icy fastnesses.

Descending one night into a canyon to find some sort of shelter, his spirits and those of his men were uplifted by the return of a separated division of his party, under Topographer Preuss. They had been in charge of the howitzer, but were compelled by rough going to leave it behind. For the very last time Frémont sent out and salvaged it. After dragging it laboriously through the appropriately named Devil's Gate, "a narrow strip of prairie about fifty yards wide, between walls of granite," he recorded that "a very steep hill" (it was really the spike of a giant peak) proved "the last and fatal obstacle to our little howitzer, which was finally abandoned at this place."

Although he grieved somewhat over his loss, his men must have chanted *Te Deums* under their breath. But even now the brass gun was not dead, only sleeping; a malevolent djinn whose wraith would later wreak mischief, in contributing toward Frémont's court-martial.

He now missed a second chance to utilize a good pass, the "Sonora," by turning down, instead of up, the West Walker River. Sonora Pass was only a dozen miles away, but nobody knew it. He was confused by some Washoe Indians, who not only misled but exasperated him. To his offers of blankets and beads if they would guide him, they replied by staring at him as if he were mad, and by stretching their arms upward, full length, to suggest the depth of the snows. Due to their misguidance, he presently found himself down to his former level, and close to a former position. It was on the last day of January that he braced himself again to seek a pass through the icy summits. But at last he found a guide, a young Washoe named "Melo," or "Friend." It was great while it lasted! Melo promptly prinked himself out in his gaudy new garments, and filled his lean belly with pine-nuts. The white men, craving something more succulent, killed a dog that had followed them, and the fastidious Frémont concedes that "the meat looked very good spread out on the snow," but it was not for him. Fortunately, some Washoes strayed in with rabbit meat.

Although he did not know it, more than a month still lay between him and Sutter's Fort. He apprehended something of the truth on the night of February 4, by the light of a camp-fire built in the lee of an enormous pine. "This was one of the bitterest nights of the journey," he wrote for Jessie. "Two Indians joined our party here; and one of them, an old man, immediately began to harangue us, saying that ourselves and animals would perish in the snow; and that if we would go back, he would show us another and a better way. He spoke in a very loud voice, and there was a singular repetition of phrases and arrangement of words which rendered his speech striking. With the aid of signs, we comprehended the old man's idea. 'Rock upon rock—snow upon snow—snow upon snow,' said he; 'even if you get over the snow, you will not be able to get down from the mountains.' He made us the sign of precipices, and showed us how the feet of the horses would slip."

Next day Frémont wrote that the night had been too cold for sleep, and they were all up by dawn. Melo was standing by the fire, with all his finery on. "Seeing him shiver, I threw on his shoulders one of my own blankets. We missed him a few minutes afterwards, and never saw him again. His bad faith and treachery were in perfect keeping with the estimate of Indian character which a long intercourse with this people had gradually forced upon my mind."

On February 6 the Colonel took Kit Carson and Broken Hand and one or two others out on a reconnaissance. After a stiff climb they reached a peak from whose top Kit swore he could recognize the California Coast Range. This so heartened them that they spent a week in the most exhausting labor, sledding their supplies across an ice-filled basin to a pass that they hoped might prove the right one, and setting up "Long Camp." Their sufferings were aggravated by snow blindness, an extremely painful affliction. Luckily, they discovered in their equipment some black silk handkerchiefs —of all things!—which, tied over their eyes, alleviated the pain.

On the night of February 13 Alexis Godey was given permission, in response to his pleading, to kill the dog "Klamath," which had once been a roly-poly puppy. He prepared it Indian fashion, scorching off the hair and washing the skin with soap and snow, and then cutting the body into pieces laid out upon the snow, so that "we had tonight an extraordinary dinner," Frémont wrote; "pea-soup, mule, and dog!"

On February 20, all the baggage and animals having at last been brought across the basin to Long Camp, Frémont joyfully recorded an encampment "with the animals and all the matériel . . . on the summit of the PASS in the dividing ridge. . . . The temperature of boiling water gave for the elevation of the encampment 9,338 feet above the sea.[13] This was 2,000 feet higher than the South Pass in the Rocky Mountains, and several peaks in view rose several thousand feet still higher. Thus, at the extremity of the continent, a range of mountains still higher than the great Rocky Mountains themselves! This extraordinary fact accounts for the Great Basin, and shows that there must be a system of small lakes and rivers here scattered over a flat country, and which the extended and lofty range of the Sierra Nevada prevents from escaping to the Pacific Ocean."

Thus it may be seen that Frémont, adventurer though he was by temperament, was a scientist first. This achievement of the long-sought pass was the apex of his career as Pathfinder of the West.

Either Kit Carson himself or some later adventurer carved Kit's name upon a tree, and today tourists read a bronze inscription set into a boulder:

ON THIS SPOT, WHICH MARKS THE SUMMIT
OF THE KIT CARSON PASS, STOOD WHAT
WAS KNOWN AS THE KIT CARSON TREE ON
WHICH THE FAMOUS SCOUT, KIT CARSON,
INSCRIBED HIS NAME IN 1844 WHEN HE

[13] Later fixed at 8,634 feet.

GUIDED THE THEN COLONEL JOHN C. FRÉMONT,
HEAD OF A GOVERNMENT EXPLORING EXPEDI-
TION, OVER THE SIERRA NEVADA MOUNTAINS

Obviously, the "Native Sons" responsible for this monument were partial to Kit.

7

"WE now considered ourselves victorious over the mountain," Frémont wrote next day, "having only the descent before us, and the valley under our eyes. . . . But," he ruefully
added later, "this was a case in which the descent was *not*
facile"—referring to the famous line in Virgil, *Facilis de-
scensus Averni*. On February 24 he wrote, "Another horse
was killed tonight, for food. My favorite horse, Proveau, had
become very weak, and was scarcely able to bring himself
to the top. I left Jacob (Dodson) to bring him on, being
obliged to press forward with the party, as there was no
grass in the forest. We grew very anxious as the day advanced and no grass appeared, for the lives of our animals
depended on finding it tonight. They were in just such a
condition that grass and repose for the night enabled them
to get on the next day." Although a little grass was found,
February 29 proved to be one of the very worst days. The
party lay shut up in a narrow ravine, resting the weary
animals, and waiting for the most enfeebled ones to catch
up. The French voyageur Derosier volunteered to go back
for Proveau, but remained away so long that Frémont and
Kit went out to search,—finding the horse but not the voyageur. Next day, March 1, Charles Towns, whose mind was
obviously affected by the hardships he had suffered, "went
to swim in the river as if it were summer, and the stream
placid, when it was a cold mountain torrent foaming among

the rocks." When Derosier at last came back into camp he sat down before the fire and began to wander so in his speech that it was clear that he, too, had become deranged. "Hunger and fatigue, joined to weakness of body, and fear of perishing in the mountains, had crazed him. The times were severe when stout men lost their minds from extremity of suffering, when horses died, and when mules and horses, ready to die of starvation, were killed for food. Yet there was no murmuring or hesitation."

But meanwhile, on that same critical first day of March, the luck had turned. Poor Derosier found camp pitched on a hill near a pleasant stream, flowing between flowery banks *westward.* Preuss now got lost, and gave Frémont another bad fright, but after he rejoined the party, their spirits rose. Their road led along a ridge inclining toward a river, "a broad and plainly beaten trail," fragrant with flowering shrubs. By and by it descended directly to the stream, and the travelers entered the most beautiful valley they had ever seen. They encamped in the evening on the river bank, at a spot which so pleased Frémont that he called it "The Beautiful Camp." The undulating river-banks were shaded with great trees, which seemed to form an unbroken grove over the country. A grassy sward extended into the very stream.

By March 6 the remaining horses had so recuperated that the men were able to mount and ride them again. "We traveled rapidly," wrote Frémont, "over four miles an hour; four of us riding every alternate hour. Every few hundred yards we came upon a little band of deer; but we were too eager to reach the settlement, which we momentarily expected to discover, to halt for any other than a passing shot. In a few hours we reached a large fork, the northern branch of the river, and equal in size to that which we had descended. Together they formed a beautiful stream, sixty to one hundred yards wide, which at first we took to be the Sacramento.

. . . We made an acorn meal at noon, and hurried on; the valley being gay with flowers, and some of the banks being absolutely golden with the California poppy *(Eschscholtzia crocea)*." Frémont, with about half of his party, now pressed on more eagerly than ever. The river swept round in a large bend to the right, and the hills lowered down.

Gradually entering a broad valley, they came unexpectedly into a large Indian village, where the people not only looked clean, but actually wore cotton shirts. The Indians crowded round the strangers, who were inexpressibly delighted to find one who spoke a little Spanish, but who at first alarmed them by saying there were no whites in the country! "But just then a well-dressed Indian came up, and made his salutations in very well-spoken Spanish. In answer to our inquiries, he informed us that we were upon the *Rio de los Americanos,* and that it joined the Sacramento River about ten miles below. Never did a name sound more sweetly! . . . To our eager inquiries he answered, 'I am a *vaquero* (cowherd) in the service of Captain Sutter, and the people of this *rancheria* work for him.' Our evident satisfaction made him communicative; and he went on to say that Captain Sutter was a very rich man, and always glad to see his country people. We asked for his house. He answered that it was just over the hill before us, and offered, if we would wait a moment, to take his horse and conduct us to it. . . . In a short distance we came in sight of the fort."

8

EARLY next morning, Frémont was off with provisions and fresh horses to the relief of Broken Hand and the remainder of the party. The next day he found them, "and a more forlorn and pitiable sight than they presented cannot well be imagined. They were all on foot—each man weak and emaciated—leading a horse or mule as weak and emaciated as themselves." Many animals had slipped over precipices, some with their valuable packs, including rich stores of botanical specimens. Of the 104 horses and mules with which he left The Dalles, only thirty-three now survived, thirty-four having been lost in crossing the Sierra. Soon a campfire was blazing, and a bountiful spread of beef, bread, and salmon relieved the famine.

On the next day, March 8, 1844, the whole reunited party encamped at Sutter's Fort; the famed second expedition had reached its western terminus.

"The Duke of New Helvetia," walking just outside his fort that day in March, got a sudden shock, and Sutter was not easily shocked. "Two human skeletons," as his biographer puts it, "wearing Scotch caps and little else, rode up to him on phantom horses. They were John Charles Frémont, the leader of a United States exploring expedition, and his mountain guide Kit Carson."

Elsewhere in his *Sutter,* J. P. Zollinger[14] says that Sutter and Frémont had much in common. "Both were self-willed romantics, hypersensitive and temperamentally top-heavy; both were arch-civilians hungry for the glories of a military career for which they were peculiarly unfit. Sutter, however, with his *sturm und drang* over, and his position in the world assured, was beginning to stand on formality."

It is at least evident that the temperaments and habits of these two men postulated a clash, however friendly their first meeting.

Their differences outnumbered their resemblances. Sutter was a German-Swiss reincarnation of Sir John Falstaff, with-

[14] See Acknowledgments.

out the old knight's loyalties. Like Falstaff, he might be called a fat, humorous, sensual pretender; a swindler and an amusing liar; and something of a coward. But he was also an empire builder.

Instead of a German-Swiss *papiermeister* as a parent, Frémont prided himself on an elegant and educated French father, and was himself about as different from his California host as a French Charlestonian can be from a "Dutch Charley"—to use the phrase of the forty-niners. Frémont, the Protestant "husband of one wife," found the Catholic proselyte Sutter, with a *frau* and four children over in Switzerland, "the sultan of a hundred squaws," an offense to his fastidious taste, to say the least. A stern disciplinarian, the Fort's loose life soon repelled him, and he gladly pitched tent with Kit Carson in the clean outdoors near their men, where they subsisted on soldiers' fare. Frémont's faults were serious and many, but most of them were not Sutter's faults; so that these two men, as already remarked, were foredoomed to collision.

A close observer has described the opulent and always hospitable Sutter as "a man of medium or rather low stature, but with a marked military air. He wore a cap, and a plain blue frock coat; a moustache covered his lips. His head was of a very singular formation, being flat and well-shaped behind, and rising high over the crown, with a lofty and expanded forehead," from under which protruded large chinablue eyes. In marked contrast is Bayard Taylor's portrait of Frémont, sketched a few years later, of a slight man all wire and fire: "I have seen in no other man the qualities of lightness, activity, strength and physical endurance in so perfect an equilibrium. His face is rather thin and embrowned by exposure; his nose a bold aquiline and his eyes deep-set and keen as a hawk's. Rough camp life has lessened in no degree his native refinement of character and polish of manners. A stranger would never suppose him to be the Columbus of our central wilderness, though when so informed, would believe it without surprise."

No narrative could better prove the necessity of a "Columbus of our central wilderness" than Sutter's personal account of his own roundabout way to northern California. Having left St. Louis on April 11, 1838, with seven men and an Indian boy who had originally belonged to Kit Carson, he took six months merely to reach Oregon. Learning at Fort Vancouver that his most practicable route to California even from there was by way of Honolulu, he got to the Islands on a lumber sloop of the Hudson's Bay Company, in December, with only one man of his original seven, and the little Indian. But he was just in time to be too late, barely missing a California-bound ship. To get back to the American coast he now bought the cargo of a ship bound to Alaska, where, at Sitka, he enjoyed a month of social jollity with the Russians. Then he re-embarked on his chartered brig *Clementine,* entering the Golden Gate July 1, 1839, only to be told that in order to land he must sail on down to Monterey and report to Governor Juan Alvarado. His manners being as ingratiating as his promises were grandiose, he wheedled that official into a promise to endow him, later, with eleven square leagues of fertile land in the Sacramento Valley, a square league equaling 4,483 acres. Another Mexican official, Manuel Micheltorena, subsequently granted him twenty-two leagues more, so he became far and away the most important land-holder in California, at a highly strategic point controlling the whole interior. But he did not find rest for the sole of his foot at the *embarcadero* of his famous Fort until August 13, 1839, a year and four months out of St. Louis, a journey of 10,071 miles, a gigantic zigzag by both land and water. Surely, a pathmarker such as Frémont was a necessity, if northern California were to be preempted by settlement, as Oregon had been.

But Frémont did not tarry long at Sutter's Fort. "A few weeks," he tersely said, "were utilized to obtain some knowledge of the bay and the dependent country. Its broad gates lay open to that trade of the Pacific for which we had been searching a way across the continent."

When he turned homeward Sutter accompanied him and his party some distance down the San Joaquin Valley, and as they finally vanished in a cloud of dust he waved a flourish of farewell. Nor was that all. The Pathfinder now rode a magnificent iron-gray four-year-old stallion, presented by Sutter to console him for the loss of Proveau. This wonderful horse, one of the star horses of American history, wins an honored place in Benton's *Thirty Years' View* under his full name, *El Toro del Sacramento,* though Frémont called him "Sacramento" for short. He won his name as a colt by his feat in swimming the mighty river at the end of a grilling all-day journey. Born near the Tulare lakes from the pure wild California stock that roamed in huge herds through the San Joaquin Valley, it is probable that he was caught while still very young by the horse-thieving Indians of the Tulare region and traded to Sutter, whose skillful *vaqueros* broke him in. But his spirit was never broken. Kit Carson once told a newspaperman, "I owe my life to them two, Colonel Frémont and Sacramento," an episode that will be narrated later (see page 101). On another occasion, the explorer and some members of his party, galloping through a forest, suddenly came on an enormous uprooted oak. Without hesitating, Frémont urged Sacramento on, and the beautiful stallion cleared the whole green mass in a bound. Kit Carson, amazed, called out, "That horse will break your neck some day!" "But," Frémont adds, "it never happened to Sacramento to hurt his rider." [15]

On reaching the banks of the Kansas at the end of July, 1844, still astride Sacramento, he discovered that for months his safety had been a matter of national concern, as he was long overdue. Not since he left The Dalles in the preceding November had any word come from him. Alarm had become so grave that the Secretary of War planned a rescue expedition of dragoons, but was dissuaded when reminded that if the Pathfinder himself could not make his way home, certainly untried dragoons could not find him.

Steamboating down the muddy, snag-filled river, he reached the junction of the Missouri and Mississippi late on the 6th day of August, too excited to sleep as the boat neared St. Louis, where Jessie had anxiously awaited him for months. They had been months of sadness for her and her father, Nicollet and Hassler and Senator Linn having all passed away. But her anxiety for her husband outweighed everything, and the absence of her father in Washington deprived her of his sturdy comfort. To her mother and her St. Louis kinfolk she seemed as if wasting away. Her biographer says that as early as February she began active preparations for her husband's return. Each night a table was set with his supper, and his bed made ready. Fresh wood was piled near the fire-place, and a lamp set in the window to burn all night. As summer advanced, she lost weight alarmingly, but kept up her vigil.

On the evening of August 6, just after she had arranged the lamp and the supper-table, word came that her Cousin Anne's husband, the Presbyterian parson, was thought to be dying. Black Gabriel, the Benton coachman, drove her to the manse; here she kept night-watch until nearly dawn,

[15] John A. Hussey in *The Western Horseman,* November-December, 1937.

when she lay down for a little rest. Meanwhile, Frémont had come ashore at 3 a.m., many duties having detained him on the steamboat. No vehicle being visible, he ran all the way to the Benton home. It was closed and dark, so he threw a handful of gravel up against Gabriel's window over the carriage house. Gabe, a notorious tippler, looked down and saw in the moonlight the Captain in uniform, but thin as a shadow. Sure he was talking to a ghost, he answered a whispered inquiry with word that "Miss Jessie am at Miss Anne's." Frémont, fearful of disturbing a house of sickness, but dead tired, made his way to a bench in front of the Barnes Hotel, and threw himself down on it. One of the hotel people presently saw a man in an officer's uniform on the bench outside, and hospitably invited him to a bed. Frémont, who had not slept on a bed for eighteen months, gratefully accepted, and was soon drenched in sleep. Meanwhile, Gabe's ghost story had seeped through the city, Frémont being a celebrity, and it finally reached Jessie, some time after sunup. Luckily, however, Frémont's arrival coincided with sunup, and Jessie's long vigil was over.

9

BEFORE leaving for Washington with Jessie and Lily, the new national hero sent *El Toro del Sacramento* to a veritable horse-heaven in the famous bluegrass region of Kentucky, where Old Bullion owned a farm. As special attendants familiar with his lordship's ways went two Indian boys, Juan and Gregorio, waifs that had joined the returning party. A little Chinook Indian, also an uninvited attaché, went to a Quaker family in Philadelphia, while Pablo, a Mexican orphan, became at first a pet of the Bentons, and later, according to Frémont, the bandit Murieta.

The whole country impatiently awaited publication of a

complete report of the odyssey, or second expedition, although it knew in a general way what had been accomplished. The first expedition, besides clarifying the road to Oregon and making it attractive to settlers, had demolished the legend of the great American Desert, and advertised in its place the fertility of a vast stretch of prairie. This second one now disclosed to restless multitudes "a shining new land of flowers, sunshine, and wealth." It put California on the map.

Without doubt Frémont disclosed to Benton and other interested statesmen, although privately, the cruelty of certain sorts of Californians when *Americanos* fell into their power, as with the Patties in San Diego, and Governor Juan Alvarado's victims in Monterey.[16] Further, he undoubtedly reported the plots of the French and British, and the ambitions of the Duke of New Helvetia and his rival, "Doctor" John Marsh, all of which had their part in the Bear Flag Revolt that was to make the third expedition, politically, the climax.

Frémont's and Benton's first official calls were on General Winfield Scott and Secretary of War Wilkins. Scott had already met the explorer, but Wilkins could hardly credit his eyes "to see the leader of such an expedition in the person of such a stripling," to quote Jessie. Her plan to collaborate in the formal report deeply pleased her father, but he needed all his diplomacy to persuade Mrs. Benton that it would not overtax her strength.

The two co-workers were speedily so beset by lion worshipers that they could not collaborate at all until Jessie rented a cottage as their workshop, within a block of the Benton home. Here they installed themselves secretly, as they thought, with their living-rooms upstairs, while their astronomical assistant, young Joe Hubbard, slept in the base-

---

[16] See Item 1 in the Appendix.

ment, together with the faithful Negro servant Jacob Dodson, who had accompanied both expeditions. Father Benton alone had the run of the cottage.

In connection with the astronomical observations, a ludicrous incident occurred. When about to test the accuracy of his sextant, Frémont would retire early with his alarm clock set for one a.m., when he and the two basement tenants would go out and Frémont would lie down on his back on an immense stone carriage-step in front of a nearby church —studious, but conversational. His prone position and noisy talk in front of the sacred house so shocked an elderly deacon that one morning he called on Senator Benton to say "he felt it his duty to report that Frémont and two boon companions, one of them a Negro, often came home late at night so drunk that Frémont lay on the church steps and could hardly be roused to go home."

Benton could sometimes be cruel. Instead of laughing the matter off, he sent for Frémont and Jessie, and compelled the embarrassed deacon to repeat his story despite their uproarious mirth. Benton then delivered a lecture on the rarity of Christian charity that the deacon never forgot.

After five months of uninterrupted labor—at the end of February, 1845—Jessie wrote *Finis* to her pile of manuscript, whereupon she and her husband had to possess their souls while awaiting the verdict of the War Department and Congress. At last Frémont hailed her one day, as she came in from a drive, with the joyful news that a Senate resolution had just ordered a printing of five thousand copies instead of a thousand as in the case of the first report, but that her old friend of the Bodisco wedding, Senator James Buchanan, had proposed that the number be ten thousand, and so it was.

Nor was this all. Jessie's cup brimmed over when General Scott made her husband the theme of a special report to

Congress, affirming that he had returned from his second expedition "with a name that goes over Europe and America." On Scott's recommendation, Congress conferred the double brevet of First Lieutenant and Captain "for gallant and highly meritorious services in two expeditions."

FRÉMONT'S THIRD EXPEDITION
AND THE BEAR FLAG REVOLT

I

WHEN FRÉMONT sent to the blue-grass country for Sacramento so as to unite with him again into a centaur, and ride back to Oregon and Sutter's Fort—with the faithful companionship of the Indian boy Gregorio as groom—he did so amid circumstances of mystery. His three expeditions seem progressively mysterious. The first was relatively clear, as Old Bullion wanted to improve and at the same time publicize the road to Oregon, but even so it was arranged secretly. The second one headed straight into mystery when Frémont hesitated at the base of the Sierra in the dead of winter, and then, instead of turning toward home, as he was supposed to do, struck onward through those icy ramparts. Even yet it is not known exactly why he did it—whether under secret instructions, or through sheer adventurous impulse—but it does seem clear that his daring and hardihood served to publicize northern California, just as the first expedition had publicized Oregon and the fertile plains lying between the Missouri and the Rockies. But this third expedition originated in a deep twilight of political intrigue, got itself entangled in the Mexican War, sent Frémont back to

Washington for a court-martial, and still remains, in some of its aspects, an enigma.

The present writer places its origins in Old Hickory's hand-picked president, James K. Polk of North Carolina and Tennessee, and Jessie's old friend James Buchanan, his Secretary of State, with Senator Benton and Secretary of the Navy George Bancroft assisting from the side lines—each with different political principles, although all four were Democrats.

Jessie throws as much light on the origins of the third expedition as anybody, by her penetrating pen sketches of Polk and Buchanan. The latter she pillories with the criticism, "Mr. Buchanan had no fiber in him that responded to war or combativeness in any form"—implying as a corollary that as he did undoubtedly accomplish a good deal under Polk, and, later, even defeated her husband for the presidency, his methods, since they were not militant, must have been velvet-smooth and devious.

She liked Mrs. Polk far better than the President, from the start. Calling at the White House on Inauguration Day, she and her husband had to stay and share the honors of the hour, for so the crowd insisted. Mrs. Polk, only eighteen, seemed to Jessie "a young queen." Little wonder, for did she not pour out compliments on the brevetted Captain, even adding congratulations to Jessie herself on being "so conversant with public affairs."

Within a week after Polk's inauguration, Benton and Frémont were summoned by him. This obviously meant official business, so Jessie waited excitedly. Frémont came back depressed. Perhaps he had been too frank. In stressing the importance to the United States of the whole Pacific slope, and the need of accurate knowledge about it, he called attention to the map in the Library of Congress, with its incredible caricature of the Great Salt Lake pouring itself out through three imaginary rivers. Anyhow, Polk seemed cold. Like Secretary Wilkins, he found Frémont "surprisingly young," and even remarked upon "the natural impulsiveness of youth."

"Ho!" said Jessie, when Frémont repeated this. "No doubt he still believes in his three rivers! I wish you could have reported to that young queen! Her mind is wide open to new ideas!"

But the Frémonts felt encouraged a little later by the president's attitude toward the whole Western question. The Ashburton Treaty, negotiated by Daniel Webster under Tyler, but not yet ratified by the Senate, accepted Benton's forty-ninth parallel as the boundary line in the Northwest, instead of the "fifty-four forty or fight" battle-cry of Polk's campaign, which he now repudiated. This Webster-Benton agreement duly passed the Senate, so that, by the late spring of 1845, Polk was busily conferring with Frémont and Benton and Secretary Bancroft concerning California.

Excitedly, Jessie sat at dinner at Daniel Webster's house and heard him declare that San Francisco Bay and its contiguous territory was "twenty times as valuable to us as all Texas"—a territory which had concerned President Tyler far more than Oregon or California. She saw the godlike Daniel's eyes glow over Frémont's eloquent descriptions, and set herself to fan enthusiasm wherever she found it. Soon she had the reward of being assigned to actual participation in the rapidly evolving plans. Secretary Buchanan, unable to read Spanish and mistrustful of his departmental staff, asked her to translate a "confidential" Spanish letter on the Mexican situation in California. She pleased him so much that presently she was put in charge of all the "confidential" Spanish letters. When, in July of 1845, Texas accepted America's terms of annexation, Jessie translated from Mexican journals inflammatory editorials, and even the ominous news that Mexico was mobilizing. Meanwhile, Frémont had set off in May for St. Louis and his third expedition, with the backing not only of the War Department under Secretary Marcy, but of the Navy Department under Bancroft, the great historian and the founder, that same year, of the Naval Academy at Annapolis. Benton's powerful influence as chairman of the Senate's Military Affairs Committee had engineered the necessary appropriation, $50,000. Apparently Benton and Bancroft, between them, were responsible for instructions that would carry Frémont far into alien territory. He was instructed to explore "that section of the Rocky Mountains which gives rise to the Arkansas River, the Rio Grande del Norte to the Gulf of Mexico, and the Rio Colorado to the Gulf of California; to complete the examination of the Great Salt Lake and its interesting region; and to extend the survey west and southwest to the examination of the Cascade Mountains and the Sierra Nevada."

All such signs pointed straight toward California. Exploration of the Salt Lake region and the Sierra Nevada was expected to reduce the distance to Sutter's Fort and San Francisco Bay. "Examination of the Cascade Mountains" was intended to expedite travel between Oregon and northern California. And "in arranging this expedition," Frémont later wrote, "the eventualities of war were taken into consideration."

Old Bullion's sense of justice in fighting the Polk "fifty-four forty" contention in favor of "forty-nine" as the proper Oregon boundary did not in the least dim his vision of John Bull as Uncle Sam's principal contender for the possession of California. A diligent reader of history, his *Thirty Years' View* reveals not only his knowledge of Drake's seizure of New Albion in 1579, and of Captain Cook's instructions regarding it two centuries later, but his fixed belief that England in her secret counsels still regarded New Albion as her own. Frémont, therefore, tells us flatly that "our relations with England were already clouded, and in the event of war with Mexico, if not anticipated by us, an English fleet would certainly take possession of San Francisco Bay." "My private instructions were, if needed, to foil England by carrying the war now imminent with Mexico into the territory of California."

After Frémont had left St. Louis, Jessie and her father were shocked by a letter from Sam Houston announcing Old Hickory's death at the Hermitage on June 8, at the age of seventy-eight. Three weeks later nearly all Washington marched through streets draped with crape, the flags at half-mast, to hear in Capitol Square an oration by George Bancroft in honor of Jackson as "hero and illustrious patriot."

In due course Jessie received a letter from Frémont at Bent's Fort, on the Arkansas, reporting himself and his men fit and eager. Late in August came the last letter she would receive for some time. It enabled her mind's eye to visualize her husband moving out toward the Sierra in command of sixty men, with full equipment for any emergency, including two hundred horses and feed cattle, and toward whatever complications might be woven for him by the Polk administration. As to their nature she could not even dimly guess.

2

FEW PRESIDENTS have been as lucky as Polk in the steady improvement of their historical rating. From the highly uncomplimentary "Polk the Mendacious" he rose to "Polk the Mediocre," and at last Frederick J. Turner in his posthumous history of the period characterizes him as "a serious-minded, hard-headed Scotchman," who, while he lacked the magnetic personality of a Jackson or a Clay, "lacked nothing in decision and achievement. His *Diary* reveals his conscientious hard work and compels a revision of the historical estimate of the man." [17]

John Slidell's mission to Mexico having failed through Mexican exasperation over the annexation of Texas, Polk sought a private consultation with Benton in the course of which he touched on Frémont's expedition, already far away in the West. In Polk's *Diary* this significant entry occurs under date of October 24, 1845:

I told Col. Benton that I was strongly inclined to reaffirm Mr. Monroe's doctrine against permitting foreign colonization, at least so far as this Continent was concerned. . . . The conversation then turned to California, on which I remarked that Great Brittain had her eye on that country and intended to possess it if she could, but that the people of the U. S. would not willingly permit California to pass into the possession of any new colony planted by Great Brittain or any foreign monarchy, and that in reasserting Mr. Monroe's doctrine, I had California & the fine bay of San Francisco as much in view as Oregon. Col. Benton agreed that no Foreign Power ought to be permitted to colonize California. . . . Some conversation occurred concerning Capt. Frémont's expedition, and his intention to visit California before his return. Col. B. expressed the opinion that Americans would settle on the Sacraminto River and ultimately hold the country. [18]

Even before this conversation with Benton, Polk had discussed the problem of California with the ablest man in his cabinet, George Bancroft. In view of the subsequent criticisms of Frémont by Hubert Howe Bancroft—no kin to the other—it seems appropriate to preface this story of the third

[17] *The United States, 1830-1850:* Henry Holt & Co., New York, 1935.

[18] F. J. Turner detects the connection between this confidential talk with Benton and Polk's equally confidential conversation within a week with "Lieut. A. H. Gillespie, who was to bear Buchanan's instructions regarding California to Larkin, and who was also to give verbal instructions to John C. Frémont, Benton's son-in-law." *Ibid.,* pp. 545-46.

expedition with George Bancroft's statement of its relation to the presidential policies.

In a memorandum prepared for Frémont forty years after the Bear Flag Revolt, George Bancroft wrote:

Very soon after March 4, 1845, Mr. Polk, one day when I was alone with him, in the clearest manner and with the utmost energy declared to me what were to be the four great measures of his administration. He succeeded in all the four, and one of the four was the acquisition of California for the United States. This it was hoped to accomplish by peaceful negotiation; but if Mexico, in resenting our acceptance of the offer of Texas to join us, should begin a war with us, then by taking possession of the province. As we had a squadron in the North Pacific, but no army, the measures for carrying out this design fell to the Navy Department. The Secretary of the Navy, who had good means of gaining news as to the intention of Mexico, and had reason to believe that its government intended to make war on us, directed timely preparation for it. . . . Captain Frémont having been sent originally on a peaceful mission to the west by way of the Rocky Mountains, it had become necessary to give him warning of the new state of affairs and the designs of the President. . . . Being absolved from any duty as an explorer, Captain Frémont was left to his duty as an officer in the service of the United States, with the further authoritative knowledge that the government intended to take possession of California.

In a letter to Frémont accompanying this memorandum Mr. Bancroft wrote:

No officer of the government had anything to do with California but the Secretary of the Navy, so long as I was in the Cabinet. It had been my desire to acquire California by all honorable means much before that time.

Nevertheless Frémont as an army officer was responsible to Secretary of War Marcy, and this official stated categorically

in his report for 1846 that the objects of the Captain's third
expedition "were, as those of his previous explorations had
been, of a scientific character, without any view whatever
to military operations."

Small wonder that Allan Nevins comments in his *Frémont, Pathmarker of the West* (page 204):

> It is difficult to avoid the view that Frémont served two mas-
> ters: the War Department, which thought of the purposes
> of his work as purely scientific, and Senator Benton and Secretary
> Bancroft, who had ulterior political objects for it;

and again (page 212):

> It was not a mere explorative party. One of its objects was to
> carry out a military reconnaissance in California, be at hand in
> that desirable territory if hostilities broke out, and give the Amer-
> ican settlers on the Sacramento assurances of aid.

Of the many other high authorities that might be cited
to the same effect, W. J. Ghent and LeRoy Hafen state the
case tersely in *Broken Hand* (page 164):

> Captain John Charles Frémont, with sixty well-armed men,
> was to put himself where he could watch developments in Cali-
> fornia and be ready to act should action seem warranted.

3

WITH his sixty well-armed men—too many and too well-
armed for a mere exploratory party—Frémont pressed impatiently forward on his third expedition until he got within
contact distance of Kit Carson, now a benedict ranching on
the Cimarron River, resolved no more to rove. But when his
beloved Captain's messenger appeared, Kit forgot his resolutions, sold his ranch, found a good home for his wife, and

hurried to Frémont's side. "This was like Carson," his leader commented, "prompt, self-sacrificing, and true." Kit's friend Owens accompanied him, to become, with Alexis Godey, one of the three musketeers who proved almost indispensable during the trying months ahead. Another important new aide, Edward M. Kern, replaced Preuss as topographer and artist, while Godey's friend Joseph Walker proved highly efficient as an auxiliary guide. Basil Lajeunesse and Jacob Dodson kept their attendance record unbroken, and the Delaware Indian hunters had been increased to twelve. Frémont was in absolute command of what was to all effects a little army. "His order to march marked the beginning of two crowded years whose adventures, perils, triumphs and humiliations were to make him one of the most famous figures of his generation."

On reaching the Ogden River, Frémont renamed it the Humboldt in honor of the great Teutonic scientist who, a few years later, was commanded by the King of Prussia to present the explorer (to quote Humboldt's letter) with "the grand golden medal destined to those who have labored at scientific progress." The scientific progress achieved in the third expedition consisted mainly in blazing the most feasible trail of the times across Nevada, a feat that would have attracted much more attention than it did had it not been for the political complications that dwarfed it. Previously a path-marker, in this trip across the Nevada desert from east to west, and this passage of the Sierra, Frémont really became a pathfinder, as Nevins says.

4

"SACRAMENTO" neighed his joy on December 10, 1845, as his rider, accompanied by Kit Carson and seven or eight other men, dismounted in the great *patio* of Sutter's Fort.

The owner happened to be down the river at Yerba Buena, so Frémont was greeted by the clerk John Bidwell, who had come across the plains with the Bartleson party in '41. Frémont, always imperious and now tired to boot, requested for immediate use sixteen mules, six pack-saddles, some food and provender, and the loan of the blacksmith shop. Young Bidwell, somewhat self-important and a bit tetchy, said he could supply horses but no mules. Frémont muttered something to Kit and swung back into his saddle, making for his camp in the hills. Bidwell, now worried, followed, with a companion. According to their story Frémont said stiffly that as he was an officer of one government and Sutter of another, meaning Mexico, and as difficulties now existed between the two governments, it was only natural that he should not be accommodated, or words to that effect. "On my first arrival here, last year, Sutter sent out and in half an hour brought me all the mules I wanted."

Bidwell expostulated that Sutter had suffered reverses and really had no mules, to which Frémont made no answer. When Sutter got back next day he hurriedly furnished fourteen mules, with horses, beeves, and other supplies, but at the same time got word to Commander Vallejo at the Sonoma garrison that an American party had arrived.

John Bidwell is the connecting link between the self-styled "Captain" Sutter and the self-styled "Doctor" John Marsh, both of whom had not only acquired immense domains in the two great California valleys—the Captain in the Sacramento and the Doctor in the San Joaquin—but dreamed of higher things. Sutter had long considered heading an independence movement, and had even drawn up, to be sent to Washington, a plan of conquest according to which he was to be given command of all troops and half of the conquered territory. The Doctor's plan envisaged a nation reaching beyond the Columbia River as far as the forty-ninth or even the fifty-sixth parallel of latitude. He had discussed the scheme with many settlers in the Willamette valley, up in Oregon. Nature herself, Marsh proclaimed, indicated such a development, which now seemed almost inevitable, "in spite of the cupidity of the Hudson's Bay Company and the ambitions and intrigues of the British government." He foresaw Yerba Buena as "one of the great commercial *emporii* of the world, a centre of the whaling operations on the Pacific, and the main point of communication between America and Asia." There was nothing small about the Doctor. By '46 he hoped that his plans for "The Republic of California" could be executed, as by that time disaffection against the Mexican government should have spread among the native sons sufficiently to start the movement, and enough Americans would have arrived to make it a go. Should a nation result, he might be its first president! "That idea was pleasing to the Doctor. Governor John Marsh, or, better, President Marsh! Not bad at all!" [19]

These two men, each of whom aspired to be the Sam Houston of California, possessed in common an o'ertopping ambition and remarkable executive ability. In other respects they were strikingly dissimilar. Marsh the Yankee was tight-fisted and cruel; Sutter, the Swiss, open-handed and kind. Marsh posed as a surly recluse, Sutter as every man's friend. Marsh treasured a Harvard sheepskin, Sutter's *alma mater* was the college of hard knocks. Marsh rode into Los Angeles on the Santa Fé Trail two years before Sutter sailed into Yerba Buena Cove. Marsh, needing cash and discovering the southern pueblo in need of a doctor, palmed off his unreadable Latin diploma as a physician's certificate; Sutter, who also had a way with him, wheedled Governor Alvarado at Monterey out of the promise of a vast land grant provided he would fortify the Sacramento valley against go-getting

[19] Lyman (see Acknowledgments), pp. 263-267.

Americanos. Marsh collected five hundred dollars in hides from his southern patients and then rode north and by hook and crook managed to buy the huge Ompinez *rancheria* at the foot of Mt. Diablo, renaming it "Los Meganos," the Sand Dunes. Both men promptly embraced the Catholic faith so as to fulfill Mexican requirements. Each understood the other, hence bore a mutual distrust. Both disliked Frémont, who represented law and the military power to enforce it. Sutter dissembled his dislike, Marsh revealed it.

Bidwell, with thirty other immigrants, had come to the end of his trail at Los Meganos, but hated the "Doctor" on sight; so, making his way over the hundred-mile interval to New Helvetia, he entered the service of its "Duke."

5

AFTER his tiff with Clerk Bidwell and his success with Duke Sutter, Frémont, having refitted and rested, rode south in quest of one half of his party, led by Joseph Walker; thus he was absent from the fort on the Christmas Day of 1845, when two figures appeared that were to cut deep notches in the California log. One was the forerunner of the Mormons, the Ohio lawyer Lansford Warren Hastings, who gloried in the authorship of *The Emigrants' Guide to Oregon and California,* which made him the first California booster. The second, a member of this Hastings party of ten, and a better man than its leader, became famed as a dentist, Dr. Robert Semple, as the editor of the first California newspaper and the founder of the town of Benicia, and as president of the Constitutional Convention. Wherever he rode his small mule he attracted attention, as his legs were so long that he wore spurs on his calves instead of on his heels! Boniface Brown, of Yerba Buena's only hotel, had a special bed built for him, as he was a good six foot eight, and quick on the trigger when ill served, hailing as he did from Kentucky.

Lawyer Hastings, having seen California before, and being possessed of the gift of tongues, met Elder Samuel Brannan on the border before starting west with this new party, and succeeded in firing that Mormon leader's imagination with word-pictures of a land "eminently calculated to promote the unbounded happiness and prosperity of civilized and enlightened men." The Mormons were on the move. Driven out of Missouri, Prophet Joseph Smith got them into trouble in Illinois, after they had increased their numbers to some twenty thousand, most of them living in Nauvoo. Hastings, after achieving an understanding with Sam Brannan, became the California agent of the Mormons, although not a member of their church, and selected a location for them at Montezuma, confidently expecting their entire horde to follow on. Brigham Young was to lead the overland pilgrimage from Nauvoo, and Brannan to bring a shipload from New York round the Horn, while forty thousand more were to come over from the British Isles, where Brigham Young and his fellow-prophets had won many converts.

And what was "Judge" Hastings to get out of all this? John Bidwell says flatly: "He was ambitious to make California a republic and to be its first president, and wrote an iridescent book to induce immigration." [20]

Thus the year of the Bear Flag Revolt (1846) opened with three zealous candidates in the field for the leadership of a new principality which they all hoped to people with English-speaking stock—"Captain" Sutter, "Doctor" Marsh and "Judge" Hastings—while Englishmen were plotting with the native sons for an exclusive foothold, and Mexicans such as Micheltorena were plotting against the native sons. These themselves were now so at outs with Mexico that California was in all practical respects already a little independent re-

[20] *Century Magazine*, December, 1890, p. 169 *n.*

public. The government was divided between a civil and a military chief, Pio Pico holding sway as civil governor from Los Angeles, and José Castro as military commander from Monterey.

Sutter played no favorites, merely awaiting the highest bidder. He even included France within his purview—"putting up the French front of his dual Swiss nationality," [21] when Eugène Duflot de Mofras had visited him in the interests of France, and seeking to give the impression that New Helvetia was essentially a French settlement of which France should not lose sight! Shortly after this visit of Eugène de Mofras he got an astonishing letter into the hands of General Vallejo at the Sonoma garrison, promising to be "a faithful Mexican," but warning that any steps taken against him would lead to a declaration of independence, and that the first French frigate to touch the shore of California would protect his rights!

Frémont must have known all these facts, and he soon learned of another, of which his *Memoirs* tell.[22] Down in Mexico a scheme was maturing which, by collusion between that government and certain Englishmen and the Irish priest Eugene McNamara, had as its object the colonization of California by Irish subjects of the English sovereign.

Early in 1845 McNamara asked the Mexican government for a grant of California land to be settled by Catholics. His enterprise, he said, had three objectives: to advance Catholicism, to promote the interests of his fellow-Irishmen, and to obstruct the spread of an irreligious and anti-Catholic nation, namely, the United States.

Should he receive the needful land-grant, McNamara promised to bring, in the shortest possible time, two thous-

---

[21] Erwin Gudde, *Sutter's Own Story*: G. P. Putnam's Sons, New York, 1936, p. 85.
[22] Pp. 550 ff.

and families from Ireland, with more to follow. He asked for the huge tract of land lying between the San Joaquin River and the Sierra Nevada mountains. He was fortified by the powerful support of the Archbishop of Mexico. But he became impatient, and addressed an appeal to the Mexican President: "Your Excellency knows too well that we are surrounded with a vile and skillful enemy, who loses no means, however low they may be, to possess himself of the best lands of that country, and who hates to the death your race and your religion. If the means I propose to you are not promptly adopted, Your Excellency may rest assured that before a year the Californias will form a part of the American Union."

Receiving the desired encouragement in Mexico, McNamara arrived at Santa Barbara in H. M. S. *Juno* in the same month in which the Bear Flag Revolt broke out (June, 1846), and immediately submitted his plans to Governor Pio Pico, who approved them and referred them to the departmental assembly. On the 7th of July that body, in turn, approved them, and they went back to Pio Pico for his final signature, which would have made them the law of the land. But, as will soon appear, another event occurred on July 7th, up at Monterey, which nullified the McNamara plan, together with the schemes of Frenchmen and Englishmen, as also of "Captain" Sutter, and "Doctor" Marsh, and "Judge" Hastings, and "Prophet" Samuel Brannan!

6

DURING Frémont's month of absence from Sutter's Fort (December 14 to January 14) he searched in vain for the Walker contingent of his party, and in doing so encountered "the horse-thief Indians." Under the benign dispensation of the *padres*, the American aborigines had behaved fairly well, learning and practicing the arts of civilization in the missions whose ruins still dot the King's Highway, *El Camino Real,* all the way from San Francisco to San Diego. But the "secularization" of these establishments by the secular Mexicans turned their wards back to nature. Their last state speedily became worse than their first, as they used ill the knowledge they had gained. "Knowing well the coast country," as Frémont wrote to Jessie, "and the exact situation of the missions where they had lived, and the *ranchos* and the range which their horses were accustomed to, they found it easy to drive off the animals into the mountains, partly to use as saddle-horses, but principally to eat." Of this present journey he said, "We got among the Horse-thieves . . . and fought our way down into the plain again, and back to Sutter's. Tell your father I have something handsome to tell him of some exploits of Carson."

On the day before Frémont, with Kit and their companions, got back to Sutter's, Polk the chess-player advanced his pawns away down in Texas, by ordering "Rough and Ready" Zachary Taylor to march with his troops to the Rio Grande. That step speeded up the Mexican war. Meanwhile the secret agent, Lieutenant Archibald Gillespie of the Marine Corps, was hurrying on his way to Frémont through Mexico, disguised as a Spanish-speaking American merchant in quest of health. Besides a message for Consul Larkin at Monterey, he bore secret instructions for Frémont of such importance that in order to prevent their falling into the hands of the Mexicans he learned them by rote and then destroyed them.

Frémont, restless over his failure to reunite his divided expedition, spent only five days at Sutter's before steaming in that portly gentleman's launch down the river to Yerba Buena, where Vice-consul Leidesdorff, half-Dane and half-mulatto, consented to join him on a horseback jaunt of 124 miles to Monterey. Here Consul Larkin promptly took him to pay courtesy calls not only on the *alcalde* and the prefect, but on ex-Governor Alvarado and the commanding "general," Don José Castro.

Presenting the passport with which Sutter had provided him, Frémont introduced himself as an engineer of the United States Topographical Bureau "engaged in surveying the shortest route between the Atlantic and the Pacific." His party, he said, comprised civilians as peaceable as himself. Their outfit being in tatters, they asked only for replacement, and a reasonable store of provisions. He might also like to explore a little in the direction of the Colorado River. The Mexicans, polite but clearly suspicious, gave their tacit consent.

While Frémont was refitting in Monterey, his divided party got itself reunited again, so that, by the middle of February, he found himself once more commanding some three score veterans of the plains, all of them expert marksmen. These he led for a well-earned rest to the vacant "Laguna Ranch" of the American settler William Fisher, a few miles from the present site of the Lick Observatory, and about thirteen miles from San José.

During their fortnight on this ranch Frémont and his men fraternized with "the polite, hospitable, shiftless" Californians, but extended a special welcome to all the Americans that came to call. The exaggerated impression made on one of them a little later appears in a letter to "Doctor" Marsh, which so excited the master of Los Meganos that he mounted his best mustang and set out at a gallop for Frémont's camp. But Frémont and his party were no longer there.

This letter read:

Facts, more terrible than thunder! Lightnings, hurricanes, volcanic eruptions! Hear! Hear! Great News! War! War! Captain Frémont of the United States Topographical Corps with sixty or more riflemen has fortified himself on the heights between San Juan and Don Joaquin Gomero's *rancho,* the Stars and Stripes flying over their camp. José Castro and two or three hundred Californians with artillery are besieging his position. Captain Graham and sixty or more boys are moving to his rescue. The country is in revolution, Spaniards and foreigners are enlisting under their respective banners, Frémont arrived on Wednesday of last week at San Juan. . . . He was ordered by Castro to return to the frontier. He refused, alleging he could not leave the country for two months to come. Their correspondence got warmer every day, and now Castro is in arms to drive Frémont off by force. We send this night a person to Frémont's camp to bring us better information and to know his intentions. Please forward the news immediately to the Sacramento and spare no expense. I should judge your presence here in the Pueblo [of San José] would not be amiss. Affairs are becoming serious, and I think I will see the repetition of the Texas history in this country.[23]

7

WHAT had really happened? As well as can be made out, this:

After breaking camp at Laguna Ranch, Frémont had set out in a southwesterly direction, and on March 3 he paused on the ranch of the Englishman W. E. P. Hartnell, near the present city of Salinas. Here he found himself suddenly confronted by a gaily accoutred young Mexican cavalryman, with two attendants, who curtly told him that by command of General José Castro he must immediately leave the country, and who delivered to him a written message to the same effect.

Frémont's wrath blazed up in a hot reply, and when the trio galloped away he ordered boots and saddles and led his

[23] Cited from "Marsh Papers" in Lyman (see Acknowledgments), p. 272.

men to the top of Hawk's Peak in the Gavilan Mountains, where they built a sturdy log fort above which, on March 6, 1846, they hoisted the American flag as a defiance to Castro; Frémont later writing that "the raising of this flag proved a premonition of its permanent raising as the flag over California."

It could be plainly seen from the valley below, and toward the close of its second day of defiance Frémont discerned through his glasses some two hundred troopers emerging from the environs of the San Juan mission and starting up the mountain. With forty of his men he galloped down to meet them, but when they saw him coming they retreated. Castro, characterized by Zollinger as "a choleric drunkard to whom the hatred of foreigners was as necessary for life as *aguardiente*," issued next day a face-saving proclamation, as follows:

The citizen José Castro, Lieutenant Colonel of the Mexican army and Commander-in-Chief of the Department of California:

Fellow Citizens: A band of robbers commanded by a captain of the United States army, J. C. Frémont, have, without respect to the laws and authorities of the department, daringly introduced themselves into the country and disobeyed the orders both of your commander-in-chief and of the prefect of the district, by which he was required to march forthwith out of the limits of our territory; and without answering our letters he remains encamped at the farm *Natividad,* from which he sallies forth committing depredations, and making scandalous skirmishes.

In the name of our native country I invite you to place yourselves under my immediate orders at headquarters, where we will prepare to lance the ulcer which (would it not be done) would destroy our liberties and independence, for which you ought always to sacrifice yourselves, as will your friend and fellow-citizen.

Realizing his perilous position, but resolved to maintain his dignity, Frémont on the following evening began a slow withdrawal toward Sutter's Fort, marching only about five miles a day. It was during this march that the belated "Doctor" Marsh met him on the road, "humbled and humiliated, retreating up the valley, and complaining that he had waited for Castro as long as he could and had only departed because he did not have men enough to protect his large *caballada* and the property of the United States, and that not one American had come to his assistance." [24]

The "Doctor" himself must have felt gravely troubled as he saw his dream fading out in the cold light of Frémont's realism.

8

AT Sutter's Fort the excited settlers rallied about Frémont with such enthusiasm that he must have felt requited for his isolation on the mountain top. But he decided not to tarry, as the prescribed goal of his expedition was Oregon; so on March 24 he led his men rapidly up the Sacramento valley, and presently crossed the line into Oregon.

The end of March, 1846, accordingly found him some two hundred miles from Sutter's Fort, comfortably encamped at Lassen's Ranch, but marching and counter-marching every day instead of proceeding on his way—as though he were waiting for something. He knew, indeed, that at any moment he might get word of critical Mexican-American developments. It was during this stay at Lassen's Ranch that he became angered by a very foolish letter from Sutter, demanding the return of some horses Frémont had bought from Indians; Sutter claiming them as his own, and at the same time announcing that he was "still a magistrate and officer of the

[24] *Ibid.*

Mexican Government," and deemed it his duty to lodge a protest. Frémont, just as Sutter thought, never forgave him for this. Little wonder! Sutter at one stroke accused him of buying stolen property, and declared himself a magistrate and officer of a country with which, as Frémont properly surmised, the United States was on the verge of war!

The foredoomed collision had arrived. We shall hear its repercussions soon.

Exactly a month after his departure from Sutter's Fort, Frémont finally broke camp at Lassen's Ranch, on the very day when the first skirmish of the Mexican war was occurring down on the Rio Grande, causing General Taylor to report to President Polk: "Hostilities may now be considered as commenced." But Frémont could not have known this as he journeyed northward and encamped on the night of May 8 near the shore of Klamath Lake, still waiting for the message he felt sure must come.

As he stood musing under the budding oaks in front of his campfire, he heard hoofbeats approaching through the woods, and a little later grasped the hands of two of his former voyageurs, now become California settlers. Hardy as they were, they seemed completely exhausted from their long and rapid ride, having been dispatched from Butte Creek as the advance couriers of Lieutenant Archibald Gillespie, who desired Frémont to double back and meet him, on government business requiring utmost haste. Frémont insisted that the two men get some sleep, but before dawn he picked ten of his very best men, including Kit Carson and Basil Lajeunesse, and retraced his trail to meet Gillespie.

He made a ride of sixty miles without a halt. But actually to meet men, and not miss them, was one of the hazards of this trackless region. His only aids were the defiles, or the camping grounds, where parties were compelled to pass each other; the intervals in between being almost hopeless. Weigh-

ing the probabilities carefully, he came late in the afternoon
to the beaten earth of a camping ground in a glade, and decided that if the Gillespie party had not already been killed
by the bloodthirsty Klamath Indians, this was the foreor-
dained spot where they must camp that night. He and his
men dismounted, and just as the sun went down he had the
inexpressible satisfaction of descrying four men approaching:
Lieutenant Gillespie and his escort.

It was one of the most dramatic and mysterious meetings
in the history of the Pacific Coast, as Nevins says; with its
physical background of wild forest and water, and its political background of territorial ambition and war.

Besides letters from Jessie, Gillespie delivered to Frémont
cipher letters from her father, now chairman of the Senate's
committee on military affairs, as well as a member of the
President's inner circle. Frémont later wrote that they
sounded to him as "a trumpet giving no uncertain note. Read
by the light of many discussions with himself and other
governing men in Washington, it clearly made me know that
I was required by the Government to find out any foreign
schemes in relation to California, and to counteract them so
far as was in my power. His letters made me know distinctly
that at last the time had come when England must not get a
foothold; that we *must be first*. I was to *act*, discreetly but
positively."

Gillespie also brought from Secretary of State James Buchanan a so-called letter of introduction of which Senator
Badger of North Carolina subsequently said: "Although it
purported to be a mere letter of introduction, it was in reality
an official document, accrediting the bearer of it to Colonel
Frémont, with a view to the union of the two in devising
some means to counteract the designs of the British emissaries known to be in touch with the Californians." Gillespie
further turned over to Frémont a copy of a letter he had de-

livered to Larkin, which is of such importance that the reader will find it reproduced as Item 2 of the Appendix, with its most suggestive passages italicized. Dr. Paxson says, politely, that the "guarded language was sufficient to indicate to Larkin (and of course also to Frémont) that the Administration expected him to stir up a 'spontaneous' revolt." [25] A stirred-up revolt is not spontaneous, but the Administration wished it to seem so.

Certain reflections arise from the careful reading of this important letter.

President Polk, the "serious, hard-headed Scotchman; formal, punctilious, devoted to the details of his office," as Professor F. J. Turner says, can here be seen pondering with meticulous care his next move on the international chessboard. It seems pertinent to recall, here, that exactly a week after this letter had been written for him by another canny Scot, of the clan Buchanan, the President held the significant conference with Senator Benton so guardedly recorded in his *Diary* (see page 80), during which "some conversation occurred concerning Captain Frémont's expedition, and his intention to visit California before his return"; while Senator Benton expressed "the opinion that Americans would ultimately hold the country." Obviously, the President and the Secretary of State—who distinctly instructed Lieutenant Gillespie to give a copy of this letter to Frémont as well as to Larkin—expected the explorer not only to read it very carefully, but to read between the lines, and to extract from its verbosity the essential message and act accordingly; while at the same time they wove, with many qualifying phrases, a pretty effective alibi for themselves in case anything went wrong. Besides the italicized suggestions that California might establish its independence and that its native sons might naturally desire to secure for themselves the blessings

[25] Frederic L. Paxson, *History of the American Frontier*, p. 356.

of liberty through setting up a republic, the assurance is extended that in case they should wish this republic to join the American Union "they would be received as brethren." And then note the extraordinary promise that in this event California might become "one of the free and independent States of this Union"; as in fact it did; the only instance in our history of a State springing full-orbed into our flag, instead of evolving from colony or territory. All of Mr. Buchanan's allusions to foreign encroachments are clear and unequivocal, forthright and above-board; but, while the references to "an independent republic" are distinctly equivocal in the precise meaning of that term, Frémont would have been a dunce (and nobody ever called him that) had he not grasped their purport, even without the supplementary Benton letter that he likened to a trumpet call.

In reading this Polk-Buchanan composition in the light of the events that shortly ensued, one can almost discern the Bear Flag Republic in embryo.

Secretary of the Navy Bancroft, who never wrote an ambiguous sentence in his life, addressed a letter to Frémont in later years that contrasts sharply with the Polk-Buchanan letter reproduced in the Appendix:

Not having my papers here, all I can say is, that after your interview with Gillespie, you were absolved from any orders as an explorer, and became an officer of the American army . . . and it was made known to you, on the authority of the Secretary of the Navy, that a great object of the President was to obtain possession of California. If I had been in your place, I should have considered myself bound to do what I could to promote the purpose of the President. . . . If you were left without orders from the War Department, certainly you learned through the Secretary of the Navy that the President's plan of war included the taking possession of California.

Frémont was under orders from these officials: Secretary of War Marcy, who unquestionably thought of his expedition as purely scientific; Secretary of the Navy Bancroft, whose statement speaks for itself; and the Secretary of State, whose handwriting was his own, but whose voice was the President's. Besides, had he not the "trumpet letter" from his father-in-law, the Senate's chairman of the committee on military affairs? There were three against one, plus Frémont's temperament. Leaving Gillespie's secret instructions altogether aside, it is almost inconceivable that Frémont should not have supported the Bear Flag Revolt, even if he did not instigate it.

All of the mystery of the Klamath Lake night-talk is the mystery of these "secret instructions," which Gillespie deemed so important and dangerous that during his disguised trip through Mexico he had destroyed them after committing them to memory, as already noted. In Monterey he communicated them to Larkin, who was so impressed that he used every urgent measure to speed Gillespie on his way to find Frémont, for whom they were especially intended. We shall never know what they were, but we know enough without them to clear Frémont of odium.

It is further known that Gillespie brought other exciting news. Commodore John D. Sloat, commanding the Pacific squadron, had heard of the Frémont-Castro encounter, and to protect Americans had sent the sloop-of-war *Portsmouth,* Commander John B. Montgomery, to San Francisco Bay. And General Taylor had advanced to the Rio Grande! And a proclamation had issued from Monterey declaring that no unnaturalized foreigner could hold California land, and that all such were subject to expulsion! Gillespie would also have shown Frémont a letter from Larkin declaring that Commander Montgomery had expressed the opinion "that Commodore

Sloat may by the next mail (6 or 8 days) have a declaration on the part of the United States against Mexico, in which case we shall see him in a few days to take the country." Larkin added that the Californians were deeply worried by the *Portsmouth's* presence, and that he had told Generals Castro, Carrillo, and Vallejo that the Stars and Stripes might be run up at Monterey in thirty days. "The first says, for his own plans, war is preferable to peace, as by war affairs will at once be brought to a close, and each one will know his doom. . . . I have had many of the leaders at my house to inquire into the news, and believe they are fast preparing themselves for the coming events."

10

KIT CARSON has best told the story of the tragic night in the Oregon forest:

Mr. Gillespie had brought the Colonel letters from home—the first he had had since leaving the States the year before—and he was up, and kept a large fire burning until after midnight; the rest of us were tired out, and all went to sleep. This was the only night in all our travels, except the one night on the island in the Salt Lake, that we failed to keep guard; and as the men were so tired, and we expected no attack now that we had sixteen in the party, the Colonel didn't like to ask it of them, but sat up late himself.

Owens and I were sleeping together, and we were waked at the same time *by the licks of the axe that killed our men.*

At first, I didn't know it was that; but I called to Basil Lajeunesse, who was that side, "What's the matter there? What's that fuss about?"

He never answered, for he was dead, poor fellow, and he never knew what killed him. His head had been cut in, in his sleep. The other groaned a little as he died.

The Delawares (we had four with us) were sleeping at that

fire, and they sprang up as the Klamaths charged them. One of them caught up a gun, which was unloaded; but, although he could do no execution, he kept them at bay, fighting like a soldier, and didn't give up until he was shot full of arrows—three entering his heart. He died bravely. As soon as I had called out, I saw it was Indians in the camp, and I and Owens together cried out, *Indians!* There were no orders given; things went on too fast, and the Colonel had men with him that didn't need to be told their duty. The Colonel and I, Maxwell, Owens, Godey, and Stepp, jumped together, we six, and ran to the assistance of our Delawares. I don't know who fired and who didn't, but I think it was Stepp's shot that killed the Klamath chief. Anyhow, it was at the crack of Stepp's gun that he fell. He had an English half-axe slung to his wrist by a cord, and there were forty arrows left in his quiver, the most beautiful and warlike arrows I ever saw.[26] He must have been the bravest man among them, from the way he was armed, and judging by his cap. When the Klamaths saw him fall, they ran; but we lay, every man with his rifle cocked, until daylight, expecting another attack.

As the party made its way back toward Sutter's Fort, Carson was sent on ahead to inflict reprisals on the Klamath villages, and afterward reported: "It was a beautiful sight," the thatched huts burning, and the villagers skedaddling! But at one point Kit would have been killed had not Frémont on Sacramento saved him, as already intimated. An ambushed Indian was just letting his poisoned arrow fly at Kit's heart when Kit saw him and with a lightning motion leveled his rifle and pressed the trigger. But the hammer snapped, and in the next split-second Kit would have been a goner had not Frémont spurred Sacramento and trampled the Indian into the ground. "The entire incident was over in a second, but it had been a supreme test of man and mount."

[26] Allan Nevins says they were tipped with steel heads of lancet sharpness, obtained probably from the Hudson's Bay Company, and poisoned for six inches. *Frémont, Pathmarker of the West*, pp. 250-51.

11

THE PARTY now began to hear rumors, subsequently verified, that the local authorities were negotiating with the English for naval forces "to stop the progress of the ambitions of
the Americans." And when, later, H. M. S. *Collingwood* actually put into Monterey with Admiral Seymour on board, it
seemed to Frémont, as well as to all the American settlers in
northern California, that the time had come to *act*. To cap
everything, Castro was authoritatively reported to be inciting
the savages to a murderous uprising against all the whites,
demanding, as Gillespie afterward reported to the Navy Department, not only the burning of wheat fields, cattle, and
homes, and the wholesale slaughter of the men, but "the
ravishing of the women and the destruction of the children."
As Nevins says, this threat was not to be taken lightly.

In their consequent excitement and alarm the American
settlers somehow fell under the leadership of a Massachusetts
carpenter with a flair for literary composition: one William B.
Ide of the 1845 crop of immigrants, who lived with his family
well up on the West bank of the Sacramento River, and who
is variously described by historians as "a shrewd, fussy, dog-
matic Jack-of-all-trades" and as "a man who, like Cæsar,
could 'both write and fight and at each was equally skilful.'"

Ide's account of the Revolt, which culminated June 14,
1846, was written at the time:

About forty days since, a proclamation was issued by the Spaniards, ordering all foreigners to leave the country, and forbidding
them to take any of their property with them, at the same time
threatening them with extermination should they presume to remain in the country. The immigration to the States was gone;
the company for Oregon had left us. There was now no alternative but to die silently, and singly, by the hands of our enemies,

or fly to meet the foe. Information had reached the upper end of Sacramento valley (where I resided) that 200 Spaniards were on their way up the valley for the purpose of destroying our wheat, burning our houses, and driving off our cattle. Aroused by appearances so shocking, a very few of us resolved to meet our enemy (being encouraged by the known presence of Captain Frémont's command in the valley) and dispose of our difficulties in the best possible manner. The 200 Spaniards proved to be a band of horses (about 200) guarded by a Spanish officer and 15 men, being driven up the valley as far as Captain Sutter's, thence across the river for the lower settlements, for the declared and express purpose of being mounted by soldiers and sent back to enforce said proclamation. In self-defence, those few men (viz., 12, led by Ezekiel Merritt) seized the moment and pursued those horses, captured their guard and drove the horses to the neighborhood of Captain Frémont's camp. Still writhing under the dreadful necessity above alluded to, we pursued our way night and day, adding to our number a few true hearts to the number of 34 men, until the dawn of the morning of the 14th inst., when we charged upon the Fortress of General Vallejo, and captured 18 prisoners (among whom were three of the highest officers in the Californian Government and all the military officers who reside in Sonoma), 8 field-pieces, 200 stand of arms, a great quantity of cannon, canister, and grape-shot, and a little less than 100 pounds of powder (quite too little to sustain us against an attack by the use of cannon). By the articles of capitulation, it was contemplated we were to be provisioned by the generosity of our captured general, while we can keep possession, or while opposition renders possession necessary. By another arrangement of cannon and field-pieces, we have strengthened our position and continue to hold it, under the authority of 24 well-armed men and (as we have good right to believe) the will of the people. The *Alcalde* we discharged under a new appointment, the soldiers were set at liberty, and the said officers were escorted by ten armed men to an asylum under the generous protection of Captain Frémont. This day we proclaim California a Republic.

So President Polk got his republic, but something had gone wrong with it. It was not set up by the native sons, as Buchanan had suggested, but by American settlers imperiled by Castro's frightfulness, which, many observers thought, had been instigated by foreign plotters. But the President had his "alibi" handy, so when Frémont was subsequently court-martialed in Washington in consequence of an imbroglio arising from the Bear Flag incident, the President forfeited Senator Benton's friendship by consenting to Frémont's humiliation.

But this is to run ahead of the story.

12

"IT WAS decided that the Republic must have a flag, and William Todd (a nephew of Mrs. Abraham Lincoln) set out to make one," reported James McChristian, years later.

I watched him work. A Mrs. Elliott furnished the white cloth which formed the body of the flag from a bolt of cotton she had at her home. The flag was small, about twenty inches long. For the red stripe at the bottom Mrs. Josefa Matthews, a Spanish woman, wife of an American express rider, contributed a piece of her petticoat. I stood by William Todd when he painted the flag. He got the paint from the Vallejo place.

The flag was raised about five days after Merritt and his men took possession of Sonoma.

My father and I left Sonoma after the Bear Flag Republic was started, and they sent word for us to come back in time for the flag raising. Then we learned that Torre [one of Castro's officers] and his men were about to attack the settlement and massacre the Americans. We had two cannon, and Jack Randsford, a former British man-of-war's man, was in charge of them. We had some ammunition, but no powder, and sent two men over to San Rafael to get some. They were Fowler and Tom Cowey. Cowey and my father were close friends.

We found their bodies later. Torre and his men had met them, tied them to trees, riddled their bodies with bullets and mutilated them terribly.

We pursued Torre and his band and killed three of their men in retaliation.

After the American flag had been raised in San Francisco [on July 9] Commander Montgomery sent Lieutenant Revere and his son, Midshipman John E. Montgomery, to Sonoma to replace the Bear Flag with the American Flag.

When the Bear Flag was hauled down, young Montgomery, who was just my age, took it and put it in his pocket, saying that he wanted to send it back East.[27]

13

FRÉMONT'S own troubles had begun as soon as he pitched camp at the base of the "Buttes of Sacramento" the end of May. Here settlers confirmed rumors he had heard of Castro's murderous plans, including ravages by the Indians, now immediately impending. He knew at first hand the indescribable horrors Indians could perpetrate, and promised protection. Presently he kept this promise by forestalling an Indian attack with one of his own. He had resolved to "strike them a blow which would make them recognize that Castro was far and that he was near," taking such precautionary measures as would leave no enemy in his rear to cut off supplies or break his communications with the settlers.

Accordingly, early one morning he moved stealthily out of camp with most of his men, and trailed along the western bank of the big river.

This movement was quite unexpected. Riding rapidly up-

---

[27] *San Francisco Call,* September 10, 1911. Zoeth Eldredge says that the actual killing of Fowler and Cowey, after they had surrendered, was done by a member of Torre's band named Garcia, commonly called "Four-Fingered Jack." *Beginnings of San Francisco,* Vol. I, p. 404.

river, he reached without discovery the first *rancheria* of his foes. Scouts whom he had sent ahead reported them with feathered headgear on and their faces painted black, their war color—in short, celebrating their war ceremonies.

Frémont charged his rough riders directly upon them, killing several in the ensuing scatteration. Panic-stricken, many of them jumped into and swam the Sacramento, while a few escaped into the thickets lining its banks.

Frémont spurred on toward the other *rancherias,* but news of his approach preceded him by grape-vine telegraph, for the Indians were already in flight when he rode in among them. Before the day ended he had paid visits to nearly all the *rancherias,* and dispersed their inhabitants. As he rode down a hill commanding a wide view of the plain he could see them everywhere in commotion, some running away from the river and others leaping into it. By the time he reached the last *rancheria* the broad stream was dotted with the heads of swimming Indians. He had surprised them at the very height of their engrossing ceremonies.

This sharp action prevented the massacre of the whites, and they never forgot it.

It was during these anxious days that Ezekiel Merritt brought to Frémont's camp the officers mentioned by Ide as having been captured at Sonoma: General Mariano Vallejo and his brother Salvador, his brother-in-law Jacob Leese, and a Colonel Prudon. General Vallejo had expressed a preference for Frémont as his keeper if he had to have one, but the Captain declined the honor of keeping him, on the ground of inadequate accommodations; and sent him and his companions on to Sutter's Fort, where a flag with a single star upon it denoted that Frémont claimed possession.

Affairs had now become so critical that he characteristically decided "rather to govern events than to be governed by them." He knew all the facts, as he records, but could not share them, so he assumed full responsibility for acting on his knowledge. Against the Mexican government, with which he knew he was contending, sporadic actions by the settlers could meet only a temporary success, which would turn into disaster so soon as the Mexican government's troops were brought to bear upon them. "I represented the Army and the Flag of the United States," he says, "and the Navy (through Commander Montgomery of the *Portsmouth*) was apparently co-operating. This gave to my movements the national character which must of necessity be respected by Mexico, and by any foreign power to which she might ally herself; and would also hold offensive operations in check until actual war between the governments should make an open situation."

In this emergency he did a fine and generous thing, although his enemies later tried to turn it against him. "In order to place it in the power of my government to disavow my action should it become expedient to do so, I drew up my resignation from the Army to be sent by the first opportunity to Senator Benton, for transmission to the War Department, in the event of such a contingency."

"Captain Sutter," he adds, "was an officer under the Mexican Government, and I thought it best to place in charge of the Fort Mr. Edward Kern, who is already known as the topographer and artist of my exploring expedition."

This replacement of Sutter by Kern was preceded by the inevitable clash between Frémont and Sutter. Sutter precipitated it, by upbraiding Frémont for "harsh and arbitrary" behavior. Bidwell reports that Sutter came to him immediately afterward with his big blue eyes suffused with tears, complaining that the Captain had called him a Mexican, and had even said that if he didn't like what was going on he could be ferried across the San Joaquin so as to go and join the Mexicans! Later, when Sutter complained to Carson that the

Captain seemed unfriendly, Kit merely replied, "Remember that letter!"—mentioned on page 94.

Sutter's swift recovery and his weathercock loyalty appear in *Sutter's Own Story,* [28] when he boasts that by the simple act of throwing open his gates he now renounced his allegiance to the Mexican Government and threw in his lot with the forces of the United States.

Bidwell says of General Vallejo and his companions that for want of a suitable prison they were placed in Sutter's parlor, which had but one door, guarded by a sentinel. "Frémont gave me special directions about the safety of the prisoners, and I understood him to put them under my special charge."

Bidwell must have misunderstood him, for Kern was in charge of the prisoners and of Bidwell himself and everybody else in the Fort. As Nevins puts it, Frémont had executed a double stroke: he had taken control not only of Sonoma, but of the stronghold of the redoubtable Swiss, who shortly became Kern's adjutant as a lieutenant of dragoons at a salary of $50 a month.

Although Frémont seems to have treated General Vallejo with unnecessary harshness, this genial gentleman bore no malice, but, instead, supported the American occupation. Later, he distinguished himself in the Constitutional Convention, as will appear.

14

AFTER a few days Bidwell became convinced that Kern really had charge of the distinguished prisoners, and that a new régime had arrived. He even decided to "go over and join Frémont at Sonoma." Ide, he remarked with heavy sarcasm, "nearly every day wrote something in the form of a

[28] P. 171.

proclamation and posted it on the old Mexican flag-staff," but he claimed for himself the authorship of the "Bear Flag Platform":

The undersigned hereby agree to organize for the purpose of gaining and maintaining the independence of California.[29]

But the Bear Flag Platform proper, much longer than this, was written by William B. Ide. One enthusiastic California historian says of it that "if the Bear Flag Republic had produced nothing more than this magnificent contribution to the literature of human rights, the affair had sufficient excuse for existence." Ide's document ran:

A proclamation to all persons and citizens of the District of Sonoma, requesting them to remain at peace and follow their rightful occupations without fear of molestation.

The Commander-in-Chief of the troops assembled at the fortress of Sonoma gives this inviolable pledge to all persons in California, not found under arms, that they shall not be disturbed in their persons, their property or social relation, one with another, by men under his command.

He also solemnly declares his object to be: First, to defend himself and companions in arms, who were invited to this country by a promise of lands on which to settle themselves and families; who were also promised a Republican Government: when, having arrived in California, they were denied the privilege of buying or renting lands of their friends; who, instead of being allowed to participate in or being protected by a Republican Government, were oppressed by a military despotism; who were even threatened by the chief officers of the aforesaid despotism with extermination if they should not depart out of the country, leaving all their property, arms and beasts of burden; and thus deprived of their means of flight or defense, were to be driven through deserts inhabited by hostile Indians, to certain destruction.

[29] Facsimile in *Century Magazine*, February, 1891, p. 518.

To overthrow a Government which has seized upon the property of the Missions for its own aggrandizement; which has ruined and shamefully oppressed the laboring people of California by enormous exactions on goods imported into the country, is the determination of the brave men who are associated under my command.

I also solemnly declare my object, in the second place, to be to invite all peaceable and good citizens of California who are friendly to the maintenance of good order and equal rights, and I do hereby invite them, to repair to my camp at Sonoma without delay to assist us in establishing and perpetuating a Republican Government, which shall secure to all civil and religious liberty; which shall encourage virtue and literature; which shall leave unshackled by fetters, agriculture, commerce and manufactures.

I further declare that I rely upon the rectitude of our intentions, the favor of Heaven and the bravery of those who are bound and associated with me by the principles of self-preservation, by the love of truth and the hatred of tyranny, for my hopes of success.

I furthermore declare that I believe that a Government to be prosperous and happy must originate with the people who are friendly to its existence; that the citizens are its guardians, the officers its servants, its glory its reward.

15

THE SPANIARDS, with few exceptions, could not read Ide's proclamation, but they ridiculed William Todd's grizzly bear by saying it resembled a shoat! Allan Nevins, however, correctly declares that the Bear Flag, however hastily and crudely concocted, was a symbol to which the settlers attached the utmost importance, because *it meant order*. Only one unruly member of their group dared suggest that Sonoma should be sacked, but Dr. Semple comments that "an unanimous indignant frown made him shrink from the presence of honest men."

Within a few days Frémont openly joined the group, riding to their relief on June 25 when they were menaced by Castro. He had now recruited 160 men of varied nationality, but mainly Americans, "clad in homespun, in bear or antelope skins, and not a few in war-paint; their speech a jargon of a dozen languages, their allegiance belonging to a score of nations. In the joy of brotherhood and of battle they raised above their incongruous ranks the hastily improvised likeness of a grizzly bear" [30]—improvised by an eager young frontiersman who called Mrs. Abraham Lincoln "Aunt Mary"—and the Bear Flag Republic possessed the nucleus of an army.

16

H. H. BANCROFT, who by his amazing energy and industry made himself a sort of autocrat in Californian history, clamors for attention at this point. His history denounces this band of minutemen as "vagabond settlers," whose "criminal outbreak" would not have occurred, it says, "but for Frémont's promise of active support when needed," so that the "filibuster" who "ran away in the night" from Hawk's Peak in the Gavilan Mountains "must be held responsible not only for the bloodshed and bitterness of feeling that attended the conflict of 1846-7, but for the much more disastrous state of affairs which but for sheer good luck (the simultaneous announcement of the outbreak of the Mexican War) must have resulted."

Bancroft, who came West in 1852 as a youth of twenty, ran a San Francisco book-store for many years, devoting all his leisure to collecting Californiana until he actually had some 60,000 items. Becoming absorbed in the novel history of his adopted State and section, he devoted the next twenty years

[30] Valeska Bari in *The Course of Empire*: Coward-McCann, Inc., New York, 1931, p. 64.

or so to expounding it with his own untrained pen and the
pens of hired assistants.[31] From his own printing presses he
then published, and sold by itinerant book-agents, the thirty-
nine bulky volumes that form today, together with the 60,000
items just mentioned, and many valuable manuscripts, the
"Bancroft Library" at the University of California: an ency-
clopædic collection that no student of the West can ignore.

But despite such industry and the value of much of his out-
put, Bancroft's personal equation, according to his critics, embraced factors of prejudice and even malice that must be kept
constantly in mind by every beneficiary of his labors. If this
is not done, and done scrupulously, the critics fear that the
sour fruits of numerous annotated onslaughts on Bancroft's
pet "hates" may be spread abroad to the hurt of history and
the defamation of the dead. Bancroft, with a flair for publicity that would distinguish him even today, obtained such a
vogue when his books appeared in the eighteen-nineties that
nearly every author tackling a comparatively new field accepted him at his own valuation. Even a philosophical historian like Josiah Royce, referring to him abundantly, followed in his train in vilifying the Bear Flag uprising and
Frémont as its leader.

Fortunately, just after the voluminous history appeared, a
group of venerable men who had known members of the
Bear Flag party and Frémont himself personally, undertook
rectification of the more egregious errors. Unfortunately, the
findings of this group of members of the Society of California
Pioneers were given out impermanently, in a local newspaper
and a now scarce pamphlet.

The *San Francisco Call* reported on February 5, 1894, that
indignation had led the society of the forty-niners to consider
cancellation of Mr. Bancroft's honorary membership "some

[31] These assistants are named in the Oregon *Historical Quarterly*, Vol. IV,
pp. 287-364.

months ago," but that it decided to postpone action until a committee might carefully examine certain offensive statements, and their author be given opportunity to be heard in self-justification. So the committee went to work, after writing to the historian and informing him of what was in progress, and then continued at it, said the *Call,* "hoping that the author would make some reply and attempt to defend the way he had written up some of the pioneers. But no. The first letter brought no reply. A second one may never have reached its destination, for the committee is still waiting to hear of it being acknowledged, while a third epistle has been treated with the same silent contempt, and the members of the committee have concluded that they have waited long enough, and have closed up their report, and the same will be presented at the meeting of the society tonight."

Next morning the same newspaper reported that over a hundred members attended the meeting the night before and listened with deep attention to the committee's findings. "As the various calumnies, contradictions and misrepresentations were enumerated the indignation of the silver-haired audience increased in force, until finally it burst forth in approval of the scorching contempt of the committee, which denounced Bancroft. The bitter resentment culminated after a rousing speech by Judge R. Thompson in a unanimous vote to expel Bancroft from the society. The report on the resolution to expel Bancroft was signed by William Simpson, R. Thompson, S. W. Holladay and A. S. Hall. It was adopted with a roar of approval."

Not content with this summary of their transactions, the Society of California Pioneers had the Sterett Printing Company issue a 37-page pamphlet, saying in the Introduction that "the time has at last arrived when, in the judgment of the now old men who yet compose the majority of the members of this Society, the gross mis-statements . . . should be refuted, by the publication of the testimony of living witnesses, so that testimony may go upon record and be perpetuated, and the real facts and truth of history be vindicated." The body of the text includes Dr. William Simpson's account of the Bear Flag Revolt, which is of such value that it is here summarized:

At the time of this event, there were about 1000 Americans (in a population, including Indians, of 16,000) residing in California, every one of whom had enjoyed the blessings and advantages of our system of government, and who hoped and expected at some future time to see our flag waving over the territory upon which their new homes were built. This wish was intensified by the unhappy condition of things surrounding them, and which were gradually growing worse, as their numbers increased, by the aroused jealousy and suspicion of the Mexican and California officials. It was not only the weakness and instability of the government to which they were obliged to submit, or the insecurity of property, and discouragements to industry, which the Mexican system imposed, that caused the few Americans living here at that time to wish ardently for a change. A greater and far more serious interruption in the ordinary pursuits of life was impending, and growing more threatening from day to day. Texas had recently been annexed against the remonstrance of Mexico. The mission of Mr. Slidell to that country had been without a peaceful result, and had only produced new animosity. A large American force had been ordered near the Mexican border, and by these signs, as well as others, the coming war was easily predicted. It required no more than ordinary intelligence to foresee, in the expected hostilities, the loss of California to Mexico, and its probable conquest by either the United States or England. A peaceful cession to the latter country had been discussed by the California authorities, and was growing more popular among the native Californians as the rumors of war increased, and as their animosities against the Americans became excited by the critical condition of their mother country. While it remains to this day a matter of conjecture how far England was willing to proceed in securing to herself this territory, its peaceful surrender to her by the California authorities was not likely to be refused, and the whole American colony was in suspense and excitement in dread of such an occurrence. Their fortunes were not only dangerously involved in the outcome, but, during the period of expected hostilities between the United States and Mexico, they could easily anticipate the great danger and distress awaiting them. American residents within the seaports and vicinities were assured of protection by their country's warships, of which a number were already on the coast, but those of the interior had no other treatment to expect, in the event of war, than the well known Mexican methods of retaliation and punishment, and among these one quite likely to be invoked, and actually attempted later on, was the setting upon them of the Indians, who had not yet lost their sense of obedience to the California officials, so lately holding them in authority by the influence of the missions. The necessity of an organization among the Americans living in the interior was apparent, and while considering it an event occurred, which greatly aggravated the situation, and led to an immediate coming together of a number of settlers, not for defense only, but with the further purpose of assisting to secure the territory to the United States. The event spoken of was the accidental arrival, within the borders of California, of Frémont with his band of explorers. Frémont's difficulty with Castro, the details of which are too well known to require mention here, aroused that Mexican military commander to immediately issue proclamations of a warlike character, and to begin the organization of a military force.

There were a number of threatening rumors afloat besides, which, even admitting the extravagance of some of them, we know to have been generally believed. Bancroft himself furnishes evidence of this in the publication of the testimony, in a footnote, of no less than seventeen persons living at the time. These witnesses, among whom are a committee of citizens, in a report published in 1847—W. B. Ide, H. L. Ford, Wm. Hargrave, Benj. Dowell, Marshal, Semple, Hensley, Owens, Loker, Sutter and Frémont—all of whom agreed and believed that the Mexican government had determined upon the expulsion of the Americans from the country, and that Castro was inciting the Indians against them, and threatening to burn their crops, and that they would have to leave the country or fight for their homes. Although this strong array of evidence was set forth by Bancroft for the purpose of disproval, and, as we believe, to lay the foundation of a bitter attack upon a famous pioneer, its impeachment, under his examination, can have no effect whatever to impugn the motives of the settlers in organizing the "Bear Flag Revolt," since it cannot be denied they believed the rumors and were sincerely acting under the impressions they created.

The Bear insurrection was essentially a movement of defense. The grand possibilities of the country under a better administration, which time has so fully verified, were apparent to its movers, and furnished an additional motive to assist, either by direct or remote methods, to bring the territory under the dominion of the United States. The threatened misfortune of being placed under English, instead of American rule, had its effect also to promote and excuse that severity and promptness of action, so necessary to success in such an undertaking.

In the condemnation of the "Bear Flag Revolt," Bancroft lays great stress on what he terms its embarrassment to a peaceful conquest of the country. Some latter events ought to have proved to his mind that a ready submission, by the mere raising of American flags in the seaports, was not likely to have taken place. Whoever has reckoned on such a result, has made too low an estimate of the patriotism and bravery of the people with whom we had to deal. It is reasonable to conclude that their early submission was as much due to Frémont's ever-ready opposing force at hand, interrupting the progress of their concentration and unity of action, as it was to any measured hopelessness of their situation. We have a taste of what may have occurred, in the bloody engagements of San Pasquale, Natividad and elsewhere. An invitation of departure to the Americans must have come in due time under the usages of war, and by an early successful skirmish or two, unopposed by a thoroughly organized American force, arousing thus the hopes of the natives, and stimulating their patriotism to the bitter extremity perhaps of enlisting the Indians in their behalf; the comparatively small amount of bloodshed, of which Bancroft makes such virtuous complaint, would have been but as a drop in the bucket compared with that likely to have been spilt.

The intermediary stage of independence proposed by the "Bear Revolt" was a forced extremity, owing to the position, and suggested by the then recent example, of Texas. At the time of its organization, there was no way at hand to place it under the authority of the United States, and no military authority within a thousand miles to muster it into service. Its proclamation of independence cuts but a small figure in its history, because of the willing abandonment of its flag, and the substitution of the "Stars and Stripes" within less than a month of its independent organization. Its ready mergence into the California Battalion, under the flag of the United States, and the heartfelt and genuine enthusiasm expressed by its members on the raising of the American flags at San Francisco, Monterey, Los Angeles and elsewhere, leaves no doubt of their loyalty and patriotism. Their individual careers, down to the present time, exhibit more than an average of usefulness and prominence in society.

We are therefore of the opinion that Bancroft has neither fairly nor truthfully set forth the motives and character of the "Bear Flag Revolt," in his *History of California,* and his allusion to it as the "criminal outbreak of vagabond settlers" is flagrantly and maliciously untrue.

On another page, this publication of the highly honorable Society of California Pioneers declares that throughout the Bancroft history "Frémont is constantly misrepresented, and the part that he played in the acquisition of California is constantly belittled and distorted to suit a seemingly vengeful malice existing in the mind of the historian."

Jessie, in her unpublished memoirs, says with biting sarcasm that the California historian "was frequently taken for the *Honorable* Mr. Bancroft, as I will call him by way of distinguishing him. The Honorable Mr. Bancroft was so interested by the mis-statements (of the other one) that he went to see Mrs. Polk at Nashville, Tennessee, a serious journey for a man of eighty, but he wished to refresh his memory by an inspection of President Polk's papers. Mrs. Polk gave him the whole of them, to be used as he saw fit. He intended writing an account of the way California came to be ours, but the loss of energy belonging with his great age resulted only in the statements he gave me" (see pages 81, 98).

Besides Mr. H. H. Bancroft, the *Los Angeles Star* attacked Frémont, specifically accusing him of cruelty and rapacity in his treatment of the native Californians during and after the Bear Flag Revolt. In refutation, Reuben L. Underhill cites a letter from Consul Larkin of Monterey (dated August 2, 1856) testifying that the accused lived in his house for weeks on end, at various times, and that he had found him "of reserved and distant manners, active & industrious in his official duties, anxious to finish the business on hand & before him & to be on the march to accomplish more," never coarse or profane, always "polite, kind and courteous." Larkin's verdict is emphatic: "I consider Mr. Frémont a just, correct, and moral man, abstemious, bold, and persevering." [32] And it is pleasant to quote a statement of a political opponent, James Buchanan, afterward President of the United States, that "his services were very valuable; he bore a conspicuous part in the conquest of California, and in my opinion is better entitled to be called the conqueror of California than any other man." [33]

[32] Reuben L. Underhill, *From Cowhides to Golden Fleece:* Stanford University Press, 1939, p. 252.
[33] *Frémont, Pathmarker of the West,* p. 446.

17

APART from its relation to the acquisition of California by the United States, the Bear Flag Revolt may be characterized as both a culmination and a point of departure.

It was the culmination of numerous efforts, beginning with the clutching hand of the Tsar in 1804, and coming on down through individual attempts at seizure by such little Napoleons as Sutter, Marsh, and Hastings, and the religious or nationalistic efforts of a McNamara or a Eugène Duflot de Mofras to the final determination of hard-pressed and hard-bitten frontiersmen like Ezekiel Merritt and William Ide and Dr. Robert Semple to protect themselves and their families, and at the same time save the province, in which they had cast their lot, to the nation of their birth, the culmination of numerous sporadic efforts in a final wresting of the golden pomegranate from its withered stem and proclaiming to the world its separate and independent existence, which they pledged themselves to maintain. Whether the land of their birth would consent to receive the province as a state was a different affair altogether. As a matter of fact, four years and more intervened between the first raising of the American flag over Californian soil and the admission of California into the Union. But the pioneers had done their part, and were willing to stand by this new political entity and devote themselves to its protection and development with all the zeal that characterized their kind.

Besides, this infant but opulent "republic," with all it had cost its progenitors, and all it stood for, marked a beginning as well as an end. It was a source from which a new stream of influence flowed. Here was a State which the rough and ready pioneers had molded with their own hearts and brains, and defended with their lives. While willing, even eager, to see it received into the starry field of the great flag they loved, they felt a sense of ownership in it, an intense guardianship of it, a deep-seated right to determine its ultimate destiny.

To them, it should always be remembered, California was born as a State; a Minerva, full-orbed, as they were later to express in the symbolism they embossed upon its shield. It was a State, and it was theirs; theirs to say how it should be treated, and under what escutcheon, if any except its own, it should march.

March it would, but these early American settlers would insist on determining where and how, and their spirit of ownership and independence was transmitted to their coadjutors and successors when the unbelievable magic of "Sutter's gold" in '49 brought an influx of men such as no part of the western world had ever known, with the possible exception of the Crusades.

The Bear Flag Republic, then, while short-lived as a fact, survived as an influence, and its spirit was to make itself felt in the crisis of the Civil War, as will irrefutably appear.

A ROW AND A COURT-MARTIAL

1

IMPREGNABLE during the twenty-five days of its existence, the Bear Flag Republic joyfully proved its desire to submerge its life into that of the Union when word came that (on July 7) Commodore John D. Sloat had raised the Stars and Stripes at Monterey. Frémont felt vastly relieved by this Monterey news, followed as it was two days later by identical information from San Francisco, where Commander Montgomery, on orders from Sloat, hoisted the flag on the Plaza,

which is still called Portsmouth Square in honor of Montgomery's ship. As long ago as May 31, at Mazatlan, Sloat had
been informed of the battles of Palo Alto and Resaca de la
Palma, but, with "a most unfortunate and unwarranted in-
activity," to quote Secretary of the Navy Bancroft, he failed
to carry out his clear instructions to seize California ports,
until his nerve was steadied by the news of Frémont's operations. Then, and not until then, he took "his preposterously
belated action." On July 9 he dispatched formal information
of everything that had happened to Frémont, in whose veins
ran blood instead of the enfeebled fluid of illness and senility.

On July 12 Frémont got a request from Sloat to visit him on
the flagship, which chanced to be named *Savannah* after the
city of Frémont's birth. As soon as he could make ready he
set out with his force of 160 rough-and-readys. In due time
this California Battalion, "a body unlike any other that has
ever fought on American soil," was indelibly portrayed by a
lieutenant from H. M. S. *Collingwood,* lying in the harbor
near the *Savannah,* as they rode into Monterey:

Here were true trappers, the class that produced the heroes of
Fenimore Cooper's best works. These men had passed years in
the wilds, living upon their own resources; they were a curious
set. A vast cloud of dust appeared first, and thence in long file
emerged this wildest wild party. Frémont rode ahead, a spare,
active-looking man, *with such an eye!* He was dressed in a blouse
and leggings, and wore a felt hat. After him came five Delaware
Indians, who were his bodyguard, and have been with him
through all his wanderings; they had charge of two baggage
horses. The rest, many of them blacker than the Indians, rode
two and two, the rifle held by one hand across the pommel of
the saddle. Thirty-nine of them are his regular men, the rest are
loafers picked up lately; his original men are principally back-
woodsmen, from the State of Tennessee and the banks of the
upper waters of the Missouri. He has one or two with him who

enjoy a high reputation in the prairies. Kit Carson is as well known there as "the Duke" is in Europe. The dress of these men was principally a long loose coat of deer skin, tied with thongs in front; trowsers of the same, of their own manufacture, which, when wet through, they take off, scrape well inside with a knife, and put on as soon as dry; the saddles were of various fashions, though these and a large drove of horses, and a brass field-gun [*not* the famous howitzer], were things they had picked up in California. They are allowed no liquor—tea and sugar only; this, no doubt, has much to do with their good conduct, and the discipline, too, is very strict. They were marched up to an open space on the hills near the town, under some large firs, and there took up their quarters, in messes of six or seven, in the open air. The Indians lay beside their leader. One man, a doctor, six feet six high,[34] was an odd-looking fellow. May I never come under his hands!

Admiral Seymour of the *Collingwood*[35] is reported to have said to the American commodore, "Sloat, if your flag was not flying on shore, I should have hoisted mine there!" Nevertheless, the sallow and fidgety little Sloat caught a bad case of jitters when informed by Frémont that he had assisted in the Bear Flag Revolt without specific written orders from Washington! And, having now fulfilled his own specific written instructions, albeit tardily, he was glad enough to sail away on the leave of absence for which he had applied, as soon as Commodore Robert F. Stockton sailed into Monterey harbor with the *Congress* and *Cyane* to relieve him.

Benton's view of events, from the Bear Flag Revolt to the arrival of Commodore Stockton at Monterey, is tersely presented in the *Thirty Years' View.*

He says of the Revolt:

This movement for Independence was the salvation of Califor-

---

[34] Robert Semple was really six feet eight.
[35] The British frigate *Juno* also lay near by, at Santa Barbara.

nia, and snatched it out of the hands of the British at the moment
they were ready to clutch it. For two hundred years—from the
time of the navigator Drake, who almost claimed it as a discovery, and placed the English name of New Albion upon it—the
eye of England has been upon California; and the magnificent
bay of San Francisco, the great seaport of the North Pacific
Ocean, has been surveyed as her own. The approaching war between Mexico and the United States was the crisis in which she
expected to realize the long-deferred wish for its acquisition; and
carefully she took her measures accordingly. She sent two squad-
rons to the Pacific as soon as Texas was incorporated—well seeing the actual war which was to grow out of that event—a small
one into the mouth of the Columbia, an imposing one to Mazatlan, on the Mexican coast, to watch the United States squadron
there, and to anticipate its movements upon California. Commodore Sloat, commanding the squadron at Mazatlan, saw that he
was watched, and pursued, by Admiral Seymour, who lay along-
side of him, and he determined to deceive him. He stood out to
sea, and was followed by the British Admiral. During the day he
bore west, across the ocean, as if going to the Sandwich Islands;
Admiral Seymour followed. In the night the American Commodore tacked, and ran up the coast towards California; the British
Admiral, not seeing the tack, continued on his course, and went
entirely to the Sandwich Islands before he was undeceived. Commodore Sloat arrived before Monterey on the 2d of July, entering the port amicably; and offering to salute the town, which the
authorities declined on the pretext that they had no powder to
return it—in reality because they momentarily expected the
British fleet. Commodore Sloat remained five days before the
town, and until he heard of Frémont's operations; then believing
that Frémont had orders from his government to take California,
he determined to act himself. He received the news of Frémont's
successes on the 6th day of July: on the 7th he took the town
of Monterey, and sent a dispatch to Frémont. This latter came to
him in all speed, at the head of his mounted force. The commodore learnt with astonishment that Frémont had no orders from
his government to commence hostilities—that he had acted en-

tirely on his own responsibility. . . . Uneasiness came upon the commodore. He remembered the fate of Captain Jones in making the mistake of seizing the town once before in time of peace. He resolved to return to the United States, which he did—turning over the command of the squadron to Commodore Stockton, who had arrived on the 15th. The next day (16th) Admiral Seymour arrived; his flag-ship the *Collingwood*, of eighty guns, and his squadron the largest British fleet ever seen in the Pacific. To his astonishment he beheld the American flag flying over Monterey, the American squadron in its harbor, and Frémont's mounted riflemen encamped over the town. His mission was at an end. The prize had escaped him.[36]

2

BETWEEN Stockton and Frémont a warm relationship developed—which occasionally, in fact, grew heated. The newly arrived commodore, who was not above turning to his own advantage the cordial relations between the Pathfinder and the Secretary of the Navy, added eight marines to the California Battalion and marshaled it into naval service, with Frémont as major and Gillespie as captain, before hustling all on board and weighing anchor for San Diego. Castro was reported as lined up for battle there, but the report proved false. So Stockton's horse marines struck off up the coast for Los Angeles, which they entered with a brass band August 13, 1846, "having more the effect of a parade of home guards than of an enemy taking possession of a captured town." Justin Smith, in his *War with Mexico* says that Consul Larkin "with a couple of friends took Los Angeles on the twelfth of August," [37] while the Commodore with his marines and brass band, and Frémont with a part of his battalion, came in next

[36] Thomas Hart Benton, *Thirty Years' View*, Vol. II, pp. 691-92.
[37] Vol. I, p. 337.

day; but the thirteenth is the commonly accepted date of the American occupation of the City of the Angels.

Frémont's star now rode high. The Bear Flag Revolt, with less than a dozen fatalities, had resulted in the seizure of northern California by the United States. Southern California had apparently submitted without any bloodshed at all, and would probably have remained submissive except for subsequent unfortunate engagements by Gillespie, Mervine, and Kearny. Before those occurred, Frémont, as ordered by his commodore, marched triumphantly back into the Sacramento Valley, to muster his battalion to full strength. Stockton presently appointed him military governor of the Territory of California. But like a fallen Lucifer he swiftly descended from this high estate to become scapegoat in a dispute between Stockton and Kearny—Navy versus Army—and to face the threat of court-martial. To meet this ordeal he was treated as a captive and marched all the way to Washington, tied, as it were, to General Stephen Watts Kearny's chariotwheel. Such were some of the hardships Frémont suffered in behalf of California.

El Toro del Sacramento shared them. An admirer of the horse rather than its rider says that during the course of Frémont's activities before he was marched away to Washington he had to leave his horses in the Sacramento Valley. When he needed them again a Captain Burroughs was sent to Sutter for them. "Hold well your rein," the Duke of New Helvetia called to Burroughs when delivering over Sacramento; reminding him that the spirited animal had been born near the Tulare lakes, and, if allowed loose, would seek again his old haunts. The mounts were driven without especial difficulty over the Coast Ranges and on to the plains in the region of the present city of Salinas. Here their drivers found their way blocked by a body of Californian cavalry. In the ensuing skirmish they made a brave but foolhardy charge upon the enemy. Among the Californians rode the evil villain "Three-Fingered Jack." When Jack's eyes spied Sacramento they narrowed with greed. Nothing more was seen or heard of the beautiful beast until April, 1848, when two men crossing the plain of the San Joaquin came upon a drove of wild horses that dashed away as the men approached. Leading the herd was a superb iron-gray stallion with flowing white mane and tail, Sacramento beyond doubt. For years afterward he was seen now and then upon the plains, becoming a legendary figure, famous wherever horse lore prevailed. At last, in 1855, the story came of his final run. The horse-thieving Indians built the long corral that trapped him. Chased into this corral by whooping savages, he found, too late, that it led into the swamp of Lake Tulare. "There, amid the mud and tules, the noble Sacramento, the savior of Kit Carson, the faithful trail horse of the Pathfinder, breathed his last, struggling to the end for the freedom he loved so dearly."[38]

3

KEARNY'S dispatch to the West had been bound up with the westward trek of the Mormons. Polk authorized Kearny to enlist from among them five companies of a hundred men each, for one year's service, thus forming a Mormon Battalion led by Lieutenant Colonel St. George Cooke. Meantime, in the spring of 1846, from twelve to fifteen thousand Latter-Day Saints left Nauvoo for California, under their major prophet, Brigham Young, preceded by Samuel Brannan, who sailed from New York February 4 with 238 colonists in his chartered ship *Brooklyn*. So disappointed was Brannan on finding Commander Montgomery's flag flying on the Plaza when the *Brooklyn* reached San Francisco (still called Yerba

[38] John A. Hussey, *op. cit.*

Buena), that he swore a loud oath at being three weeks too
late. If Frémont had not been expeditious with the Bear Flag
Revolt, and thus led Sloat to his flag-raising, Lansford Warren
Hastings[39] might have prevailed with his ambitious presidential plan, having Brannan's nucleus to start with, and
more, as he thought, to follow.

Sam Brannan's oath, it should be said, expressed little more
than a natural disappointment, and not a hatred of the flag.
He had counted on raising the Stars and Stripes with his own
rugged hands, or, at the worst, seizing a Mexican province
out of hand, instead of which he found himself and his co-
religionists back in the same old United States from which
they had sailed—which seemed to his adventurous spirit
pretty tame.

Recovering from his disappointment, and quickly appraising California as the true Promised Land, Sam lost little time
in riding out to meet Brigham Young's pilgrims in the wilderness so as to guide them to it. He found them in the Green
River country, and then retraced his trail with them as far as
Salt Lake, where Brigham, unmoved by Sam's eloquence, decided to remain. Deeply displeased by such stubbornness,
Sam rode back alone, and was soon vying with Judge Hastings as a Californian "realtor." [40]

Within a fortnight of the *Brooklyn's* anchoring in San Francisco Bay, General Kearny, on the Santa Fé trail with his
dragoons, somewhere between Santa Fé and San Diego, met
Kit Carson hurrying eastward with official dispatches from
Stockton and private letters from Frémont. Kearny, much
against Kit's will, compelled him to go back, sending the mis-
sives east by special courier. Now, Kit had been instructed to
report to Washington that the conquest of California was
achieved; and, while Stockton and Frémont were of an opti-

[39] P. 87.
[40] James A. B. Scherer, *The First Forty-Niner.*

mistic temperament, the conquest would actually have been achieved by the time Kit reached Washington, as the event proved. But Kearny accepted the *fait accompli* as of equal date with Kit's arrival in his camp, and, accordingly, returned all but a hundred of his dragoons to their Santa Fé garrison. He had not proceeded far on his resumed march toward San Diego when Lieutenant Gillespie met him, with word that Stockton's luck had turned against him, and that the cocky commodore was under siege at San Diego. The Mormon Battalion had not as yet come up, and Kearny seemed all too glad to welcome reinforcements to the number of Gillespie's meager escort. Soon he found himself severely punished for his misinterpretation of Kit Carson's news, in a defeat by Pio Pico at the Indian village of San Pasqual, halfway between Warners Ranch and San Diego. Sixteen or eighteen of his men were killed in this severest engagement in the entire conquest of California, and as many more wounded, besides himself. Only after Kit with two companions pluckily brought reinforcements from Stockton's command was his inadequate force extricated from mortal danger.

Sporadic engagements with Californians continued until a final battle, on January 9, 1847, led to the reoccupation of Los Angeles, where Gillespie had had to lower his flag in the previous autumn. One historian, Rockwell Hunt, says that while this "Battle of La Mesa" may seem inconsequential as a conflict, it was of vast consequence in the complete establishment of American supremacy. The Treaty of Cahuenga, signed by Frémont and Andreas Pico on January 13, sealed this supremacy.

4

A WORD must be said in extenuation of General Kearny, whom the chess-playing Polk had sent across the plains so as to make trebly sure of the golden pomegranate. Kearny finally entered San Diego humbled by defeat at the hands of foes whom he had underrated, only to find a pretentious naval officer, Commodore Stockton, claiming a command to which he also had been assigned, and to hear plaudits for an upstart explorer who had lost one of Kearny's brass howitzers in the Sierra Nevada, but was now the military governor (by Stockton's appointment) of an almost subjugated territory!

The ensuing triangular controversy still seems interminable. While this page was being written the *San Francisco Chronicle* contained a bitter comment from General Kearny's grandson, who, after reading Frémont's biography, feels that "if the circumstances in which Professor Nevins places General Frémont and Stockton are true, then Major General Stephen Watts Kearny was knave or fool."

The present writer rejects such an odious alternative, but accepts as fair and final the blessedly terse statement of Professor Frederic L. Paxson in his *History of the American Frontier:*

The resistance of the Californians to the American conquest was brief and slight. The Mexican troops were too few in number to offer serious obstruction, and the Mexican population was dispersed over too wide an area to be mobilized for defense. The bond of union with Mexico was fragile at best and was weakened by the glimpses of the outside world that Californians had gained because of their position on the Pacific. The forces of Sloat, Frémont, and the revolutionists were united in July, and Commodore Stockton who soon arrived to relieve Sloat continued active co-operation to make the conquest permanent. San Diego and Los Angeles were occupied, as well as all the places around the Bay. There was a revolt of the Spanish in southern California in the autumn, and Stockton was temporarily forced to abandon both San Diego and Los Angeles. But in December Kearny arrived by the Yuma route, and early in January, 1847, all resistance ceased. Thereafter the only trouble of the American commanders in California was whether Stockton or Kearny was in command, with authority to govern the province until the President should otherwise direct. Each had sweeping orders, from the Secretaries of War and the Navy respectively; and each was disposed to insist upon his own supremacy. They took it out upon Frémont, who had no orders at all[?], and was their junior. By giving him inconsistent commands, they forced him to disobedience; and eventually they arrested him and sent him east for court-martial.[41]

5

FRÉMONT'S court-martial—linked bitterness long drawn out—generated many poisonous sequels. The young and imperious "irregular" was adjudged guilty of mutiny and insubordination by a court of "regulars";[42] the President only partially pardoned him; Frémont, with true Charleston hauteur, indignantly rejected a pardon for an offense of which he felt himself innocent; and Senator Benton became Polk's relentless foe: all three of our *dramatis personae* running quite true to form. But Frémont had his compensations. Not only Jessie, but his old "home town" stood by him passionately. When he went south, just before his long trial, to see his dying mother, who had once been the gay young Virginian Anne Beverley Whiting, the *Charleston Mercury* (of September 21, 1847) gratified Jessie by announcing that in proof of their faith in his honor and integrity, South Caro-

[41] Pp. 368-69.
[42] It must be confessed that the "regulars" would have had to be almost superhuman not to resent the pungency of some of his statements, as when, at the close of his defense, he called the "difficulties in California" "a comedy of three errors: *first*, in the faulty orders sent out from this place; *next*, in the unjustifiable pretensions of General Kearny; *third*, in the conduct of the government in sustaining these pretensions. And the last of these errors I consider the greatest of the three."

linians, by contributions limited to a dollar for each individual, were preparing for his acceptance a special sword and belt.

The sword, formally presented soon after the next Congress opened, by a South Carolina representative, was a splendid blade, mounted with gold and silver. Round the hilt, which was shaped like the head of a palmetto tree, the State symbol, a rattlesnake was coiled, suggesting the State's old motto, *Nemo me impune lacessit*—especially applicable to Frémont. On the guard a miniature map, partly unrolled, revealed the Pacific Coast. On the solid gold scabbard two silver shields displayed respectively the name "California" and the date "1846." Still lower down on the scabbard a buffalo hunt was engraved, while between the two engravings appeared the inscription,

Presented
by the citizens of Charleston
to Lieutenant-Colonel
JOHN CHARLES FRÉMONT
A MEMORIAL OF THEIR HIGH APPRECIATION
OF THE GALLANTRY AND SCIENCE
HE HAS DISPLAYED IN HIS
SERVICES IN OREGON AND CALIFORNIA

A handsome gold-mounted belt, with the arms of the State on its clasp, was presented by the Charleston ladies. Charleston College had already forgotten its former student's "habitual irregularity and incorrigible negligence," and conferred on him its baccalaureate degree.

Bigelow characterizes the court-martial, which consumed three months of time and several tons of printing paper, as "probably the most memorable military trial ever held in the United States," adding: "The principal prosecutor was called to his last account a few weeks after the trial closed, and there are few, if any, left who care now to inquire into the motives which actuated him in the course he chose to pursue toward his gallant subordinate." The press of the country sided almost unanimously with the victimized officer, as they called Frémont, who, "like Columbus, returned from the discovery and conquest of a New World a prisoner and in disgrace." But, while he emerged from his ordeal a national hero, his fortune had been shattered, and his high-strung spirit almost broken.

During his long spiritual convalescence Jessie busied herself on a geographical memoir to accompany his new map of Oregon and California. She felt especially pleased with his notation of *Chrysopylae* at the entrance of San Francisco Bay, which thus became The Golden Gate before "Sutter's gold" was discovered. Bending over her task, one day in April, 1848, she was startled by the first note of joy she had heard from her husband's lips for months. She looked up to find him reading a letter from her father, in St. Louis. The old Trojan had been busy there, for no President Polk could play ducks and drakes with *his* son-in-law! "There are a lot of business men here," he wrote, "who want to finance a railroad to the Pacific Ocean, if you'll survey the route."

Frémont's elastic temperament reacted swiftly. Jessie thought she could actually see his shoulders straighten and his deep blue eyes light with their former fire. While he was still holding her father's letter she said, "Now I must hurry, indeed, for this memoir must be worthy of you!"

She finished it by the end of May, and on June 5 the Senate ordered the publication of 20,000 copies of the beautiful new map for which she had prepared her memoir. So the Frémont star was once more rising. But Jessie had overtaxed herself; her nervous system collapsed, and her eyes seemed on the verge of blindness from too close application to "this cursed memoir," as her husband for the moment called it.

Their son was born in July, and they named him Benton for the old man who had saved them. Elizabeth (Lily), now nearly six, bore her grandmother's name. Their thoughts turned towards a home. In fact, Frémont had longed for one while feeling "flush" in California, and had entrusted $3,000 to Consul Larkin with which to purchase a ranch, so that he now owned 44,380 acres of mountain land near the Yosemite Valley—an old Mexican land-grant known as the "Mariposas," or "Butterflies." Grandpa Benton leaped to the idea, and his friend Senator Dix of New York joined him in providing a loan for milling machinery and farming tools, to be shipped round the Horn while Frémont struck out once more upon the trail. "There will be no more long separations," he promised Jessie, after he should have finished this railroad survey.

JESSIE JOINS THE GOLD RUSH

1

OFF, THEN, to St. Louis and Buffalo by rail, and thence aboard the steamboat up to Westport, Kansas, starting point for another overland journey. "Nothing shows better the buoyant courage of the man than the fact that, a few months after the court-martial, he organized his own fourth expedition." And nothing could better prove the undaunted devotion of Jessie, the young mother of twenty-four, who, despite the sudden death of little Benton, accompanied her husband to Kansas and camped with him a while before returning to the Atlantic seaboard to make ready for her own voyage

across the Isthmus. "And so," she wrote, "with our early tea
for a stirrup cup, 'he gave his bridle rein a shake,' and we
went our ways, one into the midwinter snows of untracked
mountains, the other to the long sea voyage through the
tropics."

2

TERRIBLE as his exposure on former expeditions had been,
this fourth one was to imperil Frémont even more, due
chiefly to an error of judgment in choosing a mountain guide
to replace the faithful and expert Kit. Broken Hand had also
been unavailable, so at Pueblo, Colorado, the gate to the
Rocky Mountains, he engaged "Old Bill Williams." It was
November 25, 1848, and his former experience in the winter
Sierras should have warned him, quite apart from the character of his guide. But with a party of thirty-one men and a
hundred good mules he struck off across the St. John's Mountains, virgin territory, with a pilot afterward described by a
member of the party as an embodiment of the reckless and
extravagant propensities of mountaineers, who pursued his
perilous but lucrative vocation from an innate love of its
excitement and dangers. "He had no other care for the gains
of his labors than as a means of affording him a big spree,
and enabling him to procure more powder and lead. He was
a dead shot with a rifle, though he always shot with a 'double wabble'; he could never hold his gun still, yet his ball
went always to the spot on a single shot. Though a most indefatigable walker, he could never walk on a straight line,
but went staggering first to one side and then to the other.
He was an expert horseman; scarce a horse or mule could
unseat him. He rode leaning forward upon the pommel, with
his rifle before him, his stirrups ridiculously short, and his
breeches rubbed up to his knees, leaving his legs bare even

in freezing cold weather. He wore a loose monkey-jacket or a buckskin hunting shirt, and for his head-covering a blanket-cap, the two top corners drawn up into two wolfish, satyr-like ears, rendering his *tout ensemble* exceedingly ludicrous."

Micajah McGehee, the member of the fourth expedition who wrote it up for *The Century Magazine* (of March, 1891) dishes up horrors for those with a taste for such diet. For the present purpose it seems enough to say that in one instance the men in their extremity fed on the dead bodies of their companions. The addition made to geographical knowledge by this disastrous expedition was not great, although Frémont believed that had they not been misled by their guide they would have discovered the best of all routes to California.

The rescued remnant of his party moved in a southwesterly direction into New Mexico, where, at Taos, their leader was joyfully welcomed into the home of Kit Carson. Here while in bed with a badly frozen leg, he wrote to Jessie of the horrors his men had undergone, and also said of "Old Bill Williams": "The error of our journey was in engaging this man. He proved never to have in the least known, or entirely to have forgotten, the whole region of country through which we were to pass. We occupied more than half a month in making the journey of a few days; blundering a tortuous way through deep snow which already began to choke up the passes, for which we were obliged to waste time in searching."

It was after he left Taos, and while traveling along the south bank of the Gila River, with his party of twenty-one rescued men and sixteen animals, that on a hot forenoon he saw in the distance a cloud of dust through which he could vaguely discern the moving figures of men and women, children and dogs, mules and ox carts. He was utterly astonished, not knowing that gold had been discovered at Sutter's

Mill, and that he was witnessing the vanguard of the Gold
Rush. Jessie says that on hurrying forward he overtook a
whole community on the march, twelve hundred people in
all: babies crying, drivers bawling, mules tugging at the
lurching carts, horses saddled down with heavy packs. Spur-
ring up to the rear guard, Frémont shouted,

"Where are you going?"

"Alta California!" came the reply through choking dust.

"But why such a crowd of you?"

"*Gold!* GOLD!" came the answer.

3

JESSIE encountered the Gold Rush by sea. Although the
first nuggets were picked up at Sutter's Mill January 24,
1848, the news was disbelieved on the Atlantic seaboard until a special courier delivered into the President's hands a
tea-caddy filled with them, in the last month of that year;
whereupon the canny Scot perceived a magic formula for
populating his new province, and reported the tea-caddy
and its contents to Congress. The effect on the public was
electric. Nor was the means of their transportation lacking.
Mail service had just been established with the Pacific by
sending several brand-new steamers round the Horn to ply
between Panama City and San Francisco Bay, so that when
Jessie and Lily had crossed the Isthmus they found its western port a bedlam of gold-seekers clamoring for the next
northbound steamer. The *California* had already gone up,
and they awaited either her return or arrival of the *Panama*,
overdue from the Horn.

It was during the seven long weeks while the bereaved
young mother was lodging in Panama City with a Madam
Arcé, that she got the Taos letter from her husband reporting the death by starvation of ten of his men; cannibalism;

and his own bed-stricken plight; together with a Washington newspaper reporting a Benton interview wherein the old Senator confessed the fourth expedition a disaster, and stressed the hardships of Frémont. "My very life depends upon him about whom every fiber of my being is entwined," Jessie once wrote of her husband; so, although his Taos letter brought her "every element of torture," even in her anguish she detected one clear note of comfort: he still lived, and might even meet her in San Francisco.

With cabins for only eighty but an actual passenger list of nearly four hundred, the *Panama* at last weighed anchor, northward bound. Jessie and Lily were "accommodated" on deck with a tent improvised from an immense American flag draped over the spanker boom. Luckily, the tender-hearted young mother invited a Mrs. Gray to share her "accommodations"; luckily, because, just before the ship touched at San Diego, she went down with a hemorrhage from the lungs, and Mrs. Gray lovingly tended her in a decent cabin which a sympathetic passenger surrendered. But she was so fearful of bad news from her husband that she locked her cabin door even against Mrs. Gray as the engines stopped at the first California port, desiring that no one should witness her grief. But there came a pounding on the door as a man's voice shouted, "Mrs. Frémont, the Colonel's *safe!* He's riding to San Francisco to meet you! He didn't lose his leg—only a bad frost-bite!"

Throwing open her door, she was quickly surrounded; saying, later, "I think every man on the ship came to tell me, and say a choking word of joy for me!"

Braced as by a stimulant, she improved during the further trip up the coast; but, alas! when the *Panama* finally rounded Telegraph Hill at San Francisco, there was no Colonel Frémont to meet her.

The faithful Mrs. Gray now accompanied her to the fabu-

lous Parker House, whose ground floor commanded a rental
of $60,000 a year as a gambling saloon. Through an upper
window looking out onto Portsmouth Square, ten days after
her arrival, she heard somebody saying in the street, "Your
wife's inside, Colonel," and a moment later she was in his
arms.

4

THE YOUTHFUL and poetic Bayard Taylor came up on
the next trip of the *Panama*, sent out by Horace Greeley of
The *Tribune* to write up the American Golconda. "Of all the
marvelous phases of the Present," he wrote, "San Francisco
will most tax the belief of the Future. Its parallel was never
known, and shall never be beheld again. I speak only of
what I saw with my own eyes. Like the magic seed of the
Indian juggler, which grew, blossomed, and bore fruit before the eyes of his spectators, San Francisco seemed to
have accomplished in a day the growth of half a century."
In the matter of population alone it had grown from some
sixty inhabitants when Sam Brannan arrived to about 5,000,
to say nothing of the miners in the diggin's, including Frémont's Mariposas Ranch. One day in the United States Hotel
this new Monte Cristo, so lately sunk in peril, illness, and
despair, told Taylor that whereas the earlier findings in the
mining regions had been sparse and scattered nuggets, upon
his ranch the first continuous vein of gold had been un-
earthed. "I saw some specimens," Taylor wrote; "the stone
was a reddish quartz, filled with rich veins of gold, and far
surpassing specimens from North Carolina and Georgia.
Colonel Frémont informed me that the vein had been traced
more than a mile. The thickness on the surface is two feet,
gradually widening as it descends, and showing larger par-
ticles of gold. The dip downward is only about 20°, so that

the mine can be worked with little expense. His discovery made a great sensation, yet it was but the first of many such."

Bayard Taylor is sometimes criticized for an optimism equal to Frémont's, but he reported accurately in adding: "Many of my fellow-passengers by the *Panama* were realizing their dreams of speedy fortune. Some had already made $20,000 by speculating in town lots. A friend who had shipped lumber from New York to the amount of $1,000 sold it for $14,000. Seventy-five houses had been imported from Canton, and put up by Chinese carpenters. Washing was $8 a dozen, and, as a consequence, large quantities of soiled linen were sent to the antipodes to be purified. A vessel just in from Canton brought 250 dozen, which had been sent out a few months before. Another from the Sandwich Islands brought 100 dozen, and the practice was becoming general."

5

WHEN a boat had landed her upon Long Wharf from off the *Panama,* Jessie Frémont found herself in an immense throng of her fellow countrymen, all of them eager to learn that the discouraging rumors from Washington which had preceded her arrival were without foundation in fact, and that Congress had in some way recognized the existence of this remote territory where they wished to make their home. The crowd included some of the earlier settlers, pervaded by the spirit of the Bear Flag Revolt. There were even some Oregonians, among whom the ablest was the Tennessee-Missourian, Judge Peter H. Burnett, whom Frémont had met at The Dalles (see page 54), but who had joined the Gold Rush, together with about two-thirds of all the Oregon settlers. Burnett, an upright man though an excellent lawyer, had participated in meetings in San Francisco, San José, and Sacramento to promote a convention to frame a provisional government for California. He had also prepared for the self-styled Legislative Assembly of the District of San Francisco, which extended all the way down to San José, a remarkable "Address to the People of California."

The discovery of the rich and exhaustless gold-mines of California produced a singular state of things in this community, unparalleled, perhaps, in the annals of mankind. We have here in our midst a mixed mass of human beings from every part of the wide earth, of different habits, manners, customs, and opinions—*all*, however, impelled onward by the same feverish desire of fortune-making. But, perfectly anomalous as may be the state of our population, the state of our government is still more unprecedented and alarming. *We are in fact without government—* a commercial, civilized, and wealthy people, without law, order, or system, to protect and secure them in the peaceful enjoyment of those rights and privileges inestimable, bestowed upon them by their Creator, and holden, by the fundamental principles of our country, to be *inalienable and absolute.*

For the first time in the history of the "model Republic," and perhaps in that of any civilized government in the world, the Congress of the United States, representing a great nation of more than twenty millions of freemen, have assumed the right, not only to *tax us without representation,* but to *tax us without giving us any government at all*—thus making us feel, endure, and bear all the BURTHENS of government, without giving us even a distant glimpse of its BENEFITS. A special and separate act was introduced in the House of Representatives, at the late session of Congress, by the Committee on Commerce, and subsequently passed by both Houses, extending the revenue laws of the United States over California, and leaving the bill to organize a territorial government for this neglected people to perish at the close of the session.

Under these pressing circumstances, and impressed with the urgent necessity of some efficient action on the part of the people of California, the Legislative Assembly of the district of San

Francisco have believed it to be their duty to earnestly recommend to their fellow citizens the propriety of electing twelve delegates from each district to attend a general Convention, to be held at the Pueblo de San José on the third Monday of August next, for the purpose of organizing a government for the whole Territory of California. We would recommend that the delegates be intrusted with enlarged discretion to deliberate upon the best measures to be taken; and to form, if they upon mature consideration should deem it advisable, a State Constitution, to be submitted to the people for their ratification or rejection by a direct vote at the polls.

The present state of a great and harassing political question in the United States must certainly defeat, for several coming sessions, any attempts at an organization of a territorial government for this country [California] by Congress. In the Senate of the United States the parties stand precisely equal, there being fifteen free and fifteen slave States represented in that body. Until one or the other gain the ascendancy, we can have no territorial organization by act of Congress. All parties in both Houses of Congress admit, however, that the people of California can and ought to settle the vexed question of slavery in their State Constitution. From the best information, both parties in Congress are anxious that this should be done; and there can exist no doubt of the fact that the present perplexing state of the question at Washington would insure the admission of California at once. *We have that question to settle for ourselves; and the sooner we do it, the better.*

Imagine the excitement on Long Wharf when the passengers were unloaded from the *Panama* and the throngs then learned that another session of Congress had actually adjourned without any consideration of their needs, and that instead of the territorial governor for whom they had hoped, they were promised a tax collector! The time-honored American battle-cry of Taxation without Representation resounded, followed by the demand for an indignation meeting. Murmurs even ran through the crowd urging an independent Pacific Republic.

An indignation meeting was duly held in Portsmouth Square, on June 12. Meanwhile General Bennet Riley, the military governor, poured oil on the flames by proclaiming that "the body of men styling themselves the Legislative Assembly of San Francisco has usurped powers vested only in the Congress," and then by an act of usurpation on his own account called a Constitutional Convention, with Monterey as the place and September 1 the time. As to this, the *Annals of San Francisco* note that "the people in many parts of the country considered the interference of the military authority to be unnecessary as it was uncalled-for."

6

TWO of Jessie's fellow-passengers from off the *Panama* kept the indignation meeting of June 12 from breaking up in a brawl. The first was a dandified Georgia congressman, T. Butler King, President Taylor's personal representative, who spoke straight from the horse's mouth in assuring the people of prompt action by Congress at its *next* session, and of the President's personal desire to welcome California into the Union *as a State*. This mollified them somewhat, but King's suave persuasiveness was as nothing compared with that of a tall, imposing, not to say magnificent ex-congressman, Dr. William M. Gwin, lately of New Orleans, who had come to California with the express purpose of going back to Washington as its senator, and who at once took his first step toward that goal. In his speech at the indignation meeting Dr. Gwin cordially agreed with Judge Burnett in protesting against the assumption of civil functions by a soldier; but he then went on to counsel compliance with General Riley's proclamation in so far as it recommended the election of delegates to a convention at the place and time specified, as that would lend color to the organization of a local government under some sort of authority from the United States.

This sage advice prevailed, and on the first day of August delegates were elected throughout California, Dr. Gwin being chosen from San Francisco, as he had planned.

Thus young California was already boiling over with politics, but the *Panama* had brought out these two political cooks to watch the cauldron, subdue its bubbling, and educe a broth to nutrify the ready-made State so unexpectedly populated.

7

FRÉMONT soon removed Jessie to the late Vice-Consul Leidesdorff's comfortable adobe, which boasted the only garden in the higgledy-piggledy city, and Jessie loved gardens. No servants being available, Mrs. Gray volunteered to do the cooking and the washing, but as her charge failed to mend fast enough to suit her, she took the Colonel aside one day and said to him, "Your wife can never stand these fogs and winds; can't you take her somewhere down on the peninsula, where it's warm?"

Frémont, from previous visits to Monterey, knew it well, and that it exactly fulfilled the requirements. So, after a delightful camping trip along the peninsula, utilizing a specially built six-seated surrey with Spanish-leather cushions and spring seats easily convertible into a bed, he and Jessie and seven-year-old Lily finally found themselves established as lodgers—with whom but Madam Castro, wife of the graceless Mexican general, now said to be exiled to his native land. This genial lady made them quite at home in a long and low adobe dwelling built about a flower-filled patio, where the rolling surf played its deep accompaniment to the picturesque harmony of pine-clad hills and the silver crescent bay. Jessie thrilled to the peace and beauty of her first real Western home, and no doubt reflected, later on, that if the kindly Mrs. Gray had not caused them to live in Monterey during the meeting of the Constitutional Convention, her husband might never have gone to Washington as a senator.

But Frémont was a soldier, and Dr. Gwin a trained politician, who must now take the center of the stage. A single star adorned the Bear Flag; could it join the thirty in the national banner? That was the question Dr. Gwin set himself to answer.

PART THREE

GWIN AT MONTEREY AND WASHINGTON

CALIFORNIA'S CONSTITUTIONAL
CONVENTION

1

ON THE LONG steamer trip up the coast, Jessie became well acquainted with Dr. and Mrs. Gwin, both Southern gentlefolk, the former a native Tennesseean and the latter, his second wife, formerly famed as the Widow Logan of Bayou Sara, Louisiana, past mistress of luscious Louisiana dinners.

Gwin the Magnificent, who had known and admired Senator Benton during his own term as a Mississippi congressman, found further ground of congeniality with Jessie through their mutual devotion to Old Hickory. Gwin's father, Methodist minister after being a crack Indian fighter, had joined Jackson's Tennessee Volunteers as their chaplain at the Battle of New Orleans; but he attracted his commander's attention as a man of war rather than of peace, and had been named colonel of a regiment. Afterward intrusted with a secret horseback mission to Washington, he discharged this responsibility so well that Jackson gave him a warm friendship for fifty years. This friendship included young William Gwin, whom Jackson helped through medical and law courses at Transylvania University in Kentucky. But Old Hickory finally rescued William from medicine and law as he had rescued his father James from the ministry, and got him into politics by appointing him United States Marshal for Mississippi. During this marshalship, which extended through Van Buren's administration, Gwin had occasion to spend some time in Texas, where he learned to know Sam Houston and established a reputation as a Texan authority. Polk appointed him to supervise the construction of a magnificent Customs House in New Orleans, so that he now knew intimately four States: Tennessee, Mississippi, Texas, and Louisiana.

He delighted in telling Jessie and everybody else within hearing why he had surrendered "the most lucrative political job in the United States," and how he happened to be migrating to California in 1849.

It dated from the impressive remarks of John C. Calhoun on California, when Gwin had been a Mississippi congressman. He never forgot those remarks, and as soon as the Gold Rush began he hurried up to Washington to resign his post and settle his accounts. He arrived there on Sunday morning, March 4. All that day he consulted old congressional associates on the course to be pursued in the new territory. Shocked by congressional indifference, he happened to be standing in front of Willard's Hotel next morning, watching General Zachary Taylor's inaugural parade, when the "Little Giant," Senator Stephen A. Douglas, came along. While both of them viewed the procession Gwin told Douglas that the failure of Congress to convert California into a territory would undoubtedly provoke its settlers to make it into a State; that he was leaving Washington for California the next morning, and that he would return within a year as a Senator from the new State, and ask Douglas to present his credentials. Gwin had such assurance that when Douglas got his breath back he said, "God bless you, and I believe you will!"

2

IN General Zachary Taylor, as Roosevelt wrote in his *Life of Benton,* the Whigs chose better than they knew. Although a Louisiana slaveholder, "Old Rough and Ready" was as strong a unionist as Jackson and Houston, Benton and Frémont. In his first and only message to Congress, he stated that he would not only recommend the admission of California, but favor action by its own people in deciding for themselves the question of slavery, "the impending crisis" causing him to dread tossing another bone into the congressional pit. The wrangle over Texas had been dangerous, but, when the pro-slavery faction had won, their victory had been offset by the admission of two free States, Iowa and Wisconsin, thus giving each faction an equal number of States. This equilibrium would be upset by the admission of California as a free State, but President Taylor hoped that the autonomous settlement of the slavery question there would induce the Union at large to acquiesce with a minimum of friction. He antedated Lincoln in regarding the Union itself as the paramount political issue. While he foresaw a congressional combat as a matter of course, he thought that if his view prevailed, sectional passion might be kept within bounds.

T. Butler King of Georgia, whom he now sent out to the Coast as his personal emissary, was likewise a Southern unionist, whose personal interest in the new acquisition was inspired by a vision of sea-borne commerce. Just a year before embarking on the Pacific Mail steamship *Panama* for San Francisco, he had, as chairman of the House committee on naval affairs, offered the following resolution: "Certainty and rapidity of intercourse, only, are wanted to bring two great nations (China and the United States) together; to give them a more perfect knowledge of each other, develop their resources and build up a commerce more extensive than has probably ever heretofore existed between two nations. . . . To accomplish this, however, we must extend telegraphic wires across the continent, and establish a line of steamers from San Francisco, or Monterey, to Shanghai and Canton."

This suggests that T. Butler King might have made a good foreign minister, but it must be confessed that in the home field—assuming California to be "home"—his success was qualified. Loyal to President Taylor's wishes, but deficient in common sense and that sense of humor which always accompanies it, he paraded through the mining regions working up enthusiasm for the Constitutional Convention that was to meet at Monterey to achieve California statehood. He actually paraded, traveling with a retinue through Hell's Delight and Gouge Eye, Poker Flat and Groundhog Glory, to the huge disgust of General Persifer Smith and Commodore T. A. C. Jones and a full-blown cavalry escort forced to attend him, as presidential emissary, all through the sweltering summer of 1849. "Great is Allah" seemed to be his motto, "and I am his Mahomet." Neither to mountains nor the climate would he make the least concession. He kept exactly the same hours as in Washington, and wore the same foppish clothes, topped by an enormous hot "beaver." Guffaws echoed through the diggin's, where some of the lonesome miners are said to have run a mile to see "the King's parade" and hear the oratory.

It is not surprising that such conscientious devotion to duty, as he misconceived it, broke the health of T. Butler King, so that he was late for the Convention when it opened in September; but he had, after all, served his purpose, for no high-powered advertising agent could have succeeded better in directing widespread attention to "Colton Hall" in Monterey.

3

JESSIE'S other political fellow-passenger, Dr. Gwin, inspired a certain gentleman of the press, on arrival in San Francisco, to dilate upon "the grandeur of his exterior, and the magnificence of his person. Fully six feet two in stature, erect and stately, of herculean figure, perfect in proportions, and with a carriage and bearing commensurate, he stood among the multitude as one born to be a leader."

But even the technicolor style of Mr. James O'Meara could not do justice to Gwin's peculiar fitness for his chosen task. Schooled as an expansionist under Calhoun as well as Jackson, he would glory in the chance to enlarge the Union by the admission of a State only less large than Texas. His Texas experience, brief but intensive, had acquainted him with the pioneer psychology that he would find in California. Here, too, his training as political manipulator would find ample scope. He knew Washington well—President Taylor and powerful senators such as Clay and Calhoun, Webster and Douglas—and could be relied on to enlist their interest in his adopted home. That he would promote its material welfare was certain, as is evident from the two striking paragraphs into which he later compressed his essential creed:

Commerce is King! Wherever the flag of our country floats over the wealth, the enterprise, the industry, the agricultural products of our people, *there* is our nationality, our greatness, and our strength.

The steam engine, the telegraph wire, and the express man—these are the great civilizers of the Continent.[1]

[1] *William M. Gwin, Expansionist*, title of Miss H. McPherson's dissertation on Gwin in the Bancroft Library.

4

THE IMPRESSION Gwin made on arrival in San Francisco
was soon deepened through his impromptu judicial management in the trial of the infamous "Hounds." These were riff-
raff Tammanyites disbanded from a lately landed regiment of
"New York Volunteers," supplemented by gold-hunters into
one of those pestiferous secret orders which then cursed the
country. "Hounds" was probably chosen as their name because they resolved to hound out all non-Americans from
California and its mines. There was no organized law to
check them, so they reveled in organized lawlessness. Gun-
fire made too much noise, so they used as weapons slung
shot, bludgeon, and bowie knife. At first operating by stealth,
they soon decimated the Chileans and other South and Central Americans who had poured up the Coast in the earliest
gold ships and nested under Telegraph Hill. Growing bolder,
they broke into the open. Parading to a mass attack on their
victims with a fife and drum corps, they slashed and blud-
geoned in "Little Chile," finally entering a tent with only
women in it. Having outraged a mother and her daughter,
they killed the former, and it was this heinous crime which
aroused Sam Brannan, who had his good points, to action.
Next morning the Mormon Prophet mounted a barrel at the
corner of Clay and Montgomery streets and began exhorting
the gold seekers surging by. His deep voice and passionate
oratory stopped them, and when he had knotted a hundred
or so grim-faced men into his followers he led them up to
the Plaza and there formed a temporary band of regulators.
By sunset ringleaders of the pack of Hounds were kenneled
in the hold of a warship anchored in the Bay, since no prison
existed, and a heavy bag of gold dust had been filled for
their wounded and pillaged victims. But Brannan was not

through. Rough and ready, he called for the improvisation of a grand jury to try the prisoners, and it was on the bench with two associate justices in this makeshift trial that Gwin proved his quality. Young Hall McAllister, who had also come out in the *Panama,* began his distinguished legal career as chief prosecutor, but a whole battery of counsel was meticulously provided for the Hounds. Nine were found guilty as charged, and, so far, so good. But when it came to the punishment, sentiment split; "some were for hanging, others for whipping and banishment, still others for banishment accompanied by the warning that their return would mean execution," as McAllister said. It was Gwin who proposed this last-named punishment, and persuaded his colleagues to agree. Although the Mormon Prophet vented his disgust that "convicted criminals should be returned to the States with their voyages paid for," opinion generally lauded the wisdom of Gwin in ridding the community, temporarily, at least, of organized lawlessness without making the community lawless itself.

This affair proved three things: the extreme need of political organization in California, the ability of the immigrants to provide it, and the sagacity of Gwin.

THE LOCAL STRUGGLE FOR STATEHOOD

I

WHEN the Monterey Convention assembled, Gwin reported early, and Jessie soon asked him to dinner. In fact, with her health recovered and Gregorio manifesting genius as a cook,

her rented home soon became social headquarters for delegates from all over the territory, including the redoubtable
Sutter; politics so pervaded the air, presently, that Jessie
vowed she could actually *smell* Washington. Her big living-
room, with its whitewashed adobe walls hung with color
prints, the windows curtained with brocade, and a huge
grizzly rug fronting the fireplace, became such a popular
salon that General Riley, Southern-bred, used to tell political
interviewers, "If you want the inside, go see Miss Jessie."

Next to her own hospitality and that of the Larkins, well-
bred Americans most relished that of Doña Angustias de la
Guerra, admired by the Californians for her abounding
charity and by Jessie for her social charm. "Magnificent!"
she once called her, "combining the wisdom of a Queen
Isabella with the tact of the Duchess of Alba!" Bayard Taylor found this remarkable Spanish woman well versed not
only in her native literature, but in the novels of Scott and
Cooper, through translations. She often surprised him with
the aptness of her literary allusions.

Both ladies attended the opening of the Convention, Jessie
marveling at the thin length of Dr. Semple unfolding in order
to preside, and also at George Washington, thoroughly executed in oil by a native artist, just behind his chair. Semple,
with a flash of insight, said the Convention had assembled
"to make something out of nothing, to construct organization
and form out of chaos." But he frankly acknowledged, Gwin
informs us, that he had never before "seen the inside of a
legislative assembly, and knew no more about the rules of
proceedings than a child does in learning his A B C's."

"Colton Hall," named for Monterey's first Yankee *alcalde*,
and chosen for the Convention, had recessed the school conducted there for the children of the 1500 Monterey inhabitants by another Yankee, the Rev. Samuel Willey, who later
said that if Chaplain Colton could have foreseen the destined

use of his fine municipal hall he could hardly have bettered
it. Its masonry was the work of the better half of the New
York Regiment whose riff-raff had joined the Hounds. The
Convention met in its upper story, a huge room, sixty by
twenty-five feet, railed midway to exclude spectators. Opposite the front end of this railing a big door opened on a
balcony, where members not debating would refresh themselves on the September afternoons with the breeze from
the beautiful bay.

The debates surprised Jessie, as they surprised Bayard
Taylor, by their ability. Taken as a body, she thought the
delegates reflected honor on California, and need not suffer
by comparison with any State convention ever held. Perfect
harmony of feeling prevailed between the conquerors and
the vanquished. Of the 48 members, 36 were Americans,
but of the seven Californians some had received the unanimous American vote, such as General Vallejo of Sonoma,
Antonio Pico of San José, and Miguel de Pedrorena of San
Diego.

General Vallejo's Spanish temper flared up only once during the sessions, when the design for a coat-of-arms was
being discussed. In its background, a Major Garnett had
sketched the Sacramento River, crowded with ships, backed
by the Sierra Nevada, and over-arched by thirty-one stars
and the Greek word *Eureka;* in its foreground, a miner at
work and bunches of grapes; near its center, a helmed Minerva with spear and shield; which was all very well. But old
settlers clamored for a Grizzly guarding Minerva's shield,
whereupon Vallejo, remembering Sonoma, cried out with
biting irony that the Ursus of the Sierra should at least have
his neck securely encircled by a lariat, held in a *vaquero's*
hands! The bear went in, but the famous Bear Flag itself
was not made the official State flag until many years later.

Bayard Taylor laughed with Jessie at some of the crudities

of backwoods delegates, as when one of them opposed a constitutional provision that citizens charged with criminal offenses must be tried by a jury of their peers. He moved to strike out "peers," crying, "I don't like that word! 'Tain't

American! What do we want of peers in this kentry? This ain't no monarchy! We ain't got no house of parleyment! I vote fer no sich law!"

But Chairman Semple atoned for such illiteracy by championing the cause of higher education, arguing at one point that California might develop a university second to none, if she came down with the dust. "Why," he exclaimed, "we could bring the president of Oxford University over here if we paid him enough!" Occasionally he bungled a ruling, but on the whole presided well. William G. Marcy, a son of the Secretary of War under whom Frémont had served, was made secretary. J. Ross Browne, one of Bayard Taylor's literary and travel cronies, happened in, and accepted Gwin's nomination as shorthand reporter. His *Report of the Debates*, published at Washington in 1850, is the standard source book.

The personnel included such able men as James M. Jones of Kentucky and Louisiana, who frequented the Castro house so as to familiarize himself with Frémont's maps; the Virginian Charles T. Botts, pronounced by Chaplain Willey "a thorough gentleman, a born lawyer, a fluent and graceful speaker"; and William E. Shannon, a native Irishman who had come out with the New York Volunteers. Of the thirty-six Americans twenty-two hailed from the North and fourteen from the South, New York leading with eleven, New England following with six, and Maryland with five. Besides Shannon the Irishman, there were a Scot and a Frenchman, both old settlers. Of the Californians only two understood English, so that the Englishman W. E. P. Hartnell (see page 92) was engaged as interpreter, at $23 a day. One of his misinterpretations caused a flare-up, when Dr. Gwin was understood by "the dignified and handsome Señor Carrillo" of Los Angeles to say that a Constitution must be made *not* for the native sons, but for Americans, who comprised four-fifths of the population. Carrillo retorted, through Mr. Hartnell, that he was quite as good an American as Gwin, who thereupon apologized with such urbanity as to win the Californian's friendship.

Possibly this was the youngest body of men ever assembled in a State convention. Jones, the youngest and ablest member, was only twenty-five, nine men were under thirty, twenty-three between thirty and forty, twelve between forty and fifty, including Gwin, who was forty-four. Only four were over fifty. Fourteen were lawyers, if we count Gwin as one, eleven were farmers, eight merchants, three soldiers, and two printers. One delegate gave his profession as elegant leisure. Gwin found that they were unacquainted; none even knew the others' names until they met at Monterey. And they evinced, so he said, a strange distrust of motive. The old sections sent members dead set against a State. They suspected the newcomers, who formed such a vast majority of the population, while as for himself, he was considered a Goth or Vandal, harboring "the most dangerous designs against their property in the form of a State government."

2

AS Frémont did not belong to the Convention, he spent much time on his Mariposas ranch, some 140 miles northeast of Monterey, near the Yosemite Valley. It was a charming spot, where, an editor wrote, "waters as bright as moonbeams" poured down from "mountain springs as pure as the sheeted snow." Giant pines, six to eight feet through, shot 200 feet or so toward the sky. Under a famous oak a tribe of Chauchile Indians had been wont to gather in councils, or to worship their tribal god. The walls were the snow-capped mountains, the climate was as mild as Switzerland. Streams flashed with salmon trout, crimson clover diffused a rare perfume. Frémont built a pleasant house for Jessie and Lily, who sometimes accompanied him on camping trips in the famous six-seated surrey. He renamed the neighboring village of Princeton "Mount Bullion," after Father Benton. Some thirty Mexicans worked his mines, at first washing out such quantities of gold that it was sent down to Monterey in hundredweight buckskin bags worth as much as $25,000 each, and stored in an adobe godown behind Madam Castro's dwelling.

Incidents on the ranch revealed the Frémonts' view of slavery. The strong young Negro, Saunders, was offered to them at the bargain price of $1,700, but in lieu of buying him they gave him a chance to purchase freedom by washing gold. Jessie scorned a Texan's offer of a young mulatto woman, and when the couple were told that they might become the richest people on earth by developing slave labor in the mines, they exploded with indignation. Such incidents impressed the delegates, and when they heard of Benton's endangering his career back in Missouri through opposing slavery, fifteen of them marched to the Castro dwelling to hear "Tom Benton's daughter" belaud her father.

Naturally, such influence told, but even the Frémonts saw their hopes exceeded by the *unanimous* passage, within a week of the Convention's opening day, of Shannon's amendment to the Bill of Rights, affirming that *"neither slavery nor involuntary servitude, unless for the punishment of crimes, shall ever be tolerated in this State."* The delegates themselves were astonished when this unanimous vote was announced, "especially in the case of Dr. Gwin," wrote that gentleman himself; "but the reverse was true. He migrated to California from one of the largest slaveholding sections of the South for the express purpose of withdrawing himself and his family from that part of the country where slavery existed."

The Rev. Mr. Willey, American chaplain of the Convention, [2] who took Spanish lessons from Jessie and kept her posted when she could not attend a session, reported eloquently of the vote on slavery: "There was no sign of the amazing importance of that decision, so easily reached in that little, far-off town on that day. The convention went on about its ordinary business as if nothing unusual had hap-

[2] A Californian, Padre Antonio Ramirez, alternated with Mr. Willey in opening the meetings with prayer.

pened. The outside world was quiet; the forenoon sun had melted away the usual morning ocean fog, and the deep, unceasing roar of the surf came up from the circling shore of the bay, and everything seemed peaceful—but something had taken place there, that morning, that was soon to convulse the nation!"

To the mines must go the main credit for such a remarkable victory. As Bayard Taylor wrote with capital letters, mining had made LABOR RESPECTABLE. "May it never be otherwise," he added, "while a grain of gold is left to glitter in Californian soil!"

Were the rough-handed miners sentimental? Not a bit of it! "Who wants to work with a nigger beside him?" one of them asked. Young Jones expressed the same idea for the intelligentsia in the diggin's when he said on the floor of the Convention, "There is now a respectable and intelligent class of population in the mines, men of talent and education; men digging there in the pit with spade and pick who would be amply competent to sit in these halls. Do you think they would dig with the African? No sir, they would leave this country first."

But in apportioning credit, President Taylor must not be forgotten. T. Butler King had so thoroughly disseminated the old statesman's views, as expressed on page 142, that members were powerfully influenced by their paramount desire to get California admitted into the Union *as a State,* and believed this might not be possible unless they settled this question of slavery for themselves.

However, they went further than this. Few acts of the Convention are more impressive than the rebuff to color prejudice conveyed in the rejection of an attempt by a Missouri delegate, "General" McCarver of Sacramento, to saddle Shannon's prohibition of slavery with an embargo on the entrance into California of free Negroes. McCarver was even backed up at one time by a proposal that Indians and their descendants should be ineligible to the suffrage, but the proponents beat a hasty retreat on discovering that several of the Californian delegates were part Indian, and one a full-blood. Shannon's clear-cut declaration stood.

3

GWIN swayed the Convention from its beginning. On its very first day he offered a resolution for a State Constitution, involving appointment of two delegates from each of the ten districts.

This proposal for a State instead of a Territory evoked immediate opposition from Southern California, which comprised the "cow counties," so called by the northerners because cattle-grazing formed the main pursuit of the land barons residing there. These land barons foresaw big taxes were a State set up, whereas the Federal government would have to pay for the upkeep of a Territory. Other considerations entered into this ancient feud between "Superior" and Southern California, a feud which still dramatizes itself in the rivalry between San Francisco and Los Angeles; but taxes seem to have been the sharpest. Delegate Carrillo of Los Angeles County sought to counter Gwin's advocacy of a State by proposing that the province be divided politically, as it was physically, by the Tehachapi Mountains, which run east and west between the eight important counties of Southern California and the fifty to the north of the range. "All north of that line," Señor Carrillo argued, "might have a State government, and all south thereof a territorial government." He and his colleagues, the Convention journal reports, were under instructions to vote for a Territorial organization.

Gwin courteously but firmly argued against the proposed division, and finally had his way.

On the committee to formulate the Constitution he was named first by Semple, and Myron Norton, also of San Francisco, second; Norton becoming chairman, however, through the prevalent suspicions of Gwin. Undismayed by this rebuff, on the third day of the session, when the Convention had resolved itself into Committee of the Whole to consider a constitution, Gwin presented his specially printed copies of the new and brief constitution of Iowa. When suspicious members wondered whether they hadn't better examine *all* the State constitutions, "and skim off the cream," he urbanely explained that he would like nothing better, but that he had already examined all of them himself, had resided in three of the older States, preferred the constitution of Iowa to any and all others, and now presented it "as a matter of convenience."

In the long run he won this point also, Iowa influencing California's constitution more than any other State. Next came New York, which had the largest number of delegates.

In no respect did Gwin's masterful hand manipulate the framework of the Constitution more advantageously for the State than in connection with the banks. Here he clearly emulated his old friend and patron, Andrew Jackson. His antipathy to such bankers as Nicholas Biddle and such banks as the one over which Biddle presided had been fortified by his personal experience of the panic of 1837. As he told the delegates, in warning them of loose banks and wildcat currency, the land had been flooded with "post notes, corporation and individual tickets, certificates of deposits," and it would be a "spectacle" could he exhibit before them the variety of trashy money once in circulation. He had seen a curio collection of about a hundred different specimens, and if he could only exhibit them now they would be a powerful argument against banking establishments in *any* form.

Sherwood of New York opposed this extreme view, claiming that the abundance of precious metals in California demanded at least some authorized place or places of deposit, instead of leaving citizens to the mercies of "irresponsible private establishments."

This bank debate finally narrowed down to a tug-of-war between New York and Iowa, the majority of the committee favoring adoption of the first four sections of Article VIII of the New York constitution, while Gwin headed a minority report favoring two sections of the constitution of Iowa. He vigorously attacked majority members for having "cunningly devised" a scheme that would end in "a monied oligarchy" in California, declaring that what might be tolerable in the Empire State would there be intolerable. "Our country is like a blank sheet of paper upon which we are required to write a system of fundamental laws. Let the rights of the people be guarded in every line we write, or they will apply the sponge to our work." As an experienced politician he never forgot that any instrument the Convention might adopt would have to be ratified—or rejected—at the polls.

The issue was settled by so amending the majority report as to protect the State from such wildcat currency as Gwin dreaded. Further, rigid constitutional restrictions controlled the organization of all corporations, and the forthcoming legislatures were enjoined against the authorization of paper money in any form.

4

DUELING, which in spite of Gwin was to become a popular outdoor sport in the California of the '50s, received his special attention in the Convention, when young Jones and H. A. Tefft threatened an encounter. In averting this, he insisted, as a sort of connoisseur in duels, on a constitutional section denying duelists the right to hold office or the privilege of the polls. As with slavery, his experience of Louisiana dueling had turned him against it; he sincerely desired to protect his adopted home from its evils. Shannon wanted to table the section and leave the matter to the legislature; Hastings objected to it on practical grounds. "A citizen of California might be tried and punished in another State for fighting a duel there," said the Mormon agent, "but if he should ever return to California he would be condemned again, without trial, by the State Constitution." Furthermore, "this would violate the clause in the United States Constitution which provided that no person, after acquittal, should be tried for the same offense again." Others opposed the measure for other reasons.

Some of the remarks on dueling warrant quotation for their human interest. Said Gwin:

As I was in some degree instrumental in having this section drawn up, I feel bound to defend it. Although I have been often twitted upon this floor as having a great deference for precedents, still I adhere to this: that when we have the deliberate judgment of those who have great experience on any subject, we are bound to pay deference to their opinions; and I say that there is no State which has had more experience on the subject of dueling than Louisiana. . . . If you go through the cemetery of New Orleans, you will see the whole earth covered with tombstones of the victims of honor. It is a wonderful and a melancholy sight. It is said to have been the practice of the French population to go out almost every morning to fight with small swords or pistols. The practice of dueling has not sprung up here in California yet, and it is to be hoped that it never will. . . . Sir, I have all my life lived in States where dueling was countenanced; and I have had sad cause to know and feel its evil consequences. It is one of the most important provisions in our Constitution that this practice shall be forever prohibited here. I hope this convention will insert the section and make it, by an overwhelming vote, a part of the fundamental law.

Semple relinquished the chair to oppose the section because he believed in making the punishment fit the crime, and deemed denial of the suffrage and the right to hold office as too severe a punishment even for the duelists.

So far as I am individually concerned, dueling is unconstitutional. My own constitution forbids it! I have resolved never to fight a duel if I can honorably get out of it. . . . I have an instinctive dread of death. I dislike the idea of dying; but give me my choice, whether I shall be branded with infamy, prohibited from holding any office under the Government, from that of Governor down, and never more have the privilege of choosing at the ballot-box the men who shall preside over me, and I should choose death in preference! The idea of hanging is a little more elevated, but to me more honorable and more to be desired than such a punishment as this. I would dislike very much to fight a duel, because I might be killed. I consider that one of the strongest objections to the practice. To me it is a constitutional objection; but I think to be shot down, or to be hung, is preferable to disfranchisement. I am opposed to disproportionate punishments.

Semple's half-humorous argument amused, but did not prevail. The penalty was deleted, and the section became a dead letter.

Gwin himself, a few years later, fought a farcical duel that tickled Jessie immensely. It has passed into Californian folklore. His foe was the politician Joseph McCorkle, his field a marsh just north of the San Francisco presidio. Mrs. Gwin, once a resident of Bayou Sara, Louisiana, was familiar with duels despite her piety, and a galloping courier kept her apprised of events. After the exchange of the first shots—by rifles, at thirty paces—she was dramatically informed by an excited horseman, "First fire exchanged and no one hurt!" "Thank God!" the lady exclaimed as she fell on her knees, calling her children about her in a family thanksgiving, while the courier galloped back to the fray. Again he appeared, and announced, less noisily, "Second fire exchanged and nobody hurt!" "Praised be the Lord!" exclaimed Mrs. Gwin, letting it go at that. When for the third time he entered the mansion and reported sedately, "Third fire exchanged and no one hurt," Mrs. Gwin replied merely, "That's good." On reporting for the fourth and final time, he came in without saying anything, and was asked to stay for dinner. The Gwin table being a famous one, he sat down with gusto to a feast of *gumbo aux herbes* and all the good things that go with it. When at last he pushed back his chair and remarked, with the sigh of the overfed, "By the way, Mrs. Gwin, the fourth fire was exchanged and nobody hurt, and what do you think of that?" the Louisiana lady replied in a tone of disgust, "I think there's been some mighty poor shooting!"

5

THE BOUNDARY question at the Convention proved to be Banquo's ghost.

"The Gwin-Halleck proposal" was so named because Lieutenant Henry W. Halleck, Governor Riley's secretary and a man of force, who later became Lincoln's chief of staff, agreed with Gwin that California should retain the same great area it had under Mexico, but persuaded him to accept an amendment empowering the first of the legislatures to change to the restricted Sierra Nevada boundary if Congress should so prefer. "A conspiracy!" whispered suspicious delegates, "Old Gwin has hypnotized the Governor's own secretary to support some nefarious plot in preference to the Governor's own plan!"

The slavery issue got itself entangled in the boundary dispute, notwithstanding the unanimous antislavery declaration. Gwin's numerous critics among the more dramatic historical writers, who insist on casting him as "arch-villain in the Southern plot," soft-pedal his vote against slavery, but play

CALIFORNIA AS GWIN DESIRED IT

up his struggle for an eastern boundary line that would have made California more than double its present size, and as Frémont and Preuss had drawn it on their 1848 map. Captious critics still scent a proslavery intrigue. The southern boundary line would have been projected as far eastward as the present city of Phoenix, Arizona, and thence the eastern boundary, as favored by Gwin, would have run north through Utah to the neighborhood of Bear Lake, near the intersection of Idaho and Wyoming. Thus his proposed new State would have swallowed all of Nevada, with large parts of Arizona and Utah, and would have reached eastward to the foothills of the Rockies. But Riley, in his official proclamation, had assumed the Sierra Nevada as the eastern boundary, or virtually the present area. The Convention's committee on boundary, which included "Judge" Hastings, "Captain" Sutter, and Hugo Reid of Los Angeles, not only favored this much smaller area, but opposed Gwin's larger one for three reasons: it was too big for satisfactory representation in a legislature, it would invite subdivisions that might break the coast line, and the Mormons, some 20,000 of whom would be absorbed, were unrepresented in the Convention.

Other eastern lines were proposed, but the tussle finally settled down to one between the Gwin-Halleck proposal and the boundary as we now know it.

Chairman Semple, who as a Kentuckian was suspected of pro-slavery leanings, sought light on the vexatious problem from the specially illuminated mind of the Honorable T. Butler King. "For God's sake," the President's emissary responded, "Leave us no territory to legislate upon in Congress! *The great object in our formation of a State government is to avoid further legislation.*[3] By adopting this course there could be no question as to our admission, and all subjects of minor importance could be settled later."

Semple's report of this conversation met the fate of so many good intentions. "The artful proslavery Gwin" had won the Kentuckian over! "Had he not come out in the *Panama* with T. Butler King, winning him over during the voyage? Wasn't the President himself a Louisiana slaveholder, just like Old Gwin?" The natural and simple argu-

[3] Author's italics.

ment of the proponents of the larger area, quite truthfully stated by King, was rejected by over-suspicious delegates, who envisaged Gwin as a devilishly cunning Mephistopheles, a reputation he still bears. True, "he was too shrewd a politician to hope to commit the new territory to slavery" openly and at the outset, wrote one imaginative son of the Golden West, for "the spirit shown at public meetings of settlers and miners, which he had attended, proved that slavery would not be tolerated. Hence, instead of pressing the slavery issue, he devoted his energies to securing the best ultimate advantages" for slaveholders. California had a long coast line, and her area while she was Mexican had been popularly supposed to extend eastward all the way to the Rockies. What more simple and logical maneuver than to secure the admission of this immense area as "free" territory, and afterward persuade Congress to split it horizontally, giving the lion's share to the slaveholders? The most natural division line would be the Western equivalent of the historic Mason and Dixon parallel of 36° 30', the line drawn with such monotonous regularity by John C. Calhoun and his followers. "In this work Gwin betrayed masterly political manipulation. He made an easy conquest of Butler King and Halleck, and these allies he used to win over the suspicious native Californians."[4]

The simple truth is that both groups of the Convention leaders sincerely sought the plan most likely to win congressional approval to the admission of California as a State. There was merely an honest difference of opinion. But this difference stubbornly persisted, despite adoption of the Gwin-Halleck boundary by the Committee of the Whole, by a vote of 19 to 4, on September 24, 1849.

One argument against the larger area stressed the fact that it would take in the many Mormons at and near Salt

[4] *Century Magazine*, September, 1890.

Lake, who were unrepresented in the Convention. Gwin
ridiculed this objection:

It is a new doctrine that every man within the borders of a
new State must be represented in a State convention; a new
doctrine, never known or preached before! Besides, are not the
Mormons a peculiar people? Have they not sought their present
site for the express purpose of getting out of the reach of government?

But Hastings, who had come to California as a special Mormon agent, made the telling point against the inclusive area:

Suppose these two propositions are brought up before Congress at the same time; we applying for a State, and they for a
Territorial government, both propositions coming from the same
area. Can we be admitted into the Union, claiming the same
area, at the same time that they call for a Territorial government over it? No, Sir!

Arguments of equal weight against the Gwin-Halleck
measure continued to be heard before it reached the Convention floor for final action, sixteen days after adoption by
the Committee of the Whole.

During the prolonged debate, Gwin disclosed his real
reason for desiring the larger area. In language that ranks
him among the foremost of Western boosters, he said he
would like to see at least six States fronting on the Pacific,
as that would mean a dozen Senators in Congress from the
Pacific Slope.

It is notorious, Sir, that the State of Delaware, smaller than
our smallest district, has as much power in the Senate as the
great State of New York. . . . The past history of our country,
Sir, develops the fact that we will have State after State here—
probably as many as on the Atlantic side—and as we accumulate

States, we accumulate strength; our institutions become more powerful to do good, and not to do evil. I have no doubt the time will come when we will have twenty States this side of the Rocky Mountains. I want the power, Sir, and the population!

Whatever may be thought of his judgment, Gwin was by no means a secret schemer in the Convention, but the outspoken champion of "Manifest Destiny." And in justice to him it should be remembered that the paramount question of slavery for all the vast territory favored by the Gwin-Halleck measure had already been settled by *all* of the Convention's votes, including his own. Whatever size Congress might assign to "California," slavery and involuntary servitude had been excluded from its territory forever.

6

AS the boundary debate progressed, advocates of the Gwin-Halleck measure warmed to the antislavery issue. By congressional acceptance of their larger area, involuntary servitude would be excluded from a vast expanse of the newly expanded Union, instead of from California only, as we know it today. Members went even further. In a crucial debate lasting from the evening of October 8 through the afternoon session of October 10, Sherwood of New York said that while it was a matter of little importance "whether for a year or two we possess that barren desert between the Sierra Nevadas and New Mexico, it is a matter of great importance to the people of the United States, and to the perpetuity of the American Union and its institutions, that we should settle this slavery question, and prevent a division between the North and the South."

Chaplain Willey comments at this point that while all would have united on the Sierra Nevada line if personal preferences alone had been considered, delegates contending for the larger area "argued that we should be more surely admitted by Congress if in our action we settled the question of slavery for the whole territory, thus relieving that body of all necessity of debate or action concerning it, and some went so far as to say that in thus gaining admission to the Union with the larger boundary, and removing the great cause of discord, we might be saving the Union itself from dissolution!"

Lieutenant Halleck closed a powerful appeal for his and Gwin's measure by a glancing stroke at the delegate who claimed that he scented a political deal, and declared, "that its very terms were dictated to this Convention by political emissaries of General Taylor, and that it was carried through the Committee of the Whole by direct interference and log-rolling." Such charges Halleck denounced as scarcely worthy of notice. Those making them, he said, only lowered themselves in the estimation of all respectable members.

But the respectable members themselves, who cast no aspersions as to log-rolling, declaimed with just as much fervor against the big area as Halleck and Gwin for it. Botts of Virginia said he could "hardly keep cool" when the subject was broached. He perceived just as clearly as Gwin and Halleck and Sherwood that the paramount purpose was to choose the boundary line most likely to win the approbation of Congress, and for that very reason opposed them. They stood no chance whatsoever of securing a State with the Rocky Mountains as eastern boundary! "Sirs, I can tell you this will not be the means of your admission. You will never get into the Union with this boundary. Or, if you do, it will be only to sit amongst its ruins, like Marius among the ruins of Carthage!"

When the question was finally called, the ballot showed 29 to 22 in favor of the Gwin-Halleck proposal. Chaplain Willey records the first scenes of disorder. "Many members rose to their feet, excitement prevailed, all was confusion, tables were overturned, some cried one thing and some another."

Amid such confusion the session adjourned. Overnight Monterey hummed like an angry hive.

7

NEXT MORNING, after Chaplain Willey had sought to soothe the delegates with his opening prayer, young Jones of Kentucky and Louisiana arose for his virgin speech on the boundary question, which he desired to reopen so as to advance an entirely new proposal. To everybody's surprise, what he proposed was an absolute reversal of the Gwin-Halleck measure: to choose the Sierra Nevada boundary, but to put up to Congress the preferential choice of the larger area.

The object of his frequent calls at the Castro home was now disclosed. He had studied the Preuss maps to such good purpose that he made perhaps the most solid speech of the entire Convention. He began:

I am now going to recur to a subject which has created a great deal of excitement among members of this House. I allude to the boundary question, upon which the vote was last night taken. I have not yet spoken upon it, and I trust I will be indulged. . . . I will move a reconsideration of the vote of last night for the express purpose of offering *this* proposition to the House: that we shall take the Sierra Nevada line; but, if Congress will not admit us with that line—if it is an insuperable barrier to our admission—then we provide for this difficulty by saying we will take a larger. . . . We tell the Congress of the United States what our choice is. We tell them what we want. If we cannot get in under that line, we say, in order to conciliate the opponents of the smaller line, "You may admit us under the larger line." We give them no choice [besides] the two. We do not give them the right to carve out the territory here as they please. We tell them precisely what the alternative is. There is nothing indefinite about it. . . . If they contend that we cannot divide the territory, if they compel us to come in with the large boundary, where are the great and "insuperable" difficulties which will fall upon the [unrepresented] inhabitants? . . . We could, within one or two years, or even six months, divide them off, and put them into a separate State [a Mormon State].

With a fighting edge to his voice, young Jones next gave warning:

If gentlemen see fit to maintain the doctrine that we should not take any means of avoiding difficulty [with the Federal government], but hold ourselves a sovereign and independent State, I am willing to meet them before the people of California on that question. The compromise which I propose is in the following words:

Jones then outlined precisely the boundary as it today exists, and as described (in his own words) in the Constitution of 1849, Article XII, and in the present Constitution, Article XXI. As the alternative, he proposed that the Convention send to Congress an equally precise outline of the Frémont-Preuss map, which he also presented.

8

AS Jones sat down, the impression he made was obvious. But the first delegate to set off the fireworks, General McCarver, claimed the real authorship of the Jones compromise for himself; then, with a capacious gesture, generously waived the claim, actually moving a suspension of the rules. A long wrangle ensued, with Dr. Semple getting tangled in his rulings; but a good many sensible speeches got themselves heard, including Gwin's.

Gwin indicated compliance with the Jones plan *if need be.*
"Congress has the right to settle our boundary," he con-
ceded. "It is a right which they will insist upon, and which
they have always refused to surrender. Inasmuch as this territory and New Mexico have been bought from Mexico by
the Government of the United States, and $15,000,000 paid
for it, they are clearly entitled to say where our boundary
shall be." Referring to Señor Carrillo's preference earlier in
the sessions for a territorial form of government, and even
hinting that slavery might be desired south of the Tehachapi
mountains, he elicited a vigorous denial from the Señor of
both these implications, which was what Gwin wished.

Jones's oblique reference to the Mormons now brought
Hoppe of San José to his feet, with the horrified cry, "I say,
Mr. President, let us exclude the Mormons, whatever we do!
Their influence would be most injurious. They would make
the taxes of this State burdensome to every man in it. No
citizen of California desires that we shall have any social
or political connexion with them!" Botts indulged in some
sarcasm at Jones's expense, and declared himself utterly
unable to become party to the imposition of a government
upon a people—the Mormons—without their consent. Botts
spoke for a number of equally determined members.

Some of these, alarmed by the impression Jones had made,
and fearing that Congress might adopt the larger area as an
alternative, now played a trump card. Needing every vote
they could gather, and knowing Lippitt of New York to be on
their side and also an excellent speaker, two of them hurried to his lodging where he was laid up with "a nervous
headache of uncommon violence," and begged for his aid.

Lippitt protested, but as he was among the chronic critics
of Gwin as the California Machiavelli, and easily discerned
a fine Italian hand in this novel duplex proposal, he swigged
down a stiff dose of laudanum and permitted himself to be

hustled into Colton Hall, where he delivered a good speech of which he later denied all recollection, saying that whatever virtue it possessed was all due to laudanum!

This laudanum oration sufficiently bolstered up the protest of Botts as to veer the Convention temporarily away from the bicephalous proposal of Jones, but it also provided the shrewd Irishman, Shannon, with the opportunity to involve native sons in a long discussion of maps. Jones, a map specialist, jumped at the suggestion that a certain authentic Mexican map might convince Congress that "California," as Mexico once knew it, comprised only the smaller area—at the same time reasserting that his sole aim was to avoid congressional friction. But the trend toward clarity was suddenly altered by Hill of San Diego, who hopelessly complicated matters by proposing a new, restricted boundary all his own; and as Lippitt's laudanum speech had not only unsettled the Convention on the Jones plan but consumed a lot of time, the wearied and exasperated delegates adjourned for lunch.

9

WHEN they met again at three o'clock lunch had not mollified them. After Editor Gilbert of San Francisco made a long speech, the unquenchable General McCarver of Sacramento demanded the same privilege. Refusing to be shouted down by loud cries for the question, he declared, "If the District of Sacramento is to be cut off from her proper representation in this Convention, whilst San Francisco is allowed to be heard on all occasions, I want to know it! I want the people of Sacramento to know it!" Cries for the question grew louder, and great confusion ensued, amid which the McCarver voice could be heard—"I will not be insulted! If this House is to stamp me down and allow other individuals to speak as often as they please, I shall no longer remain here!"

This drew loud applause, and after McCarver strode from Colton Hall his colleague McDougal, tongue in cheek, hoped that "the General might be pardoned, for it is a matter of personal feeling with him ever since the sad fate of his Free Negro project; the news brought down from San Francisco on that melancholy occasion has made him very sore."

But the General's withdrawal had at least broken the quorum, and Semple had to order his sergeant-at-arms to round up absentees. Then, at long last, after Semple had got tangled again in his rulings, and been reversed, a ballot was taken on the Jones bill, and it was voted down, 31 to 13. Two Spanish gentlemen now became involved in personalities over the weird Hill bill, which, in the ensuing confusion, was actually adopted, 24 to 22. But Gwin was on the job. He now moved that the bill be engrossed for a third reading, and got the attention of the Convention for his acid comment that he would rather have no boundary at all than the one proposed, and voted against his own motion; which, thus defeated 29 to 20, killed the Hill bill.

Meanwhile Botts and Lippitt had been talking to Jones, with the result that he regained the floor and sought the adoption of the *first half* of his original measure, thus eliminating the possibility of a large area altogether. Sherwood of New York, still loyal to the Gwin-Halleck measure, interposed with a motion for its final adoption, but was voted down, 24 to 18.

The larger boundary was now as dead as the Hill bill. Jones's proposal next came before the House, and that young gentleman enjoyed the distinction of determining the boundaries of the State of California, his proposal carrying by the handsome vote of 32 to 7. Gwin suavely voted Aye, while the less urbane Halleck and Sherwood apparently didn't vote at all.

Professor Cardinal Goodwin, in the course of the most painstaking and conscientious study of the boundary debates that has been made, reinforces Chaplain Willey's opinion of their non-sectional character. In so doing he opposes by name such historians as Hunt, Coman, and Royce, all of whom were misled by H. H. Bancroft. Summing up, Professor Goodwin says:

The usual supposition has been that the extreme eastern boundary was supported by proslavery men for the purpose of making California so large that a subsequent division, by an east and west line, would result in the establishment of two large States on the Pacific, one to be dedicated to freedom and the other to slavery. This view, however, is not substantiated by facts. . . . The motive which seems to have actuated them [the Southerners] was a desire to obtain immediate admission to statehood.

10

ITS big question settled, the Convention devoted its last three days to routine matters; some of them highly important, including adoption of the Declaration of Rights as a whole, and constitutional sections regulating or affecting education, suffrage, the executive and legislative departments of government, and the judiciary. Gwin exercised his talents to the last, not forgetting, when Semple's worn-out strength provided an opening, to move that "Mr. J. A. Sutter be requested to address Governor Riley on behalf of this Convention, when it shall wait upon him in a body after the adjournment *sine die.*" Gwin seldom lost an opportunity to do a personal kindness, and it became one of Sutter's proudest reminiscences to tell how he discharged this honor.

Bayard Taylor vividly depicts Sutter in the Convention's closing hour. When, on the afternoon of October 13, the first of a salute of thirty-one guns boomed from the nearby fort, "he was the old soldier again," says Taylor, not knowing that he had never been a soldier! He sprang from his seat, and, waving his hand round his head, as if swinging a sword, cried: "Gentlemen, this is the happiest day of my life! It makes me glad to hear those cannon; they remind me of the time when I was a soldier! Yes, I am glad to hear them— this is a great day for California!" As if recollecting himself, he sat down, tears streaming from his eyes.

The members, with one accord, gave three tumultuous cheers, which were heard from one end of the town to the other. While they signed the Constitution, gun followed gun from the fort, the echoes reverberating thunderously about the bay, until finally, as the loud voice of the thirty-first was heard, there was a shout, "That's for California!" and everybody joined in "three times three" for the new star in the constellation.

Editor Gilbert of San Francisco told in his paper of a gallant incident occurring in the harbor simultaneously. As the firing of the national salute of thirty-one guns proceeded, and the signing of the Constitution went on, the commander of an English bark in port hoisted at his peak the American flag above that of all the other nations, making, at the very moment the thirty-first gun was fired, a line of colors from the main truck to the vessel's deck; thus atoning, forever, for the dubious behavior of other British ships previously anchored in Monterey harbor.

The charter that was signed during this hour, which was to remain California's fundamental law for thirty years, justifies Professor Goodwin's tribute:

Within its articles were embodied those provisions for personal freedom and individual protection for which the English race has contended since the meeting of king and nobles at Runnymede, and the sections comprising the completed document were based on models embodying fundamental laws and principles whose soundness had been thoroughly tested. A unique situation had called the members of the Convention together, and they met it, usually, in an admirable manner. . . . Representing all sections of the Union, they had to a wonderful extent laid aside sectional prejudices and given the new State a thoroughly liberal Constitution. The clauses protecting the property of wives, providing for the election of a judiciary, and prohibiting slavery, and at the same time refusing to provide against the immigration of free Negroes, pledged the State to a progressive policy, and "gave the most magnificent illustration of the wonderful capacity of this people for self-government."[5]

"The Constitution of today," adds Miss H. M. McPherson in her unpublished dissertation on Gwin, "not only carries the original structure, but contains many of the provisions." The Constitution of 1849 is reproduced as Item 3 of the Appendix.

11

JESSIE was in the Convention hall when young Jones's proposal carried. Outside, she stood with the crowds on the afternoon when the last signature had been set to the Constitution and somebody unfurled a flag from the balcony of Colton Hall. Laughing and crying with the others, and all unconscious of what would so soon come to her under the new régime, she finally returned to her Castro home to dress for the ball toward which each delegate had contributed his $25, and at which each guest had been requested to appear in gala costume. Ruefully she now recalled her Washington

[5] The final quotation is from Von Holst's *Constitutional and Political History of the U. S.*, Vol. III, p. 463.

ball-gowns of tulle and satin, as she got into her red brocade basque and the navy-blue skirt made over from a riding-habit; but at least it was all hers, as she laughingly said on reading Bayard Taylor's facetious description, "The dark-eyed daughters of Monterey, Los Angeles and Santa Barbara mingled in pleasing contrast with the fairer bloom" of the American belles. "The variety of features and complexions was fully equaled by the variety of dress, of which scarcely one seemed to belong entirely to the wearer, and I thought if the clothes had the power to leap severally back to their respective owners, some dancers would have been in a state of utter destitution."

Taylor must have had himself in mind, thought Jessie, "since he, not a large man, danced all evening in a pair of pinned-over pantaloons lent him by an officer who weighed two hundred pounds!"

12

THE Convention story would be incomplete without a post-script from Jessie's Spanish student, Chaplain Willey. In the following January two delegates from "the State of Deseret" presented themselves as the legislature assembled at San José, California's first capital. They said their people also had held a constitutional convention, and ratified a constitution at the polls. But on hearing of California's convention, the Mormons had sent these delegates to Monterey with the request that the California boundary be large enough to take in the State of Deseret. Arriving after the Monterey convention adjourned, they went on to Monterey, asking whether the legislature couldn't do something for them. "Of course," said Chaplain Willey, "their mission was in vain. But what if they had arrived a little earlier, and had been present at the Convention in September, and had made their request there? Almost certainly, Gwin's 'larger boundary' would have been adopted. It is very plain that it was a narrow escape for California from Mormon complications."

The legislature assembled only after State-wide elections had been held in accordance with the Constitution. Judge Burnett's championship of Settlers' Rights, together with his rigid honesty, made him the first civil Governor of a State that was not yet a State, his votes tallying 6,716 as against his nearest competitor, Sherwood, with 3,188, and Captain Sutter trailing with only 2,201. Yet Sutter said in his *Reminiscenses,* "They wanted to nominate me for Governor at Monterey but I declined. Subsequently I consented but then it was too late. Notwithstanding, San Francisco gave me 10,-000 votes. Burnett stumped the State and beat me. The legislature was elected, about one third of which were good men and the rest bad. They appeared in the legislative halls with revolvers and bowie knives fastened to their belts, and were drinking, rioting, and swearing nearly all the time."

Governor Burnett, on the other hand, described this legislature as "one of the best we ever had. The members were honest, indefatigable workers. They had to begin at the beginning and create an entire new code of statute law, with but few authorities to consult. Time, also, was short. Under the circumstances their labors were most creditable."

"The Legislature of a Thousand Drinks" is the unforgettable coinage of one Thomas Jefferson Green, a political adventurer from Texas, where Sam Houston had conferred on him the dubious immortality of an even more memorable epigram, "He has all the characteristics of a dog except fidelity." Green is reported by a contemporary to have regarded the first legislature as a bibulous picnic.

He had a room near the State House liberally supplied with all kinds of drinks, and after every adjournment his sonorous voice was heard crying, 'Come, let's take a thousand drinks!' Survivors of this legislature declared that Green was a seasoned vessel, and seldom appeared the worse for potations that would have put Squire Western under the table before midday. Even with the inducement of free liquor always on tap the drinking was not general. The little coterie that Green gathered about him had no influence upon the working members. Well would it have been for California had every succeeding legislature been as honest and as efficient as this pioneer body.

13

THAT it was a pioneer body, two remarkable incidents prove. One was the report by General Vallejo as chairman of a committee on the derivation of county names, in which he recited a family reminiscence "with the most tender feelings of the heart." His father, he said, was one of the many Mexicans who immigrated hither in bachelorship, when "the female sex was an oasis in the desert." While traveling near San Luis Obispo he unexpectedly met "a lady in travail, about to bring a new being into the world." As there was no one, save her husband, to assist her, he offered his services as *tenedor*. The lady was safely delivered of a girl, whereupon the gallant young *tenedor* solicited of the parents the hand of their daughter when she should be old enough to marry, and a formal agreement ensued, conditioned on the daughter's consent. Fourteen years later her faithful suitor reappeared and she accepted him, to become General Vallejo's mother! It was evidently an old Spanish custom.

The other episode seems only a little less remarkable, although of a political nature; testifying emphatically to the independence and self-assurance handed down from the Bear Flag Revolt. On February 9, 1850, seven months before the admission of the State, the first legislature resolved: "that the Governor be, and he is hereby authorized and requested, to cause to be procured, and prepared in the manner prescribed by the Washington Monument Association, a block of California marble, cinnabar, gold quartz, or granite of suitable dimensions, with the word *California* chiseled on its face, and that he cause the same to be forwarded to the Managers of the Washington Monument Association in the City of Washington, District of Columbia, to constitute a portion of the monument now being erected in that city to the memory of George Washington."

The Governor obeyed instructions, the stone was cut from a marble bed on a ranch just outside Placerville, and it is now in the monument. Is there anything more audacious in American history?

Three more audacious resolutions were adopted, one demanding of the Federal Government an improvement in the transportation of the mails and their distribution in San Francisco, the second urging Congress to undertake as soon as practicable the construction of a transcontinental railroad—not "from the Mississippi River to the Pacific Ocean," but "from the Pacific Ocean to the Mississippi River"; and the third requesting grants of land to each commissioned army officer who had faithfully and honorably completed a full term of service in the Mexican war. Each of the last two resolutions, without the slightest trace of humor, instructed the Governor to forward copies of them "to each of our Senators and Representatives in Congress," although those four gentlemen were not "in Congress" until five months after the resolutions were passed, and had a very hard time getting in at that.

Frémont had been chosen as California's first Senator on the first legislative ballot, receiving 29 of the 36 votes, a tribute to his popularity as the hero of the Bear Flag incident and subsequent conquest of the State. Gwin held a lead over

Halleck, Semple, T. Butler King and two others, until on the third ballot he received 24 votes and was declared elected. When he and Frémont later drew lots for short and long terms, Gwin drew the lucky straw for the full six-year term. In the general election of November 13, Editor Gilbert and G. W. Wright had already been chosen as representatives in the House, and the Constitution ratified by a vote of 12,061 to 811.

14

WHEN Bayard Taylor climbed aboard the overcrowded *Oregon* on the first day of 1850 he found Gilbert and Wright already there, as well as Gwin and T. Butler King. That night, when the new side-wheeler touched at Monterey, the Frémonts joined them, and also Lieutenant W. T. Sherman, who was taking Doña Angustias' two sons to Georgetown, D. C., to enter them in the Catholic college. In its treasure chest the *Oregon* carried $3,000,000 in gold-dust, a commodity much desired by the Federal treasury.

Jessie's biographer says that her pride, crucified by the indignities heaped upon her husband by General Kearny, now had its Easter. It was another of those amazing ascensions from the depths that star Frémont's career. He now enjoyed fame and opportunity as never before, and his trunks were crammed with buckskin bags of gold dust, washed out from his Mariposas mines. "He was a busy man of affairs, supervising his estate, laboring for the cause of free-soil Democracy in Washington and California, answering scientific inquiries, and keeping abreast of geographical advances. His ambitions were increasingly complex, for he hoped to be one of the statesmen of the new West and one of her business entrepreneurs as well as the pathmarker who mapped her highways." His reputation preceded him. At Mazatlan, where Bayard Taylor said goodby for a trip into Mexico, a British man-of-war not only fired a salute for the two Senators-elect, but showed special honor to the Frémonts by lowering the commander's own gig for their visit ashore.

Panama must have been Jessie's predestined purgatory, for again she suffered there such a painful illness that her life was despaired of. Frémont also went down, from trouble with his frost-bitten leg. Madam Arcé once more proved her hospitality, even providing four trusty men as palanquin-bearers for Jessie after Frémont had sufficiently recovered to devise this special means for conveying her across the Isthmus. As she was being borne away she heard one of the villagers saying, in Spanish, "Colonel Frémont will live, but *this* poor young thing!—dying so far from home and country!" The voyage up to New York only prolonged their agony, for Frémont had caught the awful Chagres fever, and a West Indian hurricane so buffeted the *Georgia* that Jessie had to be lashed to her sofa. All this so detained them that Gwin and T. Butler King and the two congressmen were in Washington long before they themselves reached New York.

When back at last in the national capital, and comparatively well again, Jessie wrote, touchingly:

No person living understands better than I the term "speechless with joy." Father, Mother, all the others in the old home greeting us, our old rooms with their heavenly smells of rose geraniums, old friends greeting us, the whole city greeting us! I took sedate little walks down Pennsylvania Avenue and across the Common in the spring twilight, but I wanted to run and shout, to hug the tree-trunks, to drop down on the ground and lay my cheek against the new grass, to kiss the crocuses and wild violets, and to float away upon that misty gray-green cloud of young leaves above me.

THE GREAT DEBATE AT
WASHINGTON

1

JESSIE WAS SOON caught up into the round of dinner parties given in honor of the two new senators without seats, from the far-away fabulous California, Land of Gold. And she was just in time for the funeral of Count Bodisco. It seemed that his union with her young friend had been happy, despite their disparity of age. Not only had he taken scrupulous and wise care of Harriet's large brood of brothers and sisters and of her parents, but he had actually requested in his will, which left everything to Harriet, that she should marry again, so as to annex somebody that would make her as happy as she had made him.

This was a handsome thing to do, and what a requital was inflicted on him at his funeral! No priest of the Greek Church being available, an old-timer of the Baptist persuasion was called in. As he rambled along in an extemporized "oration," what should he do but deplore the heresy of the creed in which "the dear departed" had been trained! A safety-valve was provided for Jessie's indignation by the Mayor of Washington, standing by, who, when the cleric went on to wonder "what the dear departed would say could he look down on us now," quickly whispered in her ear, "He would say, 'What a bad-manage-ceremony!'"

It was this same talented Mayor who left on record this charming etching of the Frémonts at one of the dinner parties:

Colonel Frémont in his correct dinner clothes was of an arresting dignity, but he looked worn and thin. His black hair, heavily streaked with gray, gave distinction to his weather-worn features. His eyes shone youthfully as he answered questions as to the possibility of the coast under a railroad project. He listened with grave reference to whoever was speaking, but under cover of general conversation he lapsed into frequent silences, his glance resting with scarcely veiled admiration on his wife as she spoke and laughed with all the sparkle of a carefree schoolgirl. When Jessie caught his glance upon her, there was an exchange which I can only describe as a mental wink; a flash of eye, a fleeting smile, discreet flirtation; throughout the long dinner.

When the Countess Bodisco put off her mourning and went about again, Jessie enjoyed her companionship in visiting the Senate gallery to hear the long debate on the admission of California, about which "sectional feeling rapidly developed, and the agitation in Congress communicated itself to the entire country," as James G. Blaine has said in his *Twenty Years of Congress.*[6]

The character and eminence of the men who took part in the discussion gave it an intense, almost dramatic interest. Mr. Clay in his seventy-third year was again in the Senate by the unanimous vote of the Kentucky legislature, in the belief that his patriotic influence was needed in the impending crisis. Webster and Cass, natives of the same New England State, Benton and Calhoun, natives of the Carolinas, all born in the same year and now approaching three-score and ten, represented in their own persons almost every phase of the impending contest. Stephen A. Douglas had entered the preceding Congress at the early age of thirty-four. . . . Jefferson Davis had come from Mississippi with the brilliant record of his achievements in the Mexican war, already ambitious to succeed Mr. Calhoun as the leader of the extreme South, but foiled in his Disunion schemes by his elo-

[6] Vol. I, pp. 88-90.

quent but erratic colleague, Henry S. Foote. William H. Seward of New York was for the first time taking position under the National Government, at the age of forty-nine. . . . Most striking of all, William M. Gwin and John Charles Frémont, men of Southern birth and proslavery training, stood at the door of the Senate with the constitution of California in their hands to demand her admission to the Union as a free State.

2

JESSIE found her father almost panic-stricken by the national outlook, but in the Senate the old Spartan never once faltered. The fact is, as Theodore Roosevelt says, he had now reached his highest stature as a statesman. When Calhoun had fathered the famous resolutions declaring that Congress lacked the power to interfere with slavery in the territories, hence the power to prevent admission of new States seeking to foster it, Benton assailed the resolutions as disunionist and inflammatory. Calhoun sent for him privately and said he expected his support "as the representative of a slaveholding State." Benton thereupon answered that Calhoun could not possibly have expected any such thing. "Then," said the angered South Carolinian, "I shall know where to find that gentleman!" "I shall be found in the right place," retorted the North Carolinian, "on the side of my country and the Union!"

This marked him off as a leader of those Southerners who held the nation above any section, even their own; who, when the Civil War forced a final decision, "furnished Farragut, Thomas, Bristow, and countless others as loyal as they were brave," according to Roosevelt.

When President Zachary Taylor, on February 13, 1850, laid before Congress the Constitution California had adopted, with its antislavery section, and recommended admission as a State, Benton aligned himself with the supporters of the President's plan, without compromise, maintaining this position to the end.

This struggle proved to be the most important, as it was the most dramatic, in the Senate's long history. Lord Bryce has written in *The American Commonwealth* that the question of the extension of slavery west of the Missouri River had become by 1850 the vital and absorbing question for the people of the United States, "and as in that year California was knocking at the doors of Congress, it had become an urgent question which evoked the hottest passions, and the victors in which would be victors all along the line."

Calhoun, too ill to meet the entire California delegation, welcomed his old friend Gwin, rallying his flagging energies to convince him that the admission of California as a free-soil State would wreck the Union. Gwin, duly impressed with the great South Carolinian's earnestness, and depressed by the gloom of his prophecies, nevertheless refused to follow his lead. This was tantamount to defection from the stronger wing of the Democratic party in Congress, and to his taking refuge with the free-soil wing, as represented by Benton and Frémont. A little later he was sent for by that inveterate compromiser, Henry Clay, of Kentucky, the State in which he had been educated. Gwin's memorandum of this interview, an important historical document, follows:[7]

When the California delegation reached Washington and asked for the admission of the State into the Union, I was in favor of its being acted on as a separate and independent measure, and with the least practicable delay. I found Mr. Clay, General Cass, Mr. Webster, Judge Douglas, and others who were the great leaders in Congress at that time, in favor of this policy. But afterwards they changed their views and I was sent for by Mr. Clay, who gave me the reason. He said he had been called upon by members of the House of Representatives and informed that

[7] *Century Magazine*, September, 1890, pp. 789-90.

a sufficient number of the members of that body from the Southern States to control its action had entered into a solemn compact, which they would execute at the risk of their lives, never to permit a bill to pass the House admitting California until the right of the South to carry their property [i.e., slaves] to the Territories of the United States was first guaranteed by law. Mr. Clay was incredulous; he thought it impossible for such a body of men to come to so desperate a resolve—which was revolution itself. He called for facts, which were furnished him; names also were given, and, if necessary to remove all doubts from his mind, it was proposed to bring each member who had entered into this league to his room to make the declaration to him in person. Mr. Clay said that then, for the first time in his life, he thought the Union in immediate peril, and that the short remnant of days left to him would see it destroyed. He at once determined upon the course he would pursue, and the first person he consulted was Colonel Benton—with whom he had been up to that time acting in full concert for the immediate admission of California into the Union—and my colleague, Colonel Frémont. The interview [with Benton and Frémont] lasted for an hour, and he exerted all the powers he possessed to induce Colonel Benton to join him in postponing the admission of the State until the question of the territorial government was settled, but in vain. Colonel Benton sternly refused, and Mr. Clay confessed to me that he did what he had never before done in his life—he implored a fellow-man to do his duty, but all to no effect. Mr. Clay then sought the interview with me; and, after [his] stating the case fully, I had no doubt of the facts, and told him that I never wished to see California *forced* into the Union in a revolutionary way which would destroy its [the Union's] existence, and that I was willing that the admission of the State should be considered in connection with all the questions that were then agitating the country.

The compromise plan to which Gwin thus agreed, and to which Daniel Webster later subscribed, was embodied in Clay's famous "Omnibus Bill," so called in ridicule by President Taylor, which precipitated the battle of the giants. Having given his word to Clay, Gwin did not permit even General Taylor to budge him, in a stormy interview wherein his support was demanded for "the President's plan."

Both Clay and Webster, two Whigs notoriously ambitious for the White House, are sometimes charged with having resented the preference of the electorate for military glory, as exemplified in the new Whig President, rather than the statesmanship by which they themselves were distinguished. At any rate, they made no effort to unite their party in support of the President's plan, but supported the Omnibus Bill introduced by Clay on January 29, 1850.

[NOTE: In the drawing made on the spot by P. F. Rothermel, Fillmore presides, while Clay is speaking. At Fillmore's left stand Calhoun, Gwin, and Dayton. Seated in front of Gwin is Seward, watching Clay. Cass sits opposite Seward, also watching Clay. Behind Cass, right to left, are Pearce, Stockton, Dickens, and Hale.

Immediately behind Clay, Chase is seated. Standing, right to left, are Smith, Soule, Douglas, and Foote (hand on desk). Seated behind Foote is Webster (head on hand). Behind Webster, in ascending scale, come King and Bell, Mangum (facing reader), then Cooper and Mason.

Standing at extreme left is Sam Houston. From left to right stand Clemens, Butler, Jefferson Davis, and Dodge. Seated at the extreme left is Benton.

Every figure in the picture is a portrait, including gallery visitors, among whom, probably, is Jessie. Frémont, if present, cannot be identified.]

The chief compromise in this hydra-headed measure sought to placate proslavery men for the admission of California with its antislavery Constitution by promising slave States a new and more stringent Fugitive Slave Law. Other olive-branch sections declared the inexpediency of abolishing the slave trade in the District of Columbia, but the expediency of restricting it; and recommended the organization of *territorial* governments in New Mexico and other portions of the great area acquired from Mexico (except California) with no provisions either for or against slavery, while ex-

THE GREAT DEBATE OF 1850. *Courtesy of Stanford Gwin*

SENATOR GWIN. *Courtesy of the University of California*

pressly denying congressional power to obstruct the interstate slave trade.

Whatever motives may be attributed to Clay and Webster, it would be hard to imagine a set of resolutions more likely to fan controversy. They were heatedly debated for three solid months before bills embodying their principles could even be framed.

3

GWIN'S friend Sam Houston, Virginia-born but now senator from his new State of Texas, was the first speaker of prominence to support Clay on the floor. Like his old leader Andrew Jackson, Houston's own watchword might well have been, *Anything to preserve the Union.* "I wish," he now said with a deep solemnity, "if this Union *must* be dissolved, that its ruins may be the monument of my grave." Later, when the Southern States were holding their convention of protest at Nashville, he repudiated the leadership of Jefferson Davis, whom he characterized as "cold as a lizard and ambitious as Lucifer."

Calhoun's opposition speech of March 4 was the last effort of his life, and the most dramatic. Schouler, a hostile critic, says that "the gloom of the sick chamber in which he prepared it deepened its raven gloss; its dismal croak was of disunion." Senator Mason of Virginia had to read it because of the author's illness, but Calhoun sat directly in front of Mason and listened "like some disembodied spirit reviewing the deeds of the flesh. It was a strangely haunting spectacle. The author turned half round, and listened as though all were new to him, moving not a muscle of his face, but keeping his immovable posture,—pale, skinny, and emaciated as he was, —with eyes partially closed, until the last words were uttered and the spell was broken."

After a long itemized indictment of the Unionist majority

in Congress for its step-by-step infringement of the constitutional rights on which the South depended if it were to stay in the Union, Senator Calhoun declared that the admission of California, with a free constitution written and ratified by its own people, had become the test question upon which everything depended.

The Executive has laid the paper purporting to be the Constitution of California before you, and asks you to admit her into the Union as a State; and the question is, will you or will you not admit her? It is a grave question, and there rests upon you a heavy responsibility. Much, very much, will depend upon your decision. If you admit her, you endorse and give your sanction to all that has been done. Are you prepared to do so? Are you prepared to surrender your power of legislation for the territories —a power expressly vested in Congress by the Constitution, as has been fully established? Can you, consistently with your oath to support the Constitution, surrender the power? Are you prepared to submit that the inhabitants of the territories possess the sovereignty over them, and that any number, more or less, may claim any extent of territory they please, may form a constitution and government, and erect it into a State, without asking your permission? Are you prepared to surrender the sovereignty of the United States over whatever territory may be hereafter acquired, to the first adventurers who may rush into it? Are you prepared to surrender virtually to the Executive Department all the powers which you have heretofore exercised over the territories? If not, how can you, consistently with your duty, and your oaths to support the Constitution, give your assent to the admission of California as a State, under a pretended constitution and government?

Having shown that all the cords that had held the Union together had been snapped, except only the political party system, and that even this had been weakened and was on the point of giving way, Calhoun asked the solemn question,

"How can the Union be saved?" and answered it concretely: "Provide for the insertion of a provision in the Constitution, by an amendment, which will restore to the South in substance the power she possessed of protecting herself, before the equilibrium between the sections was destroyed."

Benton points out that while Calhoun's speech did not specify the nature of this proposed amendment, an authentic publication soon afterward disclosed it as involving the election of two presidents, one from the free and the other from the slave States, each of whom must approve all the Acts of Congress before they could become laws. "Upon this condition alone," comments Old Bullion in his most caustic manner, "the speech declared the Union could be saved!—which was equivalent to pronouncing its dissolution. For, in the first place, no such amendment to the Constitution could be made; in the second place, no such double-headed government could work, even through one session of Congress, any more than two animals could work together in the plough with their heads yoked in opposite directions."

4

MEANWHILE the California delegation, finding itself and its cause seriously misunderstood and misrepresented, prepared a lengthy Memorial, addressed to both houses of Congress, beginning with a recital of recent events in California, including the Monterey Convention, and then stressing three points: (1) the Convention and its Constitution resulted from a spontaneous movement by the American settlers, not from executive dictation exercised through General Riley; (2) the prohibition of slavery represented the popular will almost unanimously, despite the fact that two-fifths of those voting for the Constitution were recent immigrants from slaveholding States; and (3) no proposal to project the southern boundary so as to join the Mason and Dixon Line had even come before the Convention.

The stressing of these points indicates pretty clearly the three misrepresentations most widely current in Washington.

Besides refuting these misconceptions, the Memorial went on to show that the right of suffrage and the qualifications for citizenship had been correctly prescribed, that the conclusions of the Convention had been submitted to popular vote, and that the vote of ratification was practically unanimous. The Memorial further reported that in the same election State officers had been chosen, who had entered on their duties, in which they were still engaged. It closed with the words:

This people request admission into the American Union as a State. They understand and estimate the advantages which will accrue to them from such a connection, while they trust they do not too highly compute those which will be conferred upon their brethren. They do not present themselves as suppliants, nor do they bear themselves with arrogance or presumption. They come as free American citizens—citizens by treaty, by adoption, and by birth, and ask that they may be permitted to reap the common benefits, share the common ills, and promote the common welfare as one of the United States of America.

William M. Gwin.
John C. Frémont.
George W. Wright.
Edward Gilbert.

5

WEBSTER'S "seventh of March speech" is so familiar through its magnificent oratory that to reproduce it would be superfluous. But, surprisingly enough, its essential core, without which it becomes little more than oratory, has been omitted from nearly all the published copies, even in such

scholarly works as Alexander Johnston's *American Orations,*
and in Henry Cabot Lodge's well known *Life,* a mere row of
asterisks implying a trivial omission—so unimportant did this
core of the speech seem to scholars who but recently have begun to give a due regard to those economic factors in the
determination of history which Webster's Jove-like mind
comprehended, far ahead of his time. What he really did was
to answer Calhoun's political polemic with a solidly reasoned
account of the rise of the slave power, leading to a conclusion
that seemed cogent at the time, namely, that as cotton could
not be grown in California, slavery was debarred there as by
an Act of God. His logic appeared so unanswerable that in
the end it prevailed in the Senate, securing, albeit piecemeal,
the passage of Clay's "Omnibus Bill," which included the admission of California as a State.

Webster pointed out that in the earliest years of American
history under the Federal Constitution slavery was condemned by "a general concurrence of sentiment" in all parts
of the country, South as well as North. "But soon a change
began, the North growing much more warm and strong
against slavery, and the South growing much more warm and
strong in its support." Then he took a bold stand, as broad-
minded as it was brave.

Sir, there is no generation of mankind whose opinions are not
subject to be influenced by what appears to them to be their
present emergent and exigent interests. I impute to the South no
particularly selfish view in the change which has come over her.
I impute to her certainly no dishonest view. All that has happened has been natural. It has followed those causes which always influence the human mind and operate upon it. What, then,
have been the causes which have created so new a feeling in
favor of slavery in the South, which have changed the whole
nomenclature of the South on that subject, so that . . . it has
now become an institution, a cherished institution, in that quar-

ter; no evil, no scourge, but a great religious, social, and moral blessing, as I think I have heard it latterly spoken of? This, I suppose, Sir, is owing to the rapid growth and sudden extension of the COTTON[8] plantations of the South. So far as any motive consistent with honor, justice, and general judgment could act, it was the COTTON[8] interest that gave a new desire to promote slavery, to spread it, and to use its labor. I again say that this change was produced by causes which must always produce like effects. The whole interest of the South became connected, more or less, with the extension of slavery. If we look back to the history of the commerce of this country in the early years of this government, what were our exports? Cotton was hardly, or to a very limited extent, known. In 1791 the first parcel of cotton of the growth of the United States was exported, and amounted only to 19,200 pounds.[9] It has gone on increasing rapidly, until the whole crop may now, perhaps, in a season of great product and high prices, amount to a hundred millions of dollars. In the years I have mentioned, there was more of wax, more of indigo, more of rice, more of almost every article of export from the South, than of cotton. When Mr. Jay negotiated the treaty of 1794 with England, it is evident from the twelfth article of the treaty, which was suspended by the Senate, that he did not know that cotton was exported at all from the United States. Well, Sir, we know what followed. The age of cotton became the golden age of our Southern brethren. It gratified their desire for improvement and accumulation, at the same time that it excited it. The desire grew by what it fed upon, and there soon came to be an eagerness for other territory, a new area or new areas for the cultivation of the cotton crop; and measures leading to this result were brought about rapidly, one after another, under the lead of Southern men at the head of the Government, they having a majority in both branches of Congress to accomplish their ends. . . . No man acquainted with the history of the Union can deny that the

[8] This typographical emphasis is copied from Webster's unabridged works.
[9] *Seybert's Statistics*, p. 92. A small parcel of cotton found its way to Liverpool from the U. S. in 1784, and was refused admission, on the ground that it could not be the growth of the U. S.—*Note in Webster's Works.*

general lead in the politics of the country, for three-fourths of the period that has elapsed since the adoption of the Constitution, has been a Southern lead. In 1802, in pursuit of the idea of opening a new cotton region, the United States obtained a cession from Georgia of the whole of her Western territory, now embracing the rich and growing States of Alabama and Mississippi. In 1803 Louisiana was purchased from France, out of which the States of Louisiana, Arkansas, and Missouri have been framed, as slaveholding States. In 1819 the cession of Florida was made, bringing in another region adapted to cultivation by slaves. . . . And lastly, Sir, to complete those acts of legislation which have contributed so much to enlarge the area of the institution of slavery, Texas, great, and vast, and illimitable Texas, was added to the Union as a slave State in 1845; and that, Sir, pretty much closed the whole chapter, and settled the whole account.

Webster now announced the main proposition of his speech: "There is not at this moment within the United States, or any territory of the United States, a single foot of land, the character of which, in regard to its being free territory or slave territory, is not fixed by some law, and some irrepealable law, beyond the action of the Government." This he argued with considerable length as to Texas. Coming at last to the crucial question of California and New Mexico, he said:

I hold slavery to be excluded from those territories by a law even superior to that which admits and sanctions it in Texas. I mean the law of nature, of physical geography, the law of the formation of the earth. That law settles forever, with a strength beyond all terms of human enactment, that slavery cannot exist in California or New Mexico. Understand me, Sir; I mean slavery as we regard it; the slavery of the colored race as it exists in the Southern States. California and New Mexico are Asiatic in their formation and scenery. They are composed of vast ridges of mountains, of great height, with broken ridges and deep valleys. The sides of these mountains are entirely barren; their tops capped by perennial snow. There may be in California, now made free by its Constitution, and no doubt there are, some tracts of valuable land. But it is not so in New Mexico. What is there in New Mexico that could, by any possibility, induce anybody to go there with slaves? There are some narrow strips of tillable land on the borders of the rivers; but the rivers themselves dry up before midsummer is gone. All that the people can do in that region is to raise some little articles, some little wheat for their *tortillas,* and that by irrigation. And who expects to see a hundred black men cultivating tobacco, corn, cotton, rice, or anything else, on lands in New Mexico, made fertile only by irrigation? I look upon it, therefore, as a fixed fact, to use the current expression of the day, that both California and New Mexico are destined to be free, free by the arrangement of things ordained by the Power above us. I have, therefore, to say, in this respect also, that this country is fixed for freedom, to as many persons as shall ever live in it, by a less repealable law than that which attaches to the right of holding slaves in Texas; and I will say further, that, if a resolution or a bill were now before us, to provide a territorial government for New Mexico, I would not vote to put any prohibition into it whatever. Such a prohibition would be idle, as it respects any effect it would have upon the territory; and *I would not take pains uselessly to reaffirm an ordinance of nature, nor to re-enact the will of God.*[10]

The argument almost reduces to the syllogism: slavery follows the cotton crop, California cannot grow cotton, hence slavery is no issue there. Even "the godlike Daniel" could not foresee the fallacy of his minor premise, today rendered baseless by modern irrigation methods. California now plants several hundred thousand acres to cotton, with an average yield of some 600 pounds to the acre, nearly treble that for

[10] Author's italics.

the nation at large. And the rapid increase of acreage leads the Governor to warn thoughtful citizens against "industrial peonage, a new type of slavery"! But of course these present-day facts do not in the slightest degree detract from Webster's achievement.[11]

[11] The notes he held in his hand as he delivered his speech are still preserved by the New Hampshire Historical Society, and they emphasize his main contention:

In 1789, when Constitution adopted, everybody regarded Slavery as a great evil.

The sentiment stronger in the South, or oftener expressed, because the South had more of it.

It is called now, an "Institution," a "good," a "blessing," a "Religious, moral, & social blessing"—

Then it was denominated a "blight," a "blast," a "mildew," "a curse"—
. . . ☞ The whole country unanimous, in all this.

But now: What has caused the change?

In the North a stronger religious feeling, & a horror at seeing Slavery increase—

In the South, Cotton—

In 1790-91, &c—Cotton hardly exported—vid Tables

—Sudden growth of this created eagerness for acquisition of Slave Territory—

Cession of Georgia — 1802
Louisiana—   1803
Florida—   1804
And Finally Texas . . .

Now as for California & New Mexico

This is all Free Country by the Ordinance of Nature.

There is no slave there, in our sense of that word, & never can be—

It is an Asiatic formation, & Slavery—

Immense Mountains, & deep vallies—

Especially New Mexico

—Mountains with white tops—parched vallies—no culture but by Irrigation Wilmot, here, would be perfectly without effect. . . .

I wish to be distinct—

I shall not vote for Wilmot, in New Mexico—

Nor in Texas.

As to Texas, I will not violate faith, & repeal the Law of Congress—

As to New Mexico & California—

I will not reaffirm an Ordinance of Nature or attempt to reenact the Will of God.

6

THIS speech, which the orator himself thought the most important of his life, produced diametrically opposite effects on men of opposed temperament and training. As with the Senators that heard it, so the business men and economists that read it, including those in New England, responded to it immediately with a convinced enthusiasm. Gamaliel Bradford gives it the major share of the credit for the postponement of the Civil War for ten years, or "until the growing power of the North got the immense development of the West behind it." James Ford Rhodes says that although it is generally believed that a speech in Congress does not alter opinions, this was certainly not the case in 1850. "Webster's influence was of the greatest weight in the passage of the compromise measures, and he is as closely associated with them as is their author. Clay's adroit parliamentary management was necessary to carry them through the various and tedious steps of legislation," but "it was Webster who raised up for them a powerful and much-needed support from Northern public sentiment." Testimonials of approval came pouring in, of which the most significant was the one from "eight hundred solid men of Boston, who thanked him for 'recalling to us our duties under the Constitution,' and for his 'broad, national, and patriotic views.'"

"The conservative elements everywhere rallied to his support," writes Henry Cabot Lodge in his *Daniel Webster*, "but the triumph was hollow and short-lived. He had attempted to compass an impossibility." The effect on men in whom the emotions predominated, such as preachers and poets, and the public whose emotions they swayed, was to topple him from his pinnacle of popularity and destroy his political prospects. Theodore Parker said at a public meeting in Faneuil Hall:

"I know no deed in American history done by a son of New England to which I can compare this but the act of Benedict Arnold." Emerson called the old statesman "a man who lives by his memory; a man of the past, not a man of faith and hope. All the drops of his blood have eyes that look downward." Whittier wrote his terrible poem "Ichabod"—

> *So fallen! So lost! the light withdrawn*
> *Which once he wore.*
> *The glory from his gray hairs gone*
> *Forevermore. . . .*
>
> *Let not the land once proud of him*
> *Insult him now,*
> *Nor brand with deeper shame his dim*
> *Dishonored brow. . . .*
>
> *Then pay the reverence of old days*
> *To his dead fame;*
> *Walk backward with averted gaze*
> *And hide his shame.*

7

SEWARD'S maiden speech of March 11, 1850 (four days after Webster's) brought him such fame throughout the nation that his political strength dated from it; and it grew so steadily that when Lincoln became President ten years later Seward became Secretary of State as a matter of course. He spoke more than three hours, and bored some of his auditors, but the speech was redeemed by brilliant passages. On the Admission question he said, for example:

California is already a State, a complete and fully appointed State. She can never again be less than that. She can never again be a province or a colony, nor can she be made to shrink and shrivel into the proportions of a federal dependent territory.

California, then, henceforth and forever must be, what she is now, a State. The question whether she shall be one of the United States of America has depended on her, and on us. Her election has been made. Our consent alone remains suspended, and that consent must be pronounced now, or never. I say now, or never. Our harmony cannot increase while this question remains open. We shall never agree to admit California unless we agree now. Nor will California abide delay. I do not say that she contemplates independence; but if she does not, it is because she does not anticipate rejection.

Do you say she can have no motive? Consider, then, her attitude, if rejected. She needs a constitution, a legislature, and magistrates; she needs titles to that golden domain of yours within her borders—good titles, too—and you must give them on your own terms, or she must take them without your leave. She needs a mint, a custom-house, wharves, hospitals, and institutions of learning; she needs fortifications and roads and railroads; she needs the protection of an army and a navy; either your Stars and Stripes must wave over her ports and her fleets, or she must raise aloft a standard for herself. . . .

Are we so moderate, and has the world become so just, that we have no rivals and no enemies to lend their sympathies and aid to compass the dismemberment of our empire? Try not the temper and fidelity of California—at least, not now—not yet. Cherish her and indulge her until you have extended your settlements to her borders, and bound her fast by railroads and canals and telegraphs, to your interests—until her affinities of intercourse are established, and her habits of loyalty are fixed, and then she can never be disengaged.

California would not go alone. Oregon, so intimately allied to her, as yet so loosely attached to us, would go also; and then, at least, the entire Pacific coast, with the western declivity of the Sierra Nevada, would be lost. It would not depend at all upon us, nor even on the mere forbearance of California, how far eastward the long line across the temperate zone should be drawn which would separate *the republic of the Pacific* from *the republic of the Atlantic.*[12]

[12] Author's italics.

It was the phrase *a higher law,* coined during this speech, that spread Seward's fame.

We hold [he said] no arbitrary authority over anything, whether acquired lawfully or seized by usurpation. The Constitution regulates our stewardship; the Constitution devotes the domain [i.e. the territory not formed into States] to union, to justice, to defence, to welfare, and to liberty. *But there is a higher law than the Constitution,*[12] which regulates our authority over the domain, and devotes it to the same noble purposes. The territory is a part, no inconsiderable part, of the common heritage of mankind, bestowed upon them by the Creator of the universe. We are his stewards, and must so discharge our trust as to secure in the highest attainable degree their happiness.

As Rhodes says, this remark about a higher law, while far inferior in rhetorical force to Webster's "I would not take pains uselessly to reaffirm an ordinance of Nature, nor to re-enact the will of God," was destined to have transcendent moral influence. "A speech which can be condensed into an aphorism is sure to shape convictions," and this aphorism of Seward's shaped them not only at the time, with reference to California, but throughout the troubled decade to come, with reference to the whole question of slavery.

Four great speeches, then, starred the most notable debate in all American history, those of Clay, Calhoun, Webster, and Seward; but the greatest of these was Webster's.

8

SOUTHERN extremists in the Senate were as deeply angered by the Great Compromise of 1850, and especially the admission of a free California, as were the extreme New England abolitionists. President Taylor's son-in-law, Senator Jefferson Davis, said when the Senate had decided to admit California, by a vote of 34 to 16, "It is the magnitude of the occasion which justifies the offering of a protest," which he offered at once. Signers of this protest, besides Mr. Davis, were Mason and Hunter of Virginia, Butler and Barnwell of South Carolina, Turney of Tennessee, Atchison of Missouri, and Morton and Yulee of Florida. It began:

We, the undersigned Senators, deeply impressed with the importance of the occasion, and with a solemn sense of the responsibility under which we are acting, submit the following protest against the bill admitting California as a State of this Union, and request that it may be entered upon the journal of the Senate. We feel that it is not enough to have resisted in debate alone a bill so fraught with mischief to the Union and the States we represent, with all the resources of argument which we possessed, but that it is also due to ourselves, the people whose interests have been intrusted to our care, and to posterity, which even in its most distant generations may feel its consequences, to leave, in whatever form may be most solemn and enduring, a memorial of the opposition which we have made to this measure, and of the reasons by which we have been governed, upon the pages of a journal which the Constitution requires to be kept so long as the Senate may have an existence.

The protest claimed further that the Senate by its vote had sanctioned the action of a portion of the inhabitants of California in making an "odious discrimination" against the "property" of the fifteen slaveholding States; that the equality of these States had been destroyed; and that for these and similar reasons the dissolution of the Union was threatened.

Benton cried out against this word "dissolution" with all of his old fire.

"Dissolution" to be entered on our Journal! What would our ancestors have thought of it? The paper contains an enumeration of what it characterizes as unconstitutional, unjust, and oppressive conduct on the part of Congress against the South, which, if persisted in, must lead to a dissolution of the Union, and names the admission of California as one of the worst of these measures. I cannot consent to place that paper on our Journal. . . . I deem it my sacred duty to resist it—to resist the entrance upon our Journal of a paper hypothetically justifying disunion.

In his *Thirty Years' View,* as dictated to Jessie, the old Senator added triumphantly: "The reception of the protest was refused, and the bill sent to the House of Representatives, and readily passed; and immediately receiving the approval of the President, the senators-elect from California, [Messrs. William M. Gwin and John Charles Frémont], who had been long waiting were admitted to their seats; but not without further and strenuous resistance."

9

ALTHOUGH Senator Benton apparently did not know it, the bill had not "readily passed" the House, but encountered "strenuous resistance" there, too. This included a visit to President Taylor by fellow-Whigs, Representatives Alexander Stephens and Robert Toombs of Georgia, demanding that he as their party's chief should join them in refusing admission to California unless, as a rider to the bill, Congress agreed to the recognition and protection of slaves in the other parts of the territory acquired from Mexico—such as Utah and New Mexico—on the same basis as other property. The gruff old General treated them as Andrew Jackson might have done, informing them that he would sign any constitutional law that Congress might pass, and intimating further that he might approve the application of the odious Wilmot Proviso to all the territory in question! On this, they, too, ventured to employ the menacing word "Dissolution," whereupon Old Rough and Ready shouted angrily that if it became necessary he would take the field again to enforce the laws of his country, and should they—his visitors—be taken in rebellion against the Union, he would hang them with as little mercy as he had shown to deserters and spies down in Mexico!

His last days were saddened by such dark shadows of coming events. Within a few hours of his death, on July 9, he said to his physician, "I did not expect to encounter what has beset me since my elevation to the Presidency; God knows that I have endeavored to fulfil what I conceived to be my honest duty."

After the official mourning had ended, the California fight went forward in the House, but even the most determined foes of admission perceived that they waged a losing fight. Representative Thompson of Mississippi, having proposed as a substitute for the Senate bill a southern boundary that would join the Mason and Dixon Line, with the proviso that all the southern area should be "South California," without prohibition of slavery, said on September 7:

I struggle without hope; I know the result in advance. But I have sought the floor to enable me to place on record my own opinions and views. . . . The adoption of a territorial government for South California is demanded by the people of that country.[13] The whole South (that *I* represent) asks for the division [along the Mason and Dixon Line] as an act of justice. Every consideration of sound policy demands this division. . . . By the formation of a territorial government the whole South will feel that they are not excluded by your act; that the majority here has some respect, still, for them and their rights. . . . I see that the majority are bent on their purposes. I despair of equity. I have done my utmost to ward off this blow. My counsel has been unheeded, and I am overpowered. This outrage is this day to be

[13] This was untrue.

perfected, and all I can do is to leave the people's rights in the keeping of the people. In their action I shall acquiesce with more cheerfulness than in your arbitrary course.

What the action of the people in the South would ultimately be had already been foreshadowed in the *Charleston Mercury:*

When the future historian shall address himself to the task of portraying the rise, progress, and decline of the American Union, the year 1850 will arrest his attention, as denoting and presenting the first marshalling and arraying of those hostile forces and opposing elements which resulted in dissolution.

Soon after Representative Thompson concluded his address, the Senate's admission bill passed the House by a vote of 150 to 56. This was on a Saturday; on Monday, September 9, 1850, the new President, Millard Fillmore, turned the bill into law by his signature, and California had indeed become the thirty-first State of the American Union.

Meanwhile, dissatisfaction on the Coast had become acute. For two years the people had vainly hoped that Congress would give them a territorial organization. Now another year had elapsed since the drafting of their Constitution, a year filled with wrangling and contention at Washington, including aspersions showered upon them. "It was during these months of debate and delay in Congress, while the problem of law and order and settled government was daily becoming more critical around them, that the people talked openly of declaring their independence, and of setting up a separate republic on the Pacific, thus bringing to pass the old idea of Lansford W. Hastings and of other empire dreamers in the days before the Mexican War." [14]

[14] Cleland, *History of California*, p. 260.

10

THE PEOPLE could not have chosen better than in sending
Frémont and Gwin to Washington while the question of
admission was still pending. Frémont, although a semi-
invalid, managed, with Gwin's assistance, during his twenty-
one actual working days in the Senate, to introduce eighteen
bills, including two to give his State public lands for educa-
tional uses; one to provide asylums for the insane, deaf-
mutes, and blind; one to open a wagon road across the continent; and one to regulate operations in the mines. But he
incurred enmity by voting against such items of the Omnibus
Bill as those palliating slavery in the District of Columbia
and penalizing encouragement to runaway slaves anywhere.
News of his abolitionist bent got back to California and damaged his chances of re-election among the extreme Southerners there, as did an outspoken charge against him by Senator
Foote that he had framed his mining measure to his own advantage. Characteristically, Frémont challenged Foote to a
duel. The dispute was hushed up, but not the injurious rumor,
one of a multitude provoked by his Mariposas estate. Nevins
calls Mariposas his Pandora Box, which for the next fifteen
years would continue to plague him with countless vexations,
and in the end vanish "as suddenly as a rainbow bubble."

Gwin, his congressional experience a golden asset and his
conciliatory talents "much fine gold," proved a very effective
lobbyist during the long struggle for admission. Mrs. Gwin
being as good a hostess as he was a good mixer, their well-
appointed Washington home lavished true Southern hospitality on leaders of all factions, from Jefferson Davis and Mason
and Hunter and Atchison, who signed the rejected protest, to
Hale of New Hampshire and Fish and Seward of New York.

Thus the indefatigable and influential Gwin cast two anchors to windward. As recorded, he had yielded in the beginning to Clay's persuasiveness in behalf of the Omnibus Bill; but, should admission fail under its provisions, was not his eloquent friend Seward, the new Senator from New York, lined up with Benton and Houston and Frémont to demand admission separately? The exact vanishing point where the politician merges into the statesman is hard to detect, but in so far as unsleeping watchfulness and untiring skill could make Gwin a statesman, he was one.

His most conspicuous service before keeping his promise to Senator Douglas (page 148) and becoming an actual Senator, was a letter to the Secretary of the Treasury with the following recommendations: (1) a survey of the port of San Francisco and the entire Pacific Coast from Cape San Lucas to Puget Sound; (2) the issuance of charts to both merchants and navigators; (3) the location of lighthouses at all harbors along the Coast, with a large revolving minute-light at the entrance to San Francisco Bay, fixed lights at southern and northern points, and lights also at San Pablo Straits, the Straits of Carquinez, Suisun Bay, and the head of San Francisco Bay; (4) the deepening of the channels of both the Sacramento and San Joaquin rivers; (5) the erection of marine hospitals at San Francisco and Stockton; (6) the establishment of ports of entry at San Francisco, Sacramento, San Diego, San Pedro, Santa Barbara, Santa Cruz, Bodega, and Trinidad Bay; (7) the maintenance of life-saving stations; and (8) the establishment of a mint upon a large scale and with generous equipment at San Francisco, with branch mints at Sacramento and Stockton, to benefit the mining traders. Stressing the national significance of such improvements, his letter said:

When we consider that nearly the whole products of the industry of California consist of gold, of which so many millions of dollars have been already shipped to New York, New Orleans, and other ports, augmenting the capital of our country, the value of property and the wages of labor; furnishing a vast and rapidly augmenting market for our own products and manufactures, as well as employment for our vessels; while at the same time in the purchase also of foreign imports, adding millions of dollars annually to our revenue from customs, and giving us a new export with which to sustain the balance of trade in favor of the Union, the importance of furnishing every facility to commerce with California cannot be overrated. Such facilities would not be local, but for the benefit of the revenue of the government and of the trade, industry, commerce, shipping and manufactures of the whole country.

Considering that Gwin had spent only seven months in California, of which a month and a half was absorbed by the Constitutional Convention, he had certainly proved himself "diligent in business." The Secretary of the Treasury transmitted the foregoing letter to the Committee on Commerce, which in due course reported it to the House. Thus business men in Congress and throughout the country gained information about the new State which influenced them much more than oratory. As J. Ross Browne wrote impartially in The *Overland Monthly*,[15] "The services of Dr. Gwin, whose influence in Washington was paramount in procuring the admission of California into the Union, should be gratefully remembered by citizens of this State. . . . No man ever devoted himself more ardently to its interests."

11

THE TRANSMISSION of news between the two coasts was still so slow that although President Fillmore signed the Admission Bill on September 9, California did not know of it

[15] 1st series, XV, 348.

SAN FRANCISCO'S FIRST ADMISSION DAY PARADE *as sketched by Frank Marryat*

ADMISSION DAY BALL. *From an old print*

until October 18. On that morning San Francisco woke up to the booming of guns, fired by the steamship *Oregon* as she came in through the Gate. Immediately the whole of the inhabitants were afoot, according to the exuberant *Annals of San Francisco*, and grew half wild with excitement until they learned definitely that the tidings were as they had hardly dared hope. Business of almost every description was instantly suspended, the courts adjourned in the midst of their work, and men rushed from every house into the streets and toward the wharves, to hail the blessed harbinger. When the steamer rounded Clark's Point and came in front of the city, her masts literally covered with flags and streamers, one common shout arose from "ten thousand voices on the wharves, in the streets, upon the hills, housetops, and the world of shipping in the Bay." Every public place was soon crowded with eager news-seekers, and the first papers issued from the press—within an hour after the *Oregon* appeared—brought from $1 to $5 each.

Enthusiasm mounted with the sun. Flags of all nations broke out on a thousand peaks and staffs, while two big cannon, hastily dragged into the Plaza, bellowed incessantly. When night came, all the saloons and gambling hells sparkled with their brightest lights, music blared from all their hundred bands, balls and other entertainments were hastily got up, bonfires blazed upon the fourteen hills, rockets spurted skyward until dawn.

Unsatiated with a single day and night of jubilation, the citizenry appointed October 29 as special Joy Day. A serpentine procession of various civic and fraternal orders, gay with decorations and riotous with music, wound in and out along the makeshift streets to come to a stand in the Plaza. Although Bret Harte had not yet come, his heathen Chinese had, of whom a brigade in exotic costumes carried aloft a banner with the strange device, "China Boys." On one of the floats, Miss California, "Belle of the Pacific," stood between army and navy officers, while from another the enterprising *Alta California* newspaper distributed from its trundling printing press a special ode composed for the occasion by a Mrs. Wills of Louisiana, so that nobody could have an excuse for not trying to sing it to the tune of "The Star-Spangled Banner" after the Honorable Nathaniel Bennett should have delivered himself of his oration. When he finally finished, huzzas resounded not only from the densely crowded Plaza, but from all the nearer hills, which were black with celebrants, amid whose shouting the names of Clay and Webster, Benton and Frémont, Fillmore and Gwin, could be occasionally distinguished.

In the evening, bonfires blazed again from Telegraph Hill, Rincon Point, and the islands of the Bay. As night wore on, "some 500 gentlemen and 300 ladies met at the grandest public ball that had yet been witnessed in the city, and danced and made merry until daylight, in the pride and joy of their hearts that California was truly now *the thirty-first State of the Union!"*

12

JESSIE, in Washington, celebrated the day after Admission Day by going to the Senate to glory in the sight of Senator Barnwell of South Carolina—who had fought admission to the last ditch—escorting her husband up the aisle to take the senatorial oath. Later, when the gallant Southerner paid a tribute to Frémont's "statesmanlike qualities in so prompt and clear a presentation of bills covering the immediate needs of his infant charge," Jessie took some of this compliment to herself, for she had made the final copies not only of these bills, but of thirteen others still on the docket. Letters of congratulation came pouring in from California before Congress finally adjourned, but with them came also disquieting news of Mariposas. A prompt journey West seemed clearly indicated. Frémont planned to go alone, as Jessie was again with child. But his chief of staff, as the Bentons now called Jessie, would not hear of this, as she wanted her next baby to be a Californian. So he was: John Charles, Junior, born at San Francisco in the April of 1851.

His father's infancy had been somewhat ludicrously menaced by a fracas in a Nashville inn, but there was nothing ludicrous about the turbulence into which Junior was born. When he was two weeks old the "Great Fire" occurred, so called as the fifth and largest of an incendiary series that razed large sections of the young city six times in a year and a half; the incendiaries being left-overs of the Hounds abetted by "Sydney ducks" migrating from the prison camps of Australia, lured by California's gold. Sam Brannan, the Mormon elder who had castigated the Hounds, organized a Vigilance Committee on June 9, but paid for it by losing much of his property in the sixth of the fires, on June 22. But the sixth fire was the last. Ironically, such was the spirit of the city that the only abiding achievement of the ferocious fire-fiends was the banding together of a group of pioneers almost wholly neglected by Washington except for purposes of revenue, but resolved at all costs to establish and maintain a semblance of law in a lawless community, to set up and sustain social order despite organized destruction intrenched in political corruption.

This was all to the credit of the Vigilantes, but the debit side of their ledger must be charged with enlarging the cleavage between "Yankee shopkeepers" and the "Southern chivalry," or "chivs," as North and South factions derisively dubbed each other in the prelude to war of which the hoarse notes began to be heard in California in 1851.

Frémont's amazing energy saved his rented Stockton Street

home during the Great Fire, but he was up at Mariposas when the next one came, and the faithful Gregorio saved Jessie and her baby as the house was burned from over their heads. Frémont reached them a few days later, almost frantic with anxiety, to find his little family in a cottage among the sand-dunes, Gregorio having improvised an outdoor kitchen, and the rough neighbors seeming to Jessie most touchingly kind. But she had suffered many hardships, and before '51 ended her husband came to her with shining eyes and the shouted question, "How would you like a trip to Paris?" "Splendid," she cried, looking up from her sewing, "and Charley shall get a closer peep at the Man in the Moon, too!"

Frémont threw into her lap a gaily colored packet of steamship tickets reading "From San Francisco to Chagres and thence direct to France." Thinking first of him, as always, she exclaimed, as the reality of the trip dawned upon her, "It will be your first vacation, your first rest!" "And yours," he rejoined, "the first rest you have had since you spoke those fateful words, 'Whither thou goest, I will go!'"

Before she left California to be entertained by royalty in both France and England, she saw and heard the unmistakable signs of far-off civil war.

PART FOUR

STORM SIGNALS

AN INTER-URBAN SECTIONAL
FEUD

DURING the short stay of the Frémonts in California in 1851 they heard of an amazing sectional feud across the bay from San Francisco, between the towns of Benicia and Napa, separated by a few miles of land and river.

Benicia, founded about the time of the Bear Flag Revolt by Dr. Robert Semple, got its name in an engaging roundabout fashion. "The long Doctor," foreseeing like John C. Calhoun a metropolis on the great Bay of St. Francis, and desiring to be the founder of it, had played upon the well-known gallantry of General Mariano Vallejo to obtain at a bargain price the site for his city. Madam Vallejo chanced to be named Francisca, so Semple ingratiated himself with the great Spanish landholder by proposing to name the metropolis of his dreams Francisca, a stroke that would also appropriate to his benefit, as far as he dared, the name of the bay itself. Even his audacious Kentucky imagination balked at the idea of scooping the world-famous name, complete, for a mere blueprint—if indeed he had one—and a few square miles of sand. But the hamlet of Yerba Buena jumped at the chance, through its *alcalde*, Lieutenant Bartlett, formerly of the *Portsmouth*, who had already christened the Plaza with the name of that ship, and applied the name of Montgomery, her captain, to a miry water-front. New Year's Day of 1847 was signalized by Alcalde Bartlett's official proclamation that Yerba Buena should ever thereafter be San Francisco.

Semple felt much chagrined. The name Francisca, of which

219

he had been so proud, became a boomerang. It so closely resembled the name of its renamed rival that every settler or sea captain who heard it would impute it and all his boosting of it to the impudent hamlet boomed by Bartlett. So in sheer self-defense he had shifted to Madam Vallejo's second name, Benicia.

Lieutenant William Tecumseh Sherman sided with Semple, and never forgave San Francisco's "impudence." The matter seemed to him so important that he treats of it in his dignified *Memoirs*, being convinced, as he says, that "this little circumstance was big with consequences. That Benicia has the best natural site for a city, I am satisfied; and had half the money and half the labor bestowed on San Francisco been expended at Benicia, we should have at this day a city of palaces."

Semple being a Kentuckian, his boom town, Benicia, attracted "chivs," while Napa, already established across the estuary, filled up with "Yankee shopkeepers."

In due time a "chiv" of the border ruffian type crossed over the Napa River and tried to beat up a freedman. But the black man, emboldened by his friendly environment, worsted his Benicia assailant. Some time later, when the Benician was visiting in Napa again, he became entangled in an altercation on the slavery question with the local judge. Unkindly, the judge reminded him that a former slave had once got the better of him. The Benician, handy with the bowie knife, slit the judicial throat. Promptly arrested for murder and thrust into the Napa jail, he was quickly tried by a Napa jury and lodged upstairs in the jail to await his hanging. But Benicia now gets busy. Governor McDougal, a "chiv" who lives on the Benicia side of the river, being apparently receptive to a petition for a reprieve provided some Napans sign it, one of those natural-born petition-circulators who inhabit every community promptly ferries over to Napa with a sheet of foolscap in his hand. His name is Cooper. Unkindly, the Napans tell Cooper to take his foolscap back to Benicia where it belongs. They further tell him that if he and his petition come their way again they will send him home not by the ferry but on a rail. Hastening homeward, he reports to his fellow "chivs," who hurry with him to the Governor and beg for a reprieve signed only on their side of the river. The Governor deliberates, and deliberation takes time. With a large gesture of generosity he at last consents, and on the dawn of the very day set for the hanging, the Benician sheriff, a reprieve in his pocket, hustles with his posse to the ferry landing. But the ferryman, a Napan, is on the other side, and no amount of shouting brings him over. The mounted sheriff, with his mounted posse, never before had essayed to ford the Napa River, and it takes a lot of time to find a shallow crossing. When, at last, splashed and angry, they enter the strangely empty Napa streets and reach the jail, they see upon the threshold the end of a rope, which guides them up the stairs to a heavily timbered cell, and lo and behold! Dangling from the other end of the hundred feet of hemp, which has been looped over a beam, their fellow-Benician greets them, as a local historian puts it, in a state of permanent suspense.

This was a specimen of grim political humor that Jessie never forgot.

THE GWIN-BRODERICK FEUD:
1851, 1854

SECTIONAL PASSIONS inflamed neighboring California towns against each other, a decade before the Civil War began, and even invaded political councils. Flames were fed not so much by the slavery issue itself as by the class hatred that slavery somehow engendered. One of these caste feuds involved Gwin in the bitterest struggle of his entire career, its effect persisting to this day in a damaged reputation, ninety years after the triumphant Senator's first return from Washington. While, in the June of '51, he was being acclaimed on landing at San Francisco from the Panama steamer, a Tammany Democrat stood on Long Wharf bent on challenging him to an intra-party duel without parallel in California's annals, or, possibly, in all American history.

Gwin was not the only forty-niner lured to the "land of promise" not by gold, but by ambition. David Colbrith Broderick was another, arriving like Gwin and Jessie in the June of '49, but taking his own time to "make ready" before he fired. When he did fire, the explosion was uproarious and prolonged. As with the Burns Case in New England, the Squatter Riots in Kansas and Nebraska, and the attempt of Osawatomie Brown to incite to slave uprisings in Virginia, so "the Gwin-Broderick Controversy," as it was politely called, proved to be for California a prelude to the war, therefore significant even beyond its persisting injury to the fame of one of the parties, and the violent death of the other.

The Manhattan Irishman, fifteen years younger than Gwin, was pretty nearly his exact opposite. Son of one of the stone-

222

cutters who had carved the pillars in the Senate chamber in Washington, he never forgot this fact as he plied his father's trade for five years on the New York East Side, or, later, sold grog there as his remunerative vocation, while practicing his triple avocations of boxer, fireman, and boss of the old Ninth Ward. The Bowery boys named him for Congress in 1846, but a Whig defeated him, and this stung him to a lifelong political belligerency. His Tammany leadership he determined to exchange for a senatorial toga, and California provided his chance. On leaving the East he told his friend Daniel E. Sickles, as Gwin told Stephen A. Douglas, that he would come back in a year as Senator. On arriving in San Francisco he said it more pungently: "I tell you, Sir, by God, that for one hour's seat in the Senate of the United States I would roast before a slow fire in the Plaza!" "I'll go if I have to march over a thousand corpses, and every corpse a friend!"

There you have Broderick, self-painted. He knew what he wanted, and would go any length to get it.

His first prominence in State politics was his presidency of the organizing convention of Democrats at San José during "the legislature of a thousand drinks," to which the San Francisco Tammanyites had elected him almost unanimously; for Stevenson's Regiment had set up a Tammany Hall there, and Dave Broderick quickly became its master. To achieve this he first mastered the Empire Fire Company, such companies, on account of the "fires," having become influential. Colonel Stevenson and many of the disbanded New York Volunteers aided him, hip and thigh. When Governor Burnett resigned and McDougal succeeded him, Broderick, as president pro tem of the Senate, succeeded McDougal as Lieutenant Governor.

His salaried San Francisco job was in the branch mint Gwin had established, but this took only a part of his energy, so he formed a partnership with a trained assayer and manu-

factured gold "slugs" that were much more convenient than
the buckskin pouches of gold dust, and readily passed current
at their face values of $5 and $10 each, although intrinsically
worth only $4 and $8 respectively. Along with this lucrative
side line he also manufactured the heavy kind of jewelry affected by the newly rich, wielding a sledge hammer in the
stamping press instead of the mallet and chisel of the marble
cutter.

Collision with Gwin, who monopolized Federal patronage
in the new and Democratic State, could not long be deferred.
Indeed, these two men must have collided had there been no
patronage. They were both Democrats, and there the resem-
blance ended. Comb the whole country, and two more different politicos could not have been found, thought Jessie: in
physique, temperament, breeding, political training. In appearance, Gwin was a sleek handsome mastiff, Broderick a
belligerent bulldog. Gwin was always cool and usually self-
controlled, Broderick hot-tempered and arbitrary. Gwin was
the Southern aristocrat, Broderick the Bowery boy. Gwin's
political technique always suggested the foils, Broderick's the
boxing gloves, and loaded at that. Or, to put it more simply,
Gwin always remained a fine-fingered surgeon, Broderick a
rough-handed stonecutter. To Broderick, Gwin was always
"a silk-sock Southern tyrant," any of whose utterances be-
speaking devotion to the Union or opposition to slavery
were just so much camouflage for sinister belief and conduct.
To Dr. Gwin, on the other hand, Broderick was merely a
necessary evil, such as he had sometimes encountered in
Mississippi and Louisiana and Washington. Nothing could be
more obvious than that they couldn't get on together. It
was their fate that they had to.

With Broderick, politics was war, and war what William
Tecumseh Sherman subsequently called it. But with an inborn originality Broderick scorned traditional strategy and

loved what is now known as the blitzkrieg. To gain absolute mastery of the State's Democracy, Gwin being absent in Washington, and Frémont in Europe with Jessie, he planned a gigantic blitzkrieg for the State Democratic Convention of 1854 at Sacramento, where the capital had been finally established in that year. As chairman of the Central Committee he made all the arrangements, including rental of the big Baptist church. With such aides-de-camp as the infamous "Judge" Ned McGowan, a fugitive from Pennsylvania justice; James P. Casey, whom the Vigilantes of '56 were to hang for murder; and one Billy Mulligan, Broderick chose as his GHQ the immense pulpit platform, pre-empting for his secondary aides the two Amen corners, and keeping the keys to the rear entrance in his pocket.

It was another case of "best-laid plans." The McDougal "chivs" had a good intelligence service. At the outset the Tammany plan functioned pretty well. But the rear entrance did its full duty when the Chivalry poured in through the front doors on the stroke of the appointed hour, 3 p.m. The platform and the Amen corners were already crammed with Broderick's men, with himself in the midst thereof. But things now began to go wrong. The henchman told off to rush the nomination of McGowan as permanent chairman failed of his hair-trigger duty, apparently intimidated by the walking-arsenal aspect of the "chivs." In that split second of hesitation McDougal got himself nominated. Broderick, however, ignored the "chiv" nomination, and calmly recognized McGowan's, which hadn't been made.

James O'Meara, that technicolor political reporter whose portrait of Gwin has already been presented, declares that indescribable confusion now prevailed, in the midst of which the McDougal nominator put his own motion, which he declared carried, and before Broderick could announce McGowan elected, Governor McDougal was thrusting his way to the chairman's chair upon the platform. The Amen corners now milled with impious men of both factions, "bawling, shrieking, threatening gun-play." The platform itself milled almost as violently, and it took the fiery leadership of the Supreme Court Justice, David S. Terry of Texas, to prevent McDougal's ejection from his chair. (Remember that fatal name of Terry!) So McDougal and McGowan sat there beside each other, each attempting to put the motions bawled out by their respective factions. The only officer on whom both factions agreed was a secretary. The church had a seating capacity of 400, but was jammed with 600, of whom at least a hundred continually brandished pistols, so it remains a California wonder that no massacre occurred.

From three until eight p.m. these extraordinary conditions prevailed, says O'Meara, whose Irish imagination conjured visions of Dante when darkness fell. For the church trustees refused to light it in the regular way, and the feeble glow from two candles, each held by a sturdy volunteer beside each chairman, served no more than to reveal his whereabouts. No face was visible half a dozen yards away; only at the closest range could any man be recognized. Then, after five hours of bedlam, an amazing thing happened. Somebody made a motion that got itself heard, and it was carried. In accordance with its terms, the two contesting chairmen arose from their chairs, locked arms, and proceeded peaceably down the middle aisle, followed by pairs similarly united, from the howling platform. The Amen corners followed suit, and then the body of the church. But once outside the sacred edifice the factions again separated, to meet next day in hostile camps, the "chivs" in Musical Hall and the Broderickites in Carpenter's Hall, and to nominate rival tickets to carry factional warfare into every precinct of the Democratic State. But before adjournment, and without pre-arrangement, both the "chivs" and the Broderickites remembered the damaged church, the former assessing themselves $5 each and the Tammanyites taking up a collection of $400, "a committee having reported that the building had been injured to that extent."

Gwin, in Washington when this split in his party occurred, soon became acutely aware of it, suffering a blitzkrieg on his own account. Broderick began one later in that same year of 1854 by summoning the legislature to convene ahead of time and ordering it to nominate him instead of renominating Gwin. But Broderick's knowledge of Tammany psychology did not fit the pioneers. To his surprise and chagrin, old settlers dominating the legislature rebuffed his totalitarian methods and demanded the re-election of "Old Gwin." He did succeed in blocking this move for eight months, and throughout that time California had only one Senator at Washington: an Ohio ex-congressman who had come out on the *Panama* with Jessie, and who succeeded Frémont in the Senate after Frémont's short term expired—one John B. Weller, a Southern sympathizer ingeniously called by the Unionists a Copperhead, "from a reptile which waits on the rattlesnake, the rattlesnake being emblematic of the South." [1]

GWIN JOINS DOUGLAS IN COMPROMISE REPEAL: 1854

JESSIE was in Washington with her parents when Gwin committed the first of three major political errors. Old Bullion, having lost his senatorial seat because of his opposition to slavery in the proslavery State of Missouri, had doughtily

---

[1] Goldwin Smith, *The United States:* Macmillan, New York, 1899, p. 255.

stood for a seat in the House, and won. Learning that Jefferson Davis as Secretary of War had outmaneuvered him by designating West Point regulars to outline a railway route to the Pacific, instead of his son-in-law, he had reacted in his characteristic manner by writing to Frémont to come back home and survey an independent route that he himself would finance. While Frémont was engaged on this railway expedition, Jessie aided her father in the research and actual writing required by his *Thirty Years' View.*

But important history was in the making as she wrote. On January 4, 1854, Gwin's friend Senator Stephen A. Douglas of Chicago introduced a bill of which it has been said that no act since the foundation of the government had ever equaled it in danger to the Nation, and Gwin supported him for no better reason than personal and partisan loyalty.

Douglas, ambitious for the presidency, maneuvered his repeal of the Compromise of 1850 in connection with an act carving Kansas and Nebraska into territories out of the huge slab of "bacon" known as the Louisiana Purchase. As chairman of the committee on territories, Douglas accompanied his proposal to organize the only unorganized part of the United States—a vast region of nearly half a million square miles—with a report vitally affecting slavery. By study of the Omnibus Bill of 1850 he claimed to have discovered that it did not prohibit slavery from the proposed territorial area. In fact, the essential principle of the famous Compromise, he said, was the right of every territorial community to determine for itself the character of its local institutions. He gave color to this contention by pointing out that California had come in as a free soil State because it so desired, while Utah and New Mexico had been organized into territories with no requirement as to slavery. Within a few days his ideas grew. By definitely separating Kansas from Nebraska he provided an opportunity for both the North and South factions to annex a State, thus throwing out his political anchors in two directions. He also added an amendment to his bill declaring explicitly what originally had been only implied: that even the Missouri Compromise of 1820 should be now stricken from the statute books.

A powerful debater, with a larger personal following than any Senator of his times except Clay, "the little giant" waged his warfare from January through May, and finally won, with Gwin's astute aid. His bill passed the House amid some of the wildest scenes ever known there, Old Bullion sturdily voting against it. He and Jessie saw clearly that the whole question of the extension of slavery was now thrown wider open than ever. The Compromise of 1850, although opposed for a time in the North, had in the end been accepted, and the nation had settled into a tranquillity unknown for years. As Paxson puts it, the Compromise had saved the day, and secession was averted until it was too late for it to succeed. Rhodes says that many men contemporary with the events went so far as to say that if the Compromise of 1850 and the preceding one of 1820 had not been abrogated the Civil War might have been averted altogether. At any rate, both sections were thrown into the wildest excitement by the mad action of Douglas. Men in the North who had been almost unable to swallow the new Fugitive Slave Law now felt they had been cheated. "The Fugitive law did much to unglue the eyes of men," wrote Ralph Waldo Emerson to the New York *Evening Post*, "and now the Nebraska bill leaves us staring." While the proslavery South rejoiced in an entirely unexpected triumph, handed to it by a Western senator eager for its votes, gloom and wrath overspread the entire North. Horace Greeley wrote that Douglas and President Pierce, between them, made more abolitionists in three months than Wendell Phillips and William Lloyd Garrison could have made in half a century. A new political party was born expressly to fight the extension of slavery, and Frémont became its first standard-bearer, with Jessie as his "chief of staff."

THE FRÉMONT PRESIDENTIAL CAMPAIGN: 1856

FRÉMONT'S railway expedition of 1853-54, by which Old Bullion was not seeking personal gain but the defeat of Jefferson Davis's "Cotton Kingdom" line, was in itself a sign of the widening sectional chasm. Frémont and his score of followers braved hardships almost equaling any he had ever faced, and surveyed a good route, but the impending cloud of war darkened any such enlightened project as a transcontinental road, in the North and South alike. Davis's devotion to his purpose led him subsequently to attempt transportation by camels, while Frémont wrote to a newspaper, "It seems a treason against mankind and the spirit of progress which marks the age to refuse to put this one completing link to our national prosperity and the civilization of the world. Europe still lies between Asia and America; build this railroad and things will have revolved about; America will lie between Asia and Europe—the golden vein which runs through the history of the world will follow the iron track to San Francisco."

This sounds like an echo of some of Benton's speeches, whose dream of an American-Asiatic intercourse is perpetuated by his St. Louis monument, which shows his bronze figure pointing toward the Pacific, underlined with his ringing words, "There lies the road to India!" Seeing his hopes of union with the outer world threatened by disunion at home—he lost even his seat in the House in the fall elections of 1854 on the issue of slavery—Benton prepared to take the lecture platform as a last resort to warn the people of their peril. "I will be a new Peter the Hermit," he declared, "and though you now call me mad, later you will admit I was inspired." The year 1855 found him proclaiming on every hand that the Union was in danger of dissolution, that all its friends must rally round it, and that the further extension of slavery as permitted by the Kansas-Nebraska Act must be opposed by all constitutional means. In New England he was so struck with the appreciative, listening faces of the women that he asked to be taken for the nights into the home of some mechanic rather than those who usually entertained strangers. "They only represent money," he said; "I want to see more of these women, who represent themselves, and the real life of New England."

That was a year of sorrows for him. The wife of his youth had died in the preceding autumn, and the only alleviation of this crushing blow was afforded by the presence of Jessie with her infant son Frank Preston, as she worked diligently with him on his opus. But a fire presently destroyed the old C Street house with all its lares and penates, the precious mementos of many years. President Pierce was so touched, despite political differences, that he invited him and Jessie to a temporary home in the White House. From Southern kin came distressful letters to Jessie, "Are you and Colonel Frémont with *us*, or are you following your father's views, so *strange* for a Southerner?" "The bitterness of the coming strife invaded even my guarded room," wrote Jessie, recovering from an illness, "and as soon as I could be moved, New York became our city of refuge."

But New York can be hot in summer, and while she was resting at Nantucket her husband came up from the city to tell her that he had been approached with a tentative offer of the Democratic nomination for the presidency. It was decidedly a tentative offer, with two strings tied to it: endorsement of the Kansas-Nebraska Act and the Fugitive Slave Law. Yet Edward Carrington, who knew Jessie as well as he knew her husband, but not so well as he thought he did, waved Frémont farewell to Nantucket with the jaunty words, "We Democrats are sure to win, and no woman can refuse the Presidency!" (Carrington represented a fusionist movement, designed to unite a large body of liberal Democrats with the American or Know-nothing group.)

As Frémont drew near the seaside cottage he paused to enjoy a picture: Jessie in a summer gown at a tea-table, serving her three children. Lily the motherly held in her lap the chubby pink-cheeked baby, Frank Preston, while Frémont's namesake, now a big boy, leaned against Jessie's chair as she told the thousand-and-first chapter of a whaling serial she had improvised for his delight. "As I watched that family picture," Frémont said later, "I longed for the power to make it the symbol of my Jessie's future, but I had come to impart disturbing knowledge." For already he had made up his mind, and when the two sat on Lighthouse Hill later in the evening he said, "Carrington said no woman can refuse the Presidency, but with those strings to the nomination we *must* refuse."

Afterward, Jessie recounted her own reaction: "There was no shadow of doubt in our minds. At the foot of the bluff on which the lighthouse stood were the remains of a ship embedded in the sands, the seas washing her ribs. Above, steady and brilliant, flashed out the recurring light. Here was symbol of a choice between a wreck of dishonor or a kindly light on its mission of good. With clasped hands we made our decision and turned homeward with the kindly beacon at our back."

Little could they think that the new party that was shaping itself on the principle of *No Compromise with Slavery* would come to them too. Already in 1854, just after the enactment of the Kansas-Nebraska bill, citizens of Jackson, Michigan, invited adherents of that principle to assemble there, on July 6; and in consequence of that meeting the "Republican" party came into being. Within a year "the Republican Association of Washington, D. C.," had become energetic in organizing Republican clubs in the North and West, and by the beginning of 1856 it felt strong enough to call a preliminary convention at Pittsburgh, on Washington's Birthday, when Francis P. Blair, Sr., was chosen chairman, and Horace Greeley of the New York *Tribune* began to give the movement publicity. At a mass meeting on the following evening Greeley created excitement by suggesting in his speech that the North could aid Kansas by sending well-armed emigrants into that territory. Quickly thereafter the national committee summoned a National Convention to meet at Philadelphia on the anniversary of the battle of Bunker Hill, June 17, so as to name Republican candidates for the presidency and vice-presidency of the United States.

Long before the Convention met, Blair, a veteran Washington journalist, called at the Frémont home at 56 Ninth Street, New York, to say that the Pathfinder was his choice, and that of his associates, as standard-bearer. John Bigelow of the New York *Evening Post* converted his chief, William Cullen Bryant, to the same conviction. From the outset the Frémont following included distinguished literary men, who so increased that their roster resembles a tablet from the Hall of Fame: Greeley, Dana, Bayard Taylor, George William Curtis, Henry Ward Beecher, Edward Everett Hale, R. W. Emerson, John G. Whittier, H. W. Longfellow, the aged Washington Irving, President Felton and Professor Silliman of Harvard and Yale, respectively, and so on. Leading publicists under the Frémont banner are entitled to another tablet: David Wilmot of Pennsylvania and of the antislavery

"Proviso," Wendell Phillips, Charles Sumner, George F. Hoar, Salmon P. Chase, Thurlow Weed, Carl Schurz, Schuyler Colfax, Hannibal Hamlin—and Abraham Lincoln, whose speech against Douglas at Peoria, Illinois, on October 5, 1854, had catapulted him into national fame.

Despite such brilliant supporters, Frémont's nomination faced a formidable opposition in the first nominating convention of the Republican party. The high social and trade influences of New York City and Philadelphia opposed it, while even in Boston many old Whig families of aristocratic pretensions held aloof from the new party altogether. "It is one of the curiosities of politics that this convention of honest and competent men made a nomination that Republicans have not ceased to apologize for. Yet they did but register the popular will."

Rhodes, from whom this last statement is quoted, gives much space to Frémont's nomination, reaching the conclusion that hard-boiled politicians, such as Thaddeus Stevens, had to give way to it because of popular demand; much as the master politicians at Philadelphia in June of 1940 had to accept the nomination of Wendell Willkie.

The public of 1856 was romantically minded. Ford equals any American historian in matter-of-factness, yet even this Massachusetts businessman, being above everything honest, has to set it down soberly of Frémont that "what brought him before the public mind were his daring and energetic explorations in the West; a halo of romance clung around his expeditions. A glamour was cast over his affairs of love. The story of his attachment to the daughter of Senator Benton, her devotion, and their romantic marriage crowned his heroic exploits."

Not that Senator Benton approved his son-in-law's entrance into politics! He denounced the young Republican party as "a motley mixture of malcontents with no real desire in any of them to save the Union," and wrote to a friend concerning his mortification that "Frémont has allowed himself to be got hold of: I did what I could to prevent it but in vain, telling him that my opposition would have to become public." It did, too. The whole Republican movement, he asserted publicly, accentuated sectional hostility. "Does any one really believe," he asked in the *Tribune*, "that the South would tolerate such a President as Frémont?" "We are treading upon a volcano that is liable at any moment to burst forth and overwhelm the nation."

It is doubtful whether even Senator Benton foresaw the slimy mass of vituperation that was to be poured upon the Frémonts not only from the South but from the extreme Abolitionists in the North. William Lloyd Garrison assailed Frémont for not being as intolerant as he himself was. With Garrison's support and that of his fellow extremists, the *Radical Abolitionist* ran its own ticket, headed by one Gerrit Smith. Diatribes in every issue accused Frémont of compromises with "the monstrous evil" of slavery, the exact reverse of the truth. In the South it was precisely his uncompromising stand on slavery that brought the worst abuse. Dellenbaugh prefaces his excellent work on *Frémont and '49* with the statement that its subject has not received justice at the hands of his government or of his fellow-countrymen, adding that this is partly explained by the animosities of the campaign of 1856, which left an indelible stain. "Hostile journals delineated Frémont as a shallow, vainglorious, 'woolly-horse,' 'mule-eating,' 'free-love,' 'nigger-embracing,' black Republican, an extravagant, insubordinate, reckless adventurer, a financial spendthrift and political mountebank, and it has since been difficult even for sensible people to disentangle their judgment from this fog of slander that still thickens the air. Frémont appears to have suffered from at least three causes: his success, which brought against him the subtle powers of jealousy; extravagant laudation by his friends; and his active opposition to slavery."

From the first, Jessie shared his praise and also his abuse. In no other presidential campaign has a woman so enlisted public interest. The ratification meeting in New York crowded Beecher's tabernacle to the doors, and at the close the audience marched in torchlight procession up Broadway to the Ninth Street home, in front of which, after Frémont himself had spoken, an augmented multitude shouted, "Jessie Benton," "Jessie Frémont!" She responded, and from that moment "Our Jessie" figured in the cartoons and songs and speeches and newspaper articles of the first Republican campaign, equally with her husband.

The vilest of all the attacks on Frémont came from Richmond, where Henry A. Wise disgraced an honorable Virginia name by a speech in which he vilified "a Frenchman's bastard." Jessie never did anything finer than in the reply she wrote for John Bigelow to use in the campaign biography he prepared—dealing with her husband's birth and infancy. Readers interested in one of the greatest of American women may find this self-revelation in Mrs. Catherine Phillips's definitive biography. Jessie comes into this present chapter only because it deals with her view of California's still unanswered question, now swiftly resolving itself, under her eyes, into a contest between the Stars and Stripes and the Stars and Bars.

In California itself, the question had already arrived, although the Stars and Bars, as an actual flag, was not yet devised.

California alarmed the unionists by casting her four electoral votes for the Democrats. But Frémont captured New York and ten other States, summing up to 114 electoral votes. Former President Fillmore, running on the American or Know-nothing ticket, got only 8. James Buchanan, Jessie's old beau, a lifelong machine Democrat from Pennsylvania, won the race with 174, and the Civil War was postponed until an uncompromising rail-splitter from Illinois made it inevitable, in view of what Stephen A. Douglas had done.

In this election of 1856 the Whigs simply vanished, theirs having been the party of compromise.

THE CALIFORNIA VIGILANTES OF 1856 REFUSE TO WITHDRAW FROM THE UNION

THE SAN FRANCISCO crisis of that menacing year fortunately came under the control of the greatest of all adopted Californians, William Tell Coleman, a Kentuckian, and president of the second Vigilance Committee. The gangs of robbers and cutthroats and political corruptionists necessitating that resuscitated movement for self-preservation must be charged flatly against David C. Broderick. "Not even his most adoring worshipers," it is truly written, "have been able entirely to conceal the plain fact that in the final analysis he must, more than any one man, shoulder responsibility for the municipal corruption which was the basic cause of the second uprising of a tormented and enraged citizenry. He was the one man who could have halted the thievish officials and politicians of the most corruptly governed city in the country." James King of William, before his brutal murder by one of Broderick's henchmen, wrote in his brave little reform sheet, the *Bulletin,* "If we can only escape David C. Broderick's hired bullies a little longer, we will turn this city inside out but what we will expose the corruption and malfeasance of her officiary." King died, but in his death he served the community even better than in his life, for it was his murder that brought "the Great Committee" into being, and by means of this Committee the hired bullies became extinct. To extinguish them, Coleman had to organize and drill a genuine army of six thousand men, fully equipped. After these men had done their duty, certain rabid secessionists sought to induce "the Lion of the Vigilantes" to use his army in withdrawing California from the Union.

In a book bearing the quoted name, which was coined by Robert Louis Stevenson, the present writer has told the inside story of the seditious attempt, so that here it is only summarized. The same Henry S. Foote of Mississippi whom Frémont had challenged to a duel in Washington came out to California, and in company with local secessionists approached Coleman to suggest that with his six thousand well-armed and well-trained troops—artillery and cavalry and infantry—it would be no job at all to seize the feeble Federal garrisons together with the Benicia arsenal, so as to proclaim "a Western Empire with a glorious independent future" and Coleman as its Emperor. California, these disunionists argued, should be not only physically, but politically, separated from the Atlantic seaboard States. "It was the natural location for a great Pacific Empire," they said, and "now was the most fitting time to take the initiative."

Southerners had settled in northern California at a ratio of about forty to every sixty Northerners, but many were just as loyal to the Union as Coleman. The secessionists misjudged their man. He told them that he would rather be a mere citizen of "the grand empire of the Union" than "Emperor of the Californias." When his Vigilantes had thoroughly done their work, he disbanded them, and resumed his quiet life as a merchant.

THE GWIN-BRODERICK CONTRO-
VERSY RAGES TO ITS CLOSE

IN THIS same fateful year 1856, the mad action of Douglas two years before, having already damaged the nation at large, began to ripen to its bloody fruit in Kansas; a result which Senator Gwin, unhappily, aided with his vote even when Senator Douglas had repented and refused to be a party to the Lecompton constitution as endorsed by Buchanan.

Lecompton and Topeka were two small settlements on the Kansas River only sixteen miles apart. Topeka was settled by the Emigrant Aid Company, organized in New England by such men as Charles Francis Adams and Edward Everett Hale to settle Kansas and take advantage of "popular sovereignty" to plant free labor there and vote slavery down. By the December of 1854 rich river bottoms had been occupied by several thousand settlers from free-soil States, armed with Sharp's rifles. On the other hand, proslavery Missourians swarmed across the border armed with muskets, pistols, and bowie knives, committing such excesses that an honest Democratic governor of the territory revolted, joined the free-soilers—and was relieved of office by President Pierce!

In the October of 1855 the free-soilers framed at Topeka a constitution declaring Kansas a free State, as had been done for California, got it ratified in an election in which proslavery settlers refused to vote, and sent it to Congress. But Pierce denounced the whole procedure as rebellious, saying he would suppress all such movements with Federal troops. This was the situation at the beginning of 1856, and it added fuel to the fire of that campaign.

In the May of '56, Senator Sumner of Massachusetts, in the course of a Boanergic speech on Kansas, denounced Senator Butler of South Carolina for having attacked the Topeka movement. Butler, although proslavery, was an excellent man; Sumner, even according to his friends, seemed "incapable of giving credit to another for an honest difference of opinion." Two days after his attack on Butler, one of Butler's young kinsmen, Preston Brooks, a member of the House, entered the Senate chamber after adjournment and caned Sumner while he was sitting at his desk unable to rise—caned him so heavily that Sumner's seat remained vacant for about four years, during all of which time Massachusetts stubbornly voted for him, or, rather, for his vacant chair. Feeling ran equally high in the South; costly canes were showered upon Brooks, who resigned from Congress when it requested him to do so, only to be re-elected at once.

On the day intervening between the speech by Sumner and its punishment by Brooks, the "Yankee" settlement of Lawrence, Kansas, was sacked by a mob. This incident was the beginning of civil war in "bleeding Kansas." John Brown and his sons retaliated by the massacre of Pottawatamie and, later, by night marches from home to home, calling out proslavery owners and murdering them in cold blood. In a year about two hundred men of both factions were slain, guerrilla bands traversing the country and firing when they met opponents.

Meanwhile, James Buchanan had become President. As a candidate he had promised justice in Kansas, but as President he tried to force the admission of Kansas into statehood under a proslavery constitution framed at Lecompton. This instrument was so flagrantly vicious that Senator Hammond of South Carolina, proslavery but upright according to his lights, declared that "the South herself should kick that constitution out of Congress."

The root of its rottenness lay in writing into it the words, "the right of property in slaves now in the territory shall not be interfered with," and then providing two kinds of ballots, one "for the constitution *with* slavery," the other "for the constitution *without* slavery," no opportunity being provided to vote against the constitution altogether. Thus in any case the voter cast his ballot for slavery, because protection of property in slaves was guaranteed by the constitution. The only question was that of bringing in more slaves, but even that was left open. It was a minor question anyhow, as slaves reproduce; so that the Lecompton constitution would have made Kansas automatically a slave State, despite the pretense of giving voters the right to choose.

Douglas attempted to repair an irreparable blunder by calling on Buchanan and telling him he would oppose the Lecompton constitution openly, unless it were submitted to Kansas voters honestly. Buchanan, enraged, warned Douglas that no Democratic leader ever broke with the Administration without being crushed. Douglas defied him. Soon afterward he made one of the great speeches of his career in opposing the Lecompton constitution. Seward, overjoyed, prematurely wrote to his wife that the slave power was broken. Douglas won his contention, for the constitution met defeat—not in the Senate, but in the House.

In the Senate, Broderick, who had at last achieved his supreme ambition—through succeeding John B. Weller— voted against the constitution. Gwin, alas! was once more hypnotized by a false loyalty to his friend—Buchanan—and voted for it. When the two California senators were to get back home, the blows Broderick had already struck at Gwin seemed caresses compared with those to be dealt as though with mallet and chisel.

The Frémonts meanwhile returned to Mariposas, and in

the April of 1858 word reached Jessie of her father's death, as will be recounted in the closing pages.

It was on March 4 of 1856 that Senator Hammond of South Carolina, Calhoun's successor, delivered the valedictory of the South to a government from which it would soon retire, leading Broderick, a fortnight later, to make himself a national figure by his reply.

The Hammond speech gave currency to two tremendous phrases that rang from coast to coast like fire-bells, "Cotton is King," and "mudsill." Defying the North, Hammond cried, "No, you dare not make war on cotton! No power on earth dares to make war upon it! Cotton *is* King!" And in defending slavery, this brilliant orator used the phrase that stirred the passionate Broderick to his depths:

In all social systems there must be a class to do the menial duties, to perform the drudgery of life. That is, a class requiring but a low order of intellect and but little skill. Its requisites are vigor, docility, fidelity. Such a class you must have, or you would not have that other class which leads progress, civilization, and refinement. It constitutes the very mudsill of society and of political government, and you might as well attempt to build a house in the air, as to build either the one or the other, except on this mudsill. Fortunately for the South, she found a race adapted to that purpose to her hand. A race inferior to her own, but eminently qualified in temper, in vigor, in docility, in capacity to stand the climate, to answer all her purposes. We use them for our purpose, and call them slaves. We found them slaves by the "common consent of mankind," which, according to Cicero, *"lex naturae est"*; the highest proof of what is Nature's law. We are old-fashioned at the South yet; it is a word discarded now by "ears polite"; I will not characterize that class at the North by that term; but you have it; it is there; it is everywhere; it is eternal.

After extending this idea and exchanging taunts with the other side, Hammond continued:

Transient and temporary causes have thus far been your preservation. The great West has been open to your surplus population, and your hordes of semi-barbarian immigrants, who are crowding in year by year. They make a great movement, and you call it progress. Whither? It is progress; but it is progress toward Vigilance Committees.

Now, Broderick himself had been haled before "the Great Committee" of 1856, and it is possible that this reference stung him to his eloquent retort a fortnight later. But it is more likely that the whole tenor of this essentially aristocratic speech angered him, and made him for the moment an orator.

Many Senators [he said] have complained of the Senator from South Carolina for his denunciations of laborers of the North as white slaves and the mudsills of society. . . . I suppose, Sir, the Senator from South Carolina did not intend to be personal in his remarks to any of his peers upon this floor. If I had thought so I would have noticed them at the time. I am, Sir, with one exception, the youngest in years of the Senators upon this floor. It is not long since I served an apprenticeship of five years at one of the most laborious mechanical trades pursued by man—a trade that from its nature devotes its follower to thought, but debars him from conversation. I would not have alluded to this if it were not for the remarks of the Senator from South Carolina, and the thousands who know that I am the son of an artisan, and have been a mechanic, would feel disappointed in me if I did not reply to him. I am not proud of this. I am sorry it is true. I would that I could have enjoyed the pleasures of life in my boyhood days; but they were denied to me. I say this with pain. I have not the admiration for the men of the class from whence I sprang that might be expected; they submit too tamely to oppression, and are too prone to neglect their rights and duties as citizens. But, Sir, the class of society to whose toil I was born, under our form of government will control the destinies of this nation. If I were inclined to forget my connection with them, or to deny that I sprang from them, this chamber would not be the place in which I could do either. While I hold a seat here I have but to look at the beautiful capitals adorning the pilasters that support this roof to be reminded of my father's talent, and to see his handiwork.

This was Broderick's highest moment, and brought him many plaudits. Rhodes says, "Fearless and frank, the serious and reflective cast of mind of this man, alone in the world, without relatives or family, was an added charm for those who knew best his early circumstances. In Washington, Broderick stood high." But Josiah Royce, while conceding that "Broderick's name has ever since been, for many, a name to conjure with," adds that "one asks in vain what legislative work of importance he can be said to have accomplished."

In Broderick's eyes, Gwin was just such "a wicked pro-slavery aristocrat" as Senator Hammond. But with this difference: Gwin controlled the federal patronage for the State of California!

It cannot be claimed that he dispensed it impartially. It was really the prerogative of the President, for whom he held it in trust, but he himself would have been the last man to claim that he handed out presidential favors to all Democrats equally. He was in fact so partial to the Chivalry and so indifferent to Tammany that the San Francisco customs house, the chief field of federal patronage, swarmed with Southern men, and became known as "the Virginia Poorhouse" because of the multitude of penniless men belonging to the "First Families of Virginia"—the "F. F. V."—who there found sanctuary. And Broderick did so need his share—not only as an additional reward for his devotees, but as a sheer matter of self-respect; for what must be thought of his Washington prestige when he could not even name a village postmaster? Such was his state of mind when he came to Washington. The need had smarted, the wound rankled, until at last he had proposed a deal to "old Gwin," hard pushed by Broderick's hold on the legislature, where Gwin desired a second re-election. So in a secret midnight meeting preceding the legislative voting in the January of 1857, Broderick somehow extorted from Gwin not only "An Address to the People" in which he expressed for Broderick an admiration he certainly did not feel, and renounced the Federal patronage in his favor, but also, in addition to this Address, a private letter— as Gwin regarded it—conveying the same two items in stronger terms.

Gwin cannot be defended for having bargained with Broderick over a mess of pottage. It was the third big blunder of his career. He was selling something that was not his, but the President's. The most that can be said for him is that he had undisputedly controlled all the Federal patronage for California under Fillmore and Pierce, and had got into the habit of regarding it as his perquisite; but, even so, he was now proposing to use it on a purchase-and-sale basis. To his connivance at this rank political deal he added stupidity: placing in Broderick's hands two documents that might, and did, injure him with the electorate. His public statement, which somehow got published prematurely, and which probably reached presidential ears, damaged him enough, but not so much so as Broderick's publication of the "private letter."

This breach of confidence was occasioned by the utterly unexpected refusal of Buchanan to permit Gwin to turn over the patronage to Broderick. Although the President was a Pennsylvanian and Gwin a Southerner, the two men liked each other, while neither liked Broderick. Besides, Buchanan rightly thought that he could rely on Gwin's loyal support of his policies, even in "bleeding Kansas."

The President paid for his partiality, and "through the nose." The infuriated stone-cutter struck so hard at the Kansas policy and its presidential defender that the California legislature formally denounced his language as a disgrace to the State and the Nation.

John S. Hittell, a California historian, although opposed to Buchanan politically, put the case pretty fairly: "Mr. Buchanan was doubtless wrong, at least the people have since decided that he was, but his error was that of his party, and, it may be said, that of his country; for his policy towards Kansas was nothing more than the legitimate development of the course pursued by the Democratic leaders and approved in the two preceding presidential elections. He was gentlemanly in his manners, upright in his official position, and entitled to respect in his errors of judgment."

Yet Broderick jeered at "the fading intellect, the petulant passion, and the trembling dotage of an old man on the verge of the grave."

As for Gwin and his vote for the Lecompton constitution, Broderick bottled up his wrath until the two senators were back in California, and then unstoppered it with a violent explosion. Gwin, so he now seemed to believe, was doubly damned, doubly a villain: both for supporting Buchanan in the opinion that slave property in Kansas should be protected like all other property; and for treachery, in not delivering over the California patronage. Broderick never made a fine distinction in his life, and was probably incapable of making one. He saw only one thing, like a bull with a red flag before it: Gwin had got elected with his support, but had not kept his side of the bargain.

The melodramatic James O'Meara reports:

For the first time in his life Mr. Broderick canvassed the State as a stump speaker. He was not gifted with easy speech, and had never trained himself to popular oratory. But his soul was in the contest now, and with all the fire and force of his passionate nature he sprung at once into the campaign. Gwin was the chief object of his fierce onslaught. He had come now to hate and loathe his triumphant colleague with irrepressible fury and scorn, and he cast aside all reserve, all confidences between them, and in the most expressive and most violent language he could command, he harangued the vast multitudes which everywhere gathered to see him, and to hear him, in denunciation and despisal of Gwin. Never had such a volume of vehement wrath and terrible abuse poured from the mouth of a public man, directed at another.

Gwin retaliated in kind, as best he could; saying at Yreka, in part:

Under a garb of friendship, he concerted a conspiracy against me, that is without parallel in this or any other State. He deceived me, and then tried to ruin me; but I turned upon him and his minions, and I will pursue them as long as I live. I acknowledge with shame, that for a time I was deceived by him, and I am willing to atone for it in sackcloth and ashes. He intended to defeat my nomination, while professing to be my friend. He challenged me to this discussion. We will see if he will challenge me again after what I have said tonight. He has returned home disgraced and dishonored, while I hold a position in the party that elected me of which any man may be proud. He will slander and lie upon me. It is his avocation. But I will survive it now, as I have survived it heretofore.

It was out of that mud-slinging contest that Gwin's reputation emerged "dripping with corruption," in the eyes of people infected by Broderick's passion. Broderick to his last day on earth never tired of insisting, with damnable iteration, on Gwin's "unreliability of word," "utter worthlessness of character," and "sneaking manner of acting" even on such important questions as secession and slavery. According to Broderick, Gwin was Pecksniff, Benedict Arnold, Tartuffe, and Iago, all rolled into one.

Reputation is what a man is reputed to be, character what he is. It seems time for a closer alignment of Gwin's reputation with his character. The record is clear; all one needs to do is examine it. Gwin is by no means so black as Broderick painted him. He remained a United States senator until the day after Lincoln's inauguration, when his term expired. He remained loyal to the Union during those twelve years in the Senate. Speaking at the Jackson Day banquet in New York City in 1860, he invoked Old Hickory's benediction on "the conservative masses of the nation," so as to restore peace and harmony; the central declaration of his speech being, "The Union must and shall be preserved." The *Congressional Globe* reported him as declaring in his very last speech in the Senate, "There is nothing that can be proposed here, that can by any possibility tend to quiet the country and restore the Union as it existed, that I will not sustain."

Meanwhile, on September 13, 1859, he had been delivered from the persecution of his enemy by the hand of the fiery Judge Terry who had protected Governor McDougal from ejection by Broderick's men from the Democratic love feast in the Sacramento Baptist church. The immediate occasion of the fatal quarrel seems immaterial. Terry, a Southern aristocrat like Gwin but of a different temper, endured Broderick as long as he thought he could, and then exterminated him. Punctilious according to his code, he first resigned as Chief Justice of the California Supreme Court, then polished up his dueling pistols.

The most famous duel in the State's long roster was fought in San Mateo County, ten miles from San Francisco. As John Hittell says, both men were excellent marksmen, familiar with the weapons, and brave; but Broderick, suffering from bowel trouble, was nervous, while Terry was cool. When the signal was given, both began instantly to raise their pistols, but before Broderick had brought his to position his finger pressed the trigger, and his bullet struck the ground near the feet of his enemy, who fired a second later, the ball striking the right breast and passing into the left lung, where it lodged. Terry was so cool that he saw the dust fly and the cloth bend under the bullet. He immediately said, "The shot is not mortal; I have struck two inches to the right." Broderick lingered three days, much of the time under the influence of narcotics, administered to lessen the acute pain of his wound. It was reported that on his death-bed he said, "They have killed me because I was opposed to the extension of slavery and a corrupt administration"; but he said nothing of the kind.

The farcical feud between two California villages with which this section opened occurred in 1851. During the eight years intervening between that feud and this duel the whole Nation had traveled from dangerous laughter toward a duel to the death. Broderick and Terry were individual symbols of the hosts that were soon to oppose each other under two flags, each inviting California's aid: the Stars and Stripes and the Stars and Bars.

PART FIVE

"A PACIFIC REPUBLIC" AND "THE STARS AND BARS"

THE TRAGEDY OF GENERAL
ALBERT SIDNEY JOHNSTON

ASBURY HARPENDING, an audacious and adventurous Kentuckian not quite twenty years old, told in his later years the story of some of the seditious plans in which he was a leader. One of those rare souls like Benvenuto Cellini, utterly without inhibitions and able to divest themselves of the innermost secrets of their lives down to the last shred, he boasts of having made a fortune in Mexican mining and then of invading the City of Gold, San Francisco, taking rank with the great figures of the State before he had reached his majority, and becoming "a leading actor in an unwritten page of history when the destinies of California hung by the veriest thread."

Asbury Harpending, intensely Southern, watched this thread as though he had been the spider that spun it. His brilliant brain discerned clearly what California might mean to the Confederacy about to be born. With San Francisco and its formidable fortifications in rebel hands, the outward flow of gold, on which the Union cause so largely depended, would be shut off as by the turning of a spigot. He also thought he saw how easy it would be to open and maintain connection "through savage Arizona" into Texas, which had become a Southern stronghold despite old Sam Houston's unswerving unionism.

Young Harpending talked as freely as he thought, so one afternoon he felt a tap upon his shoulder and heard the whispered summons to appear at the house of a well-known

Southern sympathizer at nine that evening. He found the house well isolated, with entrances from several directions. Its owner lived alone except for soft-footed Chinese servants, who understood little English and cared less for what might be going on. In a large room the young novitiate found a company of leading citizens of varied callings sitting at a long table. Their spokesman welcomed him, told him that he was not only trusted but deemed fit to conduct an affair of great peril, on which the South's future might depend; and asked whether he was ready to risk his fortune and his life. Harpending eagerly answered Yes, and took this oath:

Having been brought to this room for the purpose of having a secret confided to me, and believing that to divulge such secret would imperil the lives of certain Southern men as well as injure the cause of the Southern States, I do solemnly swear in the name of the Southern States, within whose limits I was born and reared, that I will never, by word, sign, or deed, hint at or divulge what I may hear tonight. Not to my dearest friend, not to the wife of my bosom, will I communicate the nature of the secret. I hold myself pledged, by all I hold dear in heaven or on earth, by God and my country, by my honor as a Southern gentleman, to keep inviolate the trust reposed in me. I swear that no consideration of property or friendship shall influence my secrecy, and may I meet at the hands of those I betray the vengeance due to a traitor if I prove recreant to this my solemn obligation. So help me God, as I prove true.

Thus Harpending became one of a society of thirty members pledged to carry California out of the Union.

The Committee of Thirty acknowledged the absolute authority of a dictator whose name was never used, but who was simply called The General. He summoned all meetings by word of mouth through a chosen member, received large contributions in private, never drew a check, settled all accounts in gold, and accounted to himself alone. Each of the thirty members was held responsible for organizing a fighting force of at least a hundred. This was not difficult, as California abounded at that time with reckless human material: ex-filibusters, ex-Indian fighters, ex-bandits, keen for any undertaking that promised adventure and profit. Each member, therefore, chose a trusty agent devoted to the Southern cause, told him to assemble a body of men for whose wage and upkeep he himself would be responsible, and, leaving the real purpose undisclosed, gave the impression of just another filibustering expedition. These "centuries" were scattered in obscure spots about the Bay, ostensibly engaged in fishing or wood-chopping or the like, but ready at any moment for obedience to "the General," who alone knew the location of the various detachments.

The plan was to paralyze organized resistance by a simultaneous attack in great force. The Regular Army seemed to Harpending "little more than a shadow." He and his associates intended to seize Alcatraz Island and the other Federal strongholds by a night surprise, and also the militia arsenals in San Francisco itself. "All of which," said Harpending in 1913, "may seem chimerical at this late day, but *then,* take my word, it was an opportunity absolutely within our grasp. At least 30 per cent of the population of California was from the South. The large foreign element was either neutral or had Southern leanings. In 1860 the ties that bound the Pacific to Washington were nowhere very strong. The relation meant an enormous loss to California. For all the immense tribute paid, the meager returns consisted of a few public buildings and public works. Besides, thousands were tired of being ruled from a distance of thousands of miles," with no railway or even telegraph connections. "Everything was in readiness by the middle of January, 1861. It only remained to strike the blow," and exactly at this moment General Albert Sidney Johnston arrived to take command of the Department of the Pacific, as though a *deus ex machina* had descended from the skies. So the thirty thought. Johnston's young fellow Kentuckian was appointed on a committee of three to go to see him.

"This was the man," said Harpending of General Johnston, "who had the fate of California absolutely in his hands. No one doubted the drift of his inclinations; no one who knew the man and his exacting sense of honor doubted his absolute loyalty to any trust. No one dreamed for an instant that his integrity as commander in chief of the army could be tampered with"; but, then, "the drift of his inclinations" was naturally Southward, and the three fools on the committee agreed with their own "General" in hoping that they might gather from the great Kentuckian "some serviceable hints for future use." The first shot of the war was not fired until April, and this was only the middle of January. Could not Johnston, without compromising himself or in the slightest degree betraying his trust, give them out of his abundant knowledge useful advice as to what to do if war broke?

"I will never forget that meeting," says Harpending, ruefully, as if rubbing a sore spot in his memory.

We were ushered into the presence of General Albert Sidney Johnston. He was a blond giant of a man with a mass of heavy yellow hair, untouched by age, although he was nearing sixty. He had the nobility of bearing that marks a great leader of men, and it seemed to my youthful imagination that I was looking at some superman of ancient history, like Hannibal or Caesar, come to life again. He bade us courteously to be seated. "Before we go further," he said, in a matter-of-fact, offhand way, "there is something I want to mention. I have heard foolish talk about an attempt to seize the strongholds of the government under my charge. Knowing this, I have prepared for emergencies, and will defend the property of the United States with every resource at

GENERAL ALBERT SIDNEY JOHNSTON

DR. GWIN IN HIS LATER YEARS. *Courtesy of Stanford Gwin*

my command, and with the last drop of blood in my body. Tell that to all our Southern friends!" Whether it was a direct hint to us, I know not. We sat there like a lot of petrified stoten-bottles. Then, in an easy way, he launched into a general conversation, in which we joined as best we might. After an hour, we departed. We had learned a lot, but not what we wished to know. The fore-knowledge and inflexible stand of General Johnston was a body blow and facer combined.

Despite this "body blow and facer combined," Harpending from that hour cherished for General Johnston an admiration only this side of idolatry. Incidentally, it may be noted that the General's baffling character, strange compound of Puritan and Cavalier, reveals itself in this drastic message to "our Southern friends," immediately followed by a chivalrous shifting of the conversation so that the three young fools might not incriminate themselves and compel their arrest as traitors; for, notwithstanding Harpending's sincere disclaimer, treason was what they had intended to propose.

It seems unfortunate that one Elijah R. Kennedy published in 1912 his *Contest for California in 1861*, containing a fierce attack on Johnston, just before Harpending's reminiscences appeared. Harpending's frank and circumstantial report of his rebuff must have precluded such an assault; although, to be sure, Mr. Kennedy had at his command, if he had cared to use it, the standard *Life*[1] by General Johnston's son, not to mention a host of other witnesses. Kennedy's book has received a wide reading, as it is the only one on its subject, and at first glance seems to have come from "one having authority." Such circumstances require a notice of it.

Mr. Kennedy first attacks Dr. Gwin, the standing pack horse for every variety of aspersion after Broderick had befouled his reputation.

---

[1] William Preston Johnston, *Life of General Albert Sidney Johnston* (1878).

Shortly after election day in 1860 Senator Gwin started for "the States." Mr. Lincoln had been elected President. The secession determination was accordingly being carried out in hostile acts, and in the most radical States steps were being taken to fulfill the threats made during the political campaign. There was no time to be lost. Buchanan was still President. What was more to the purpose, Floyd was Secretary of War. The Pacific Coast had been divided into two military departments and each was commanded by a loyal officer. Before Senator Gwin left California it was confidently and boastfully asserted that one of his first duties on arriving at the capital would be to have a "friend" placed over the Regular Army force of the coast. I am not aware of any documentary evidence that Senator Gwin undertook that matter. There may be such. In this especial matter documentary evidence is not essential. The occurrences prove the influences.

"The occurrences prove the influences" is sheer abracadabra. Mr. Kennedy, while no cavalier, surely treats "documentary evidence" cavalierly. To make up for his confessed lack of evidence, he marshals his so-called occurrences, thus:

(1) Senator Gwin arrived in Washington about the third of December [1860].

(2) It took nearly a month for a letter to go from Washington to California. Allow a few days for Gwin to impress Floyd.

(3) On the fifteenth of January, 1861, official orders from the War Department were received in San Francisco relieving the two loyal officers of their commands, consolidating the entire coast into one department, and placing Colonel (Brevet Brigadier General) Albert Sidney Johnston in command.

Now for an examination of these "occurrences."

(1) While Dr. Gwin did reach Washington early in the December of 1860, the records prove that General Johnston

had been apprised on October 30, before Gwin even left California, that he was to assume command of the Department of the Pacific.

(2) Kennedy's inverted statements seem to mean that it took a few days even for a Mephistophelian genius such as Gwin to pervert the Secretary of War to his base plot, and then a month to execute it; but as a matter of record Floyd had assigned Johnston to command the Southwestern Department, with headquarters in Texas, and he transferred him to California on request of General Winfield Scott, Chief of Staff, General Johnston approving.

(3) General Johnston and his family, accompanied by the bodyservant "Ran," whom he had manumitted before leaving Washington but who refused to leave him, reached San Francisco in the middle of January, 1861. He took over the Department of the Pacific without any friction whatsoever, from officers who presumably had received General Scott's orders beforehand.

Mr. Kennedy, however, intent upon his melodrama, hurries on, mingling truth with its opposite, after the manner of melodramas:

The blow—for blow it seemed—was not unexpected by friend or foe. It raised the secessionists to a high pitch of confidence. Loyal men were dumfounded; but what could they do? The Federal office-holders . . . were, with few exceptions or none, in sympathy with the South. The State officers and about all of their subordinates were of the same mind, together with nearly half the members of the legislature. And now, as the threatened crisis was drawing near, the Regular Army, with its control of the fortifications, garrisons, and munitions of war, was turned over to an officer *undoubtedly designated by Senator Gwin.*[2] It mattered not that Captain Winfield Scott Hancock was stationed

[2] Author's italics.

in the southern part of the State and that Lieutenant Philip H. Sheridan was at a point in Washington Territory. There was no way by which these two, and others who would be faithful, could co-operate; and they were subject to the command of General Johnston.

Of such statements one could wish, in Hamlet's phrase, that "their defeat doth by their own insinuation grow." Obviously they have been successful in wounding a great man's reputation many years after his heroic death. Insinuation was then laid aside for less subtle weapons in a renewed attack upon Gwin. Kennedy wrote:

Doctor Gwin felt sure his friends in California would carry out his arrangements. He had said in the Senate that if the Southern States went out of the Union "California will be found with the South." Being challenged for this declaration he denied having made it, but added, "If the Union is ever broken up, the eastern boundary of the Pacific Republic will be, in my opinion, . . . the Rocky Mountains."

This statement is here wrenched from its context, wherein Gwin explicitly deprecated such a contingency. Mr. Kennedy, attempting to use it as evidence, seeks to fortify it:

There is other evidence of the Senator's confidence that "his State" would secede at this time. Mrs. Clay, wife of the Senator from Alabama, in her ingenuous and charming book of reminiscences, describes the scene on Monday, the twenty-first of January, 1861, when the Senators from several seceded States bade farewell to the venerable body of which they had been members. "As each Senator, speaking for his State, concluded his solemn renunciation of allegiance to the United States, women grew hysterical and waved their handkerchiefs, encouraging them with cries of sympathy and admiration. Men wept and embraced each other mournfully."

Then, about a month later, Mrs. Clay in her Alabama home, according to Kennedy, gets a letter from a Washington friend saying that "Mrs. Gwin is packed up ready to leave. Poor thing! Her eyes are never without tears." Which is all very affecting. But as a matter of fact Mrs. Gwin's husband was not among those "Senators from several seceded States" who bade farewell on January 21 "to the venerable body of which they had been members." Gwin's State did not secede, and he remained in the Senate until his term expired, on March 5.

In his next chapter Mr. Kennedy discloses the main purpose of his book by launching an extended panegyric of his friend the London-born senator from Oregon, Edward D. Baker, whom he introduces in November, 1860, as Gwin's "Nemesis." He says: "We have just read of his [Gwin's] master stroke" in plotting in behalf of Johnston, and he was now going on to Washington "to complete the arrangement"; but his Nemesis, in the person of Baker, sailed with him.

Baker and President Lincoln had once known each other, back in Illinois, when waging campaigns together "in times when neither wit nor argument would move a crowd; when physical courage alone sufficed to control the turbulent spirits." One night when Baker was addressing a hostile audience in the Springfield courtroom, Lincoln had protected him from threats of violence by snatching up the stone water jug from the speakers' table and shouting, "I'll break this over the head of the first man who lays a hand on Baker!" Now, in 1861, when the water-jug wielder moves into the White House, his old friend Baker invokes a second service, says Mr. Kennedy; approaching him with "one supreme demand, that Johnston should be removed and the army forces on the Pacific Ocean be subject to the orders of a loyal man." For the moment, Baker has his way with the President. Lincoln had no reason to mistrust him, and, to do him justice, he was probably sincere, although gravely misinformed. Kennedy continues:

A fortnight after the inauguration General Scott wrote to Brigadier General E. V. Sumner to prepare to sail for California, "to be gone some time." The following day a formal order was confidentially issued to General Sumner directing him to "without delay repair to San Francisco and relieve Brevet Brigadier General Johnston in command of the Department of the Pacific." . . . Sumner arrived at his destination on the twenty-fourth of April, 1861, . . . called on General Johnston, gave him the President's orders and General Scott's, and remarked, "I am now in command of the Department," [and] the crisis was past.

Had Kennedy but taken the trouble to consult the *Life* of Johnston already cited, he would have found that General Johnston had on April 10, immediately after the secession of his foster State of Texas, forwarded his resignation to Washington, and that his meeting with General Sumner was cordial to a degree. Whomever else the bluff Sumner might suspect, he knew that his fellow-soldier was the model of spotless integrity. General Johnston mentioned the facts of his resignation to General Sumner, who then said: "General, I wish you would reconsider, and recall your resignation. General Scott bade me say to you that he wished you for active service, and that you should be only second to himself." General Johnston replied, "I thank General Scott for his opinion of me, but nothing can change my determination."

Had Mr. Kennedy even read General Sumner's report to the Adjutant General, dated April 28, 1861, he would have found that it read:

I have the honor to report that I arrived here on the 24th inst., and on the 25th relieved General Johnston in command of this department. My departure from New York was not known here till the night before my arrival. It gives me pleasure to state that the command was turned over to me in good order. General Johnston had forwarded his resignation before I arrived, but he continued to hold the command, and was carrying out the orders of the Government.

Colonel Munford, of General Johnston's staff during the Civil War, said after his death in a public address at Memphis:

When his resignation of command in the army of the United States was sent from California, he kept his purpose and action a profound secret. I heard him say that he believed if he had tried he could have brought nearly or quite his entire command with him, and, remarking that we needed them very much, I asked him if he did not regret not having done so. "No sir," he replied. "That army was not mine; it belonged, with all its appointments, to the Government of the United States. My position was a trust which for myself I could relinquish, but only on condition of handing over, to those for whom I held, whatever was in my hands. I waited till I had cause to know my resignation had been received in Washington, turned over the entire command to the next ranking officer, mounted my horse and started across the Plains."

General Buell, the Union victor at Shiloh, wrote to General Johnston's son after the war was over:

I did not accompany General Sumner to California in the spring of 1861, and was not there when your father turned over the command to him. I arrived, however, very soon after. I do remember that a report had some currency about that time to the effect that your father desired, or had it in contemplation, to surrender California to the cause of the Southern Confederacy. Those were days of a good deal of distrust and bitterness;

but I do not believe that any well-informed person ever gave credence to the report. For, besides the intrinsic absurdity of such a proposition, and its utter inconsistency with your father's character, there was no foundation whatever for such a report. No man who knew your father well could ever believe him capable of a base action.

Elijah R. Kennedy did not know General Johnston well, if at all. The State Library of California furnishes the information that he spent the years 1859-1862 within the State, residing at Marysville, Yuba County. It cites Volume 14 of *Who's Who* to the effect that in April, 1861, he was chosen second lieutenant of Company E, 5th California Infantry, but refused to serve. After the war he engaged for many years in the insurance business in Brooklyn, N. Y., where he also figured in local politics. "Not satisfied with these interests," said the *New York Times* on his death in 1926, "Mr. Kennedy turned author. In 1912 his book *The Contest for California in 1861* was published. During his stay in California he had been much impressed by the personality of Edward D. Baker, and it was largely because of Mr. Kennedy's anxiety lest Baker's work be forgotten that the book was written."

Affection for his old friend might have been admirable in Mr. Kennedy had he not sought to obtain an unwarranted renown for him, claiming flatly that he "saved the Pacific Coast to the Union," and claiming it at the cost of truth and justice. The charges against both Gwin and Johnston are demonstrably false, and to cap a climax of folly Baker did not even succeed in his "one supreme demand" upon Lincoln, except for a very short time. Lincoln could be fooled "some of the time," but not long. The author of the Johnston *Life* never heard of Mr. Kennedy, but a letter he received from Postmaster-General Montgomery Blair happens to show how speedily, in this case, the President was undeceived.

There is a fact in regard to your Father that I ought to mention [wrote Mr. Blair]. When General Ord came here from San Francisco, he called on me, and stated that great injury had been done your father by the manner in which he had been superseded, that he was opposed to the secession movement altogether, and that he had often heard him check persons using secession talk in his presence. . . . I immediately told Mr. Lincoln the facts, and recommended him to send your father a major-general's commission, and he at once executed the commission. I had it forwarded to your father at San Francisco. But a few days afterward I learned that he had left for Texas, and I directed the postmaster to retain the package for cancellation.[3]

Wordsworth's *Ode to Duty*, "stern daughter of the voice of God," might well have been Albert Sidney Johnston's creed. While so considerate of the three plotting fools who visited him (page 257) as to head off the incriminating confessions that might have compelled their arrest, he would have died rather than betray, even by a look, "the drift of his inclinations" so long as he belonged to the United States Army. What Kennedy says about his subsequent "violation of his oath of allegiance" is balderdash. He had already resigned from the army once, and conceived that he had the right to do so again. He resigned, on this second occasion, in obedience to duty as he saw it, *and as West Point had taught him to see it.*

Secession, like slavery, was blinked in the Constitutional Convention of 1787 with one of those compromises without which the Federal Constitution could not have been achieved. For many years after 1787 the sovereign right of

[3] *Life,* p. 267.

a State to secede was not called in question. Nobody has stated this fact more clearly than Charles Francis Adams II, an ex-Union soldier who was also a keen constitutional scholar. In his *Military Studies* he asked: "When the Federal Constitution was framed and adopted—an indissoluble Union of indestructible States—what was the law of treason? —to what or to whom, in case of final issue, did the average citizen owe allegiance? Was it to the Union or to his State?" As a practical question, seeing things as they then were, sweeping aside all "incontrovertible legal arguments and metaphysical disquisitions," Mr. Adams thinks the answer does not admit of doubt. If the question had been put in 1788, or indeed at any time anterior to 1825, "the immediate reply of nine men out of ten in the Northern States, and of ninety-nine out of a hundred in the Southern States, would have been that, as between the Union and the State, ultimate allegiance was due to the State. . . . From 1788 to 1861, in case of direct and insoluble issue between sovereign State and sovereign Nation, every man was not only free to decide, but had to decide the question of ultimate allegiance for himself; and, whichever way he decided, almost equally good grounds in justification thereof could be alleged. The Constitution gave him two masters. Both he could not serve; and the average man decided which to serve in the light of sentiment, tradition and environment. Of this I feel as historically confident as I can feel of any fact not matter of absolute record or susceptible of demonstration."

Numerous opinions might be cited to the same effect. Abraham Lincoln's view is surprising enough (*Complete Works*, Vol. I, p. 105). But a fact positively startling to us of the present day is that a textbook on the Constitution, used at West Point while Albert Sidney Johnston was a cadet there, not only took it for granted that States had the right to secede, but took it likewise for granted that in the event of secession army officers might wish to follow the State instead of the Nation, as the following citations prove:

If a faction should attempt to subvert the Government of a State for the purpose of destroying its republican form, the national power of the Union could be called forth to subdue it. Yet it is not to be understood that its interposition would be justifiable if a State should determine to retire from the Union. It depends on the State itself whether it will continue a member of the Union. To deny this right would be inconsistent with the principle on which all our political systems are founded, which is, that the people have in all cases the right to determine how they shall be governed. The States may then wholly withdraw from the Union. If the majority of the people of a State deliberately and peacefully resolve to relinquish the republican form of government, they cease to be members of the Union. The secession of a State from the Union depends on the will of the people of such State. This right must be considered an ingredient in the original composition of the general government, and the doctrine heretofore presented in regard to the indefeasible nature of personal allegiance is so far qualified in respect to allegiance to the United States.[4]

A scholarly reader of the manuscript of this present volume points out that the foregoing citations merely present the views of a single man, a Philadelphia lawyer named Rawle. This is true, but not pertinent. The point is that Rawle's *View of the Constitution* was accepted and taught in the United States Military Academy while Albert Sidney Johnston was a student there.

In the *North American Review* for September, 1904,

[4] William Rawle, *A View of the Constitution of the United States of America,* (Philadelphia, 1825) pp. 289, 290, 292, 295. See also pp. 296, 297, 298.

Major Robert Bingham of North Carolina caused a sensation by suggesting that Rawle might have been taught to Cadet Robert E. Lee. Lee, however, graduated in 1829, and his best biography, that by Douglas Southall Freeman, shows (in Volume I, page 78) that while Rawle *may* have continued in use throughout Lee's junior and senior years, it was undoubtedly used at the Academy in 1825-26. Albert Sidney Johnston graduated in 1826, and all doubt as to his indoctrination in this textbook seems to be set aside by his son's statement, "The constitutional textbook at West Point in his cadetship was, I believe, Rawle's *Commentaries*." [5]

It now becomes clear that this thorough soldier, whose background and character rendered him peculiarly obedient to military authority, had been taught by Federal authority "the doctrine of secession according to Rawle." That he would in no circumstances have done anything detrimental to the interests of the United States so long as he was in their army is not only declared by all the officers who knew him, but substantiated by his brusque treatment of Harpending. To have fallen in with young Harpending's views, as previously reported to him, would have seemed to him treasonable. Of treason he was incapable. But, after his resignation had been forwarded to Washington and received there, he deemed himself not only absolved from allegiance to the army, but felt in duty bound to follow his State instead of the Union. The flaw, if flaw it was, was not in him, but in the Constitution. But the Constitution could not have been adopted in 1787, much less ratified, had it asserted the perpetuity of the Union. This compromise, from the beginning, contained the seeds of war; a sovereign Nation and a sovereign State being in the last analysis irreconcilable.

Does it not all simmer down to the commonplace fact that we mortals are not the godlike creatures that Hamlet

⁵ *Life*, p. 257.

made us out to be, "noble in reason, infinite in faculty"? We have to learn by trial and error, and sometimes to pay dearly for our lessons.

General Johnston's military career, culminating in the battle of Shiloh, is detailed not only in the *Life,* but in such monumental works as *Battles and Leaders of the Civil War.* But for a rapid and vivid sketch of that career no guide could serve better than Asbury Harpending.

After graduating, Johnston spent seven years on the frontier, including service in the Black Hawk War. His first wife's health causing him to resign, he took her to Kentucky and ministered to her until her death. Restless, he migrated to the Lone Star Republic and enlisted in its army as a private. Within a year President Sam Houston made him its Commander in Chief. When, in consequence of the annexation of Texas, the Mexican War occurred, he re-entered the United States Army as Colonel of the First Texas Rifle Volunteers, distinguishing himself particularly at the battle of Monterey, where he had three horses shot under him. In 1855, as Colonel of the 2d United States Cavalry, his lieutenant colonel was Robert E. Lee, his majors were Hardy and Thomas. When sent later to subdue the revolted Mormons, he did so without bloodshed, and for this was brevetted Brigadier General.

After his second resignation from the army in order to follow his adopted State (of Texas), when he passed through Los Angeles on his way to Richmond he left with his brother-in-law Dr. John S. Griffin this highly important message for the Americans settled in California: "If you sympathize with either side, and feel the call of duty to take part in a sectional war, go home, and fight there if necessary; but here there should be peace. Strife here would not be North against South, but neighbor against neighbor, and no one can imagine the horrors that would ensue."

Already when the war had seemed clearly foreshadowed, his expressed preference for a Californian assignment to one in Texas arose from his punctilious sense of duty. In the event of war, says his son, he felt in duty bound to surrender the charge committed to him to the authority committing it. But in Texas he would have faced the alternative of failing in his duty either to this authority, or to the Commonwealth to which, as his adopted State, he thought he owed his first allegiance. To do the former, he said, was quite impossible, and yet on the other hand he wished not to be compelled to fight his State. This it was that led him to seek transfer from the Southwestern Department, to which he had been assigned, to the Department of the Pacific. In the latter, when the foreshadowed storm had burst, he at least escaped one horn of the dilemma, and then set out to obey "the doctrine of secession according to Rawle."

Jessie understood him perfectly. "His heart was all right but his head was all wrong," as Old Bullion had once said of Franklin Pierce. Not only was she familiar, through her father, with the dilemma imbedded in the Federal Constitution, but her early youth was partly spent near Lexington, Virginia, from whose Military Institute Stonewall Jackson was now following Robert E. Lee in siding with their State. "In those days," says the youngest member of Jackson's staff in a recently published book, "Virginia boys read the *Federalist* and all the debates of the framers of our government and Constitution. I had no more doubt of the right of a state to secede than I had of the truth of the catechism." [6]

Johnston, when saddling his horse to leave San Francisco, told his body-servant Ran to stay behind, but Ran disobeyed. A superlative cook, he could have coined money in some famous restaurant, but preferred to fight his way with "ole

[6] Henry Kyd Douglas in *I Rode with Stonewall:* University of North Carolina Press, 1940, p. 5.

Mahs' Johnston" through the bands of Apaches in Arizona, and was finally with him at Shiloh, where Asbury Harpending saw him bemoaning the fallen leader "in a wild passion of primitive grief." He found his final home in Johnston's native State of Kentucky, where a former San Franciscan, a Mrs. Hepburn, smoothed his pillow as he died. "I's goin' to meet ole Mahs' Johnston" were his parting words.

In reporting to President Jefferson Davis at Richmond, Johnston faced an ardent admirer. Davis, who had been two years his junior at West Point, had also known him in the Mexican War, and regarded him as the *beau ideal* of a soldier, unequaled in either army. Commissioning him at once as a full General, he assigned him to the Department of Kentucky. There it was his misfortune to try to guard a long weak line, stretching from the Alleghanies to the Mississippi. With a wise retreat he met the first push of the powerful Federals, and he was severely blamed by Southern editors, uninformed in strategy. This unjust blame he bore with characteristic silence. The opening of the War's second year found him joined with Beauregard at Corinth, Mississippi, where he led the offense against Grant's army.

Here young Harpending saw him, not only before the critical battle of Shiloh, but in the full tide of success next day, and then dead from his Spartan sense of duty.

Much to the youth's disappointment, he had been assigned not to Johnston's staff, but to that of Beauregard, the second in command. He longed not only to fight beside his hero, but where the battle would rage most fiercely, and he knew it would be there. Through the night of April 5 he lay restless with the troops until two o'clock, when they were called to breakfast in preparation for a surprise attack on Grant. Like so much clockwork, company after company fell into line and set out on the nine-mile march to Pittsburg Landing, near a church called Shiloh. The terrain favored them—well wooded, with ample cover. Not a word was heard as 30,000 men marched forward with scarce noise enough to stir the early morning air. Exactly at dawn they drove in Grant's pickets. Before them lay his army, getting breakfast, with officers and men off guard. As with rebel yells and fixed bayonets Johnston's men swept down, the surprise was terrible and complete. What saved the Union army from immediate and total destruction was the gunboats in the Tennessee River. Their fire, precise and deadly, gave an opportunity for recovery. Johnston trained his field artillery on them, with his sharpshooters climbing trees to pick off their gunners, so that this naval fire slackened.

Harpending took in his chief's main strategy at a glance. Grant was encamped on rising ground, across the river. Behind him, an abrupt drop led to a narrow plain, beyond which retreat seemed quite impossible. Johnston's main plan, then, was to drive in the enemy wings until the entire Union army would become a huddled mass in the hedged-in plain, at the mercy of his murderous artillery. Then it must either surrender or be annihilated.

Far into the afternoon the battle raged, and victory seemed in sight. Another hour, and Grant's rout would have been complete. Johnston's martial figure, on his pet horse "Firefly," seemed omnipresent, inspiring his eager troops. But at the moment of snatching victory he reeled and fell. It was as though his whole army had seen him fall. In the deadly pause, Beauregard took over command, obviously under a severe mental strain. To the astonishment of many, he ordered retreat. Harpending heard him say, "Tomorrow we'll be across the Tennessee River or in hell!"

But it was the Federals that crossed the river. "Early next morning General Buell came over with 35,000 fresh troops, and all day long the Confederates struggled to win their way back to their lost position." In vain. Grant won.

Thus young Asbury Harpending saw the fiercest battle of the entire Civil War, and, in his judgment, the most decisive. He thinks it practically lost the war in the West, which might have been won except for Johnston's death. This was caused by a trifling wound from a Minie ball. It severed a leg artery, which his surgeon, Dr. Yandell, could have handled easily with a tourniquet. But Johnston had ordered his surgeon to leave him that morning, so as to extemporize a field hospital for the wounded Federals, saying, "These men were our enemies a moment ago, but they are prisoners now, and you must take care of them." When Dr. Yandell expostulated, Johnston became peremptory. Even his aide who caught him as he fell could have saved him if he had known of a wound. But this Puritan-Cavalier, born in Kentucky of Connecticut stock, although painfully aware that his cavalry boot was filling up with blood, deemed it his duty to stay in the saddle at the head of his army, and did so until his drained body fell headlong.

While still a Federal officer he had told Harpending that he would defend his charge to his last drop. Now as a Confederate officer he does so.

Many years after the battle of Shiloh, the Federal government raised a shaft in honor of Johnston on the spot where he fell. And General Grant told Harpending that only Johnston's death saved his own army, adding that "he had learned a lesson in war on that fateful day, the most important in his experience."

Johnston's career seems all the more tragic because, like Lee, he deplored the secession of his State. Both men were martyrs to conscience. Those who today lightly condemn them might find it profitable to attempt a reconstruction of their times and their problems, by looking at things, for the moment, from their angle.

Johnston's frequently expressed antipathy to secession

seems in perspective to have been more than nullified by the force of his example in joining the secessionist army. Southern settlers in California might well have paraphrased Emerson and said, "What you do speaks so loud that we cannot hear what you say." His actions spoke louder than his words, and his metaphysics seemed "caviar to the general."

When Asbury Harpending got back to San Francisco from the South he threw his whole soul into secession adventures, especially in connection with the privateering scheme of his schooner *Chapman,* of which he tells the racy story in his dictated reminiscences, *The Great Diamond Hoax and Other Stirring Episodes,*—guaranteed to delight connoisseurs in the veracious picaresque. It is too rare a masterpiece to be garbled. Here one may only say that "the *Chapman* affair" awakened San Francisco to the exposed state of its harbor, so that its board of supervisors considered an appropriation of $600,000 for adequate defense after Harpending and his fellow-conspirators had been thrown into jail. Rumors spread of other privateering plots, and a sort of hysteria spread through the State. At least one historian thinks that the pendulum of opinion swung too far toward the Unionist side. "Anyone who dared to express the least disapproval of the policy of the administration was denounced by the ultra loyalists as 'secesh,'" writes Joseph Ellison. And these "secesh" were so feared that a number of San Francisco merchants, under date of August 28, 1861, petitioned the War Department in Washington "against withdrawing the able-bodied men from California for service elsewhere," pointing out that California was in need of all its able-bodied men to fight against the secessionists at home. The petition stated that the majority of the State officers were undisguised secessionists; that three-eighths of the citizens of California were "natives of the Southern States, and 'almost a unit in this crisis,' all hating the Union and all well organized." [7]

[7] *Publications in History:* University of California Press, 1927, pp. 199-201.

THE KNIGHTS OF THE GOLDEN CIRCLE AND THE KNIGHTS OF THE COLUMBIAN STAR

SECESSION sentiment had its forcing beds in the form of two secret organizations of which Asbury Harpending's "Committee of Thirty" had been but a faint foreshadowing. "The Knights of the Golden Circle" percolated across the plains and through the Rockies from Copperhead sources in Ohio and southern Indiana, while the "Knights of the Columbian Star" apparently generated spontaneously. These latter knights evolved an elaborate organization, with a governor-general for the State as a whole and lieutenant-governors and deputies for all important localities. There were 24,000 of them, each being required to equip himself with a rifle, revolver, bowie knife, and ammunition. General Sumner, shortly after succeeding Johnston, reported to Washington "deep scheming to draw California into the secession movement, in the first place as the 'Republic of the Pacific,' expecting to induce her afterward to join the Southern Confederacy." Colonel Evans at Visalia, in the San Joaquin Valley, believed there were many secessionists in the Southern counties well organized and armed, "ready at a moment's warning to take up their arms against the Government of the United States. It is an everyday occurrence for them to cheer in the streets for Jefferson Davis and follow it with groans for the Stars and Stripes. They insult soldiers by calling them 'Lincoln's hirelings.'"

Sumner's successor, General Wright, although reporting

to Washington that the rumors of secession organizations had been "highly exaggerated," nevertheless found Napa still so suspicious of Benicia that he called on the Governor to order the militia of both Napa and Solano counties to stand by to quell disturbances.

Before Sumner surrendered his command to Wright, his intelligence service obtained for him the secret pledge and constitution of the Knights of the Golden Circle, as follows:

Whereas, a crisis has arrived in our political affairs which demands the closest scrutiny and strictest vigilance of every true patriot as an American citizen; and *whereas,* we view with regret and heartfelt sorrow the existence of a civil war now waged by one portion of the American people against another; and *whereas,* we also believe that this war has been called into requisition by the present executive of the United States without the guarantee of the Constitution and without the consent of either branch of the American Congress in their legislative capacity, and believing this is an unjust, unholy, iniquitous war, therefore be it

Resolved, that we, as a portion of the citizens of the United States, will support the Constitution as it now stands, together with the amendments thereunto appended, and that we will strictly adhere to the decisions of the United States Supreme Court made under said Constitution where a difference of opinion has heretofore or may hereafter come between the citizens of one state and those of another, or between the state and the federal government, foreign citizens, subjects, etc. Second, be it further

Resolved, that we are in favor of sustaining the southern states of the American Confederacy in all their constitutional rights; that we believe an unconstitutional war is now being waged against them to subject them to a taxation enormous and unequal and to deprive them in the end of their species of property called slaves. And be it lastly

Resolved, that we mutually pledge to each other our lives, our property, and our sacred honor to sustain our brethren of the southern states in the just defense of their constitutional rights, whether invaded by the present executive or by a foreign foe.

I, ... , here in the presence of these witnesses, before Almighty God promise and swear that I will not divulge or reveal any of the secrets of this institution to any one except I know him to be a brother (or to instruct candidates). I furthermore swear that I will obey the proper authorities when ordered to do so, and that I will assist a brother of this institution in his rights, individually or constitutionally, when required of me by him, if need be with my life. All this I solemnly swear to obey under penalty of being shot.

Besides this constitution and pledge, General Sumner learned the grip, passwords, and "words of recognition" used by the Knights of the Golden Circle, who were reported to number 16,000. The words of recognition sound a bit silly: "Do you know Jones?" "What Jones?" "Preacher Jones." "Where does he live?" "At home." "Where is his home?" "In Dixie."

THE BEAR FLAG PARADE AND THE
SHOWALTER EXPEDITION

LESS THAN twenty years ago, pioneers still survived in the San Gabriel Valley who took part in the Bear Flag Parade in the town of El Monte, when some two hundred Southern sympathizers hoisted the never-forgotten symbol of California's independence and marched back and forth through the streets in the moonlight, and round and round the house of one Jonathan Tibbetts, supposed to be a Federal secret-service man. The arms they had expected from Governor Downey never arrived, or a riot and massacre might have ensued. They seem to have belonged to the Knights of the Golden Circle, which had a big lodge in El Monte. One of them, eighty-seven years old in 1924, told a historian in that year that their first purpose was to protect their property, but that if the Confederacy had captured Washington "we would have struck a blow here, for we were ready and determined and well organized."

Immediately after the election of Leland Stanford in the November of 1861 as the first Republican governor of California, one Dan Showalter organized at El Monte a group of eighteen armed men for the purpose of escaping from "the accursed State" and joining a force of several thousand Confederates, under General Sibley, that had invaded New Mexico and captured Albuquerque and Santa Fé. Showalter, although born and bred in Pennsylvania, was an ardent secessionist. As a member of the California legislature of '61 he had debated heatedly against the resolutions that placed the State squarely on the side of the Union, and now this Stanford election was more than he could bear. He and his band traveled by night and hid by day, so they would probably have effected a junction with the Confederate forces had not one of Showalter's confidential letters fallen into the hands of Major Riggs, commanding the First Volunteer California Cavalry. He trapped Showalter's band in a grove near Warner's Ranch, where at first they showed fight, but, being heavily outnumbered, at last decided to surrender. Riggs marched them to Fort Yuma, where they were imprisoned for a while, and then released.

The "Showalter Expedition," insignificant in itself, probably led to the organization of the "California Column," as it aroused the Union's supporters to the necessity of pro-

tecting the borders from invasion. The Column, consisting
of five companies of the First California Cavalry, ten companies of the First California Infantry, and a light battery
of four brass fieldpieces, together with the Fifth California
Infantry, was dispatched against General Sibley's army in
April, 1862, Brigadier General of Volunteers Carleton commanding. When Sibley heard of their approach he evacu-
ated New Mexico and retired beyond the Rio Grande, having already lost most of his supplies. All the forts and towns
in New Mexico and Arizona were reoccupied by the Union
forces, and the California Column also performed useful
service in protecting the mail routes and subduing Indian
disturbances. Rockwell Hunt says that the State furnished
to the Union two full regiments of cavalry, eight full regiments of infantry, one battalion of native Californian cavalry, and one battalion of infantry called "the mountaineers,"
besides several companies of volunteers sent to Massachusetts and to Washington Territory. California bullion was so
important that General Grant once said, "I do not know
what we could do in this great national emergency were it
not for the gold sent from California"; and Asbury Harpending must have disappointed Jefferson Davis most bitterly
by the failure of his privateering scheme.

CONFEDERATE GUERRILLAS AND
BULLION BEND

IN THE JUNE of 1864, an attempt to seize bullion for the
Confederacy by land tried to make up for the *Chapman's*
failure by sea. A modern landmark at "Bullion Bend" com-
memorates the spot, in the northern gold region some four-

teen miles above Placerville. Here, at a turn in the mountain
road, two night coaches of the Wells-Fargo Pioneer Stage
Line were held up between nine and ten o'clock at night
and relieved of eight sacks of silver bullion and the company's strong-box: treasure from the mines of Virginia City,
Nevada.

Ned Blair was driving the first coach and Charlie Watson
the second. When Watson's rearing team had almost plunged
into Blair's coach in front, he jammed on his brakes, wound
the reins round the brake-handle, jumped down, and ran on
ahead to see what was doing. Six men with sawed-off shot-
guns had already deprived Blair's coach of six sacks of bullion, but couldn't find the strong-box. One of them now
covered Watson, who coolly drawled, "Turn that thing the
other way, it might go off." When the Confederate guerrillas searched his coach, they found not only the strong-box,
but also two more bags of bullion, and galloped off with the
loot. But haste makes waste, and they had merely disarmed
the two hardy drivers; these sounded such an alarm that the
pursued horsemen hastily lightened their mounts by burying
their treasure, some in a watering-trough near the spring at
Bullion Bend, the rest underground; so that they made their
getaway with only one bar of silver and several hundred
dollars in cash. Their captain had had the nerve to give
Watson a receipt made out to Wells Fargo, acknowledging
a blank sum of cash—for Wells Fargo to fill in—"for the
purpose of outfitting recruits enlisted in California for the
Confederate States Army," and signed "R. Henry Ingrim,
Captain Commanding Company, C. S. A., June [30], 1864."
His squad was a detachment from Quantrell's band of guerrillas, bent on financing expeditions into Southern California
and Texas. So much was learned when Sheriff James B. Hume
captured a posse of eight of these guerrillas in the following
August, after Deputy-Sheriff Staples had lost his life in at-

tempting to do so. These captives were tried on a charge of second-degree murder. Their "best man," Theodore Poole, was ultimately hanged at "Old Hangtown," Placerville; Preston Hodges was sentenced to twenty years at hard labor; but the others obtained a change of venue and were acquitted.

THE HASTINGS AND TERRY PLOTS

EQUALLY abortive with the Bullion Bend plot was a much more elaborate one emanating from the always busy brain of "Judge" Hastings, who espoused the Confederate cause with such vim that he actually visited Jefferson Davis in Richmond and explained his plot to him in person. Reaching Richmond in the December of 1863, he obtained access to Davis with a self-written letter of introduction, describing him as "a prominent and influential citizen" of California for twenty years, and stressing the "necessity and feasibility" of his plot. He was to return to the Coast via Guaymas, Mexico. Being gifted with the pen, on arrival at his Los Angeles home he would publish a pamphlet boosting the mineral resources of Mexico and Arizona. He would then organize bogus mining companies headed only by "sterling Southerners," who would thereupon advertise extensively for miners, but accept only those devoted to the Stars and Bars. The bogus companies guaranteed all expenses. The "miners" would travel in small groups to avoid notice, to a rendezvous near the Colorado River. When of sufficient force, they would attack Yuma, Arizona (where Hastings had once resided), and release Showalter and his companions, who were still imprisoned in the Federal fort there.

Then they would seize three steamers plying on the river, with results that would shake the world!

Meanwhile, another group of "miners" would take ship from San Pedro, or Los Angeles harbor, for Guaymas, whence they would march in squads up through Mexico, and rendezvous near Yuma. At the opportune moment the two forces would combine, attack the fort, and then move overland from the Rio Grande to El Paso, where they would enter the Confederate service.

The Hastings pamphlets were to be distributed by secret organizations in California, and it seems likely that Hastings was an emissary to Jefferson Davis from the Knights of the Golden Circle. His statement said, "I can raise in California from 3,000 to 10,000 superior troops, and every six months I can throw an additional force into Arizona from California, during this unholy war," and concluded with his only stipulation, that the Confederacy should finance his plan, which, however, "would not require a very large expenditure, as most of the men would supply their own horses."

The stipulation balked the plot. Jefferson Davis, after a ten-day consideration, referred the Hastings offer to his secretary of war, who was feeling poor, and said so. Hastings, writing to Davis on January 11, 1864, regretted "to learn that the government cannot enter upon the enterprise, for lack of funds." But even this did not dismay him. He submitted another plan: to return to California via Mexico, perfect the secret organizations, and then raise 1,500 men "without the financial support of the Confederacy," if its president would only promise reimbursement in case of his success.

He was too late. The Confederacy now faced far more pressing problems than recapture of its road to the Pacific, as proposed by Hastings. Gettysburg had been lost, Vicksburg had fallen. A Los Angeles historian deems it fortunate for California and Arizona that Hastings delayed his visit to Jefferson Davis, "for if he had arrived in Richmond earlier in the war, when the Confederacy was in the first flush of its early successes, his plans might have been adopted, and history for Southern California and Arizona might have had to be written differently."

This same historian reports that the notorious Judge David S. Terry, who among his many exploits had killed Broderick in a duel, reached Houston, Texas, some six months after the collapse of the Hastings plot, commissioned by Jefferson Davis to raise a brigade "for the rescue of Arizona." That Terry sought to revive the Hastings plan seems proved by a letter from one J. A. Roberts, who wrote after Davis himself came to Houston in 1864: "Terry has represented to Davis that if the road was opened to California he could get in California an army of from 20,000 to 30,000 men." It also appears that Terry, like Hastings, relied on the Knights of the Golden Circle. But both men were too late.

WILD TALK

ODDLY ENOUGH, it was not Southerners, but two Ohio politicians, Colonel John B. Weller and Milton S. Latham, who had first given official utterance to separatist sentiments, although not necessarily or altogether in a Southward direction. After Broderick had defeated Weller for re-election to the Senate, Weller in turn succeeded the "Know-nothing" J. Neely Johnson as Governor of the State, taking office on January 8, 1858, and serving two years. In his message to the legislature of January, 1860, just before relinquishing office, Weller expressed deep concern lest the Union be dissolved, but assured his hearers that California would not and should not interfere:

Standing upon the compromises of our venerated fathers, she says to the South as well as to the North, We are ready with our lives to protect all your institutions against aggression, come from whatever quarter it may; but before all, if the wild spirit of fanaticism which now pervades the land should destroy this magnificent confederacy—which God forbid—she will not go with the South or the North, but here upon the shores of the Pacific found a mighty republic which may in the end prove the greatest of all.[8]

Congressman John C. Burch was so moved by Lincoln's election that in the autumn of that same year he wrote for the *San Francisco Herald* a letter of which Latham had approved, expanding Weller's republic so as to include Oregon, New Mexico, Washington, and Utah with California, and declaring that this new political entity should "raise aloft the flag of the 'bear' surrounded with the hydrapointed cactus of the Western wilds, and call upon the enlightened nations of the earth to acknowledge our independence—the youthful but vigorous Caesarian Republic of the Pacific."[9]

Latham had succeeded Weller as Governor, but after less than a week in office he resigned to take the dead Broderick's seat in the Senate. Of less grandiose views than either Burch or Weller, but with proslavery leanings, his separatism reverted to the old plan of dividing Southern from Northern California along the backbone of the Tehachapi Mountains,

[8] *Senate Journal,* 1860, pp. 37-45, 59-65, cited in Theodore Hittell's *History,* IV, 255.
[9] *Publications in History,* p. 181.

and providing the counties of the South with an independent form of government that would restore the national equilibrium through the setting up of a new slave State.

It remained for the Virginian Edmund Randolph, who had once been the friend of Albert Sidney Johnston, and whose mind had become unsettled by a rebuff from Johnston, to deliver the most vitriolic political address in the history of the State; one given before the "Breckinridge Convention" assembled in Sacramento shortly after the secession of Virginia, which had occurred April 17, 1861. After announcing his personal party platform as one of opposition to President Lincoln's policy and the war, Randolph said:

If that be the Democratic party represented by yourselves, then I am with you. If it be any other party, under any other name, represented by anybody else under God's heaven, then I am with *them*. My thoughts and my heart are not here tonight in this house! Far to the east, in the homes from which we came, tyranny and usurpation, with arms in its hands, is this night, perhaps, slaughtering our fathers, our brothers, and our sisters, and outraging our homes in every conceivable way shocking to the heart of humanity and freedom. To me, it seems a waste of time to talk. For God's sake, tell me of battles fought and won. Tell me of the usurpers overthrown; that Missouri is again a free State, no longer crushed under the armed heel of a reckless and odious despot! [10] Tell me that the State of Maryland lives again; and oh! let us read, let us hear, at the first moment that not one hostile foot now treads the soil of Virginia! If this be rebellion, then I am a rebel. Do you want a traitor, then am I a traitor! For God's sake speed the ball; may the lead go quick to his heart, and may our country be free of this despot usurper that now claims the name of President of the United States! [11]

[10] Frémont, commanding the Department of the West.
[11] Winfield Davis, *History of Political Conventions in California* (1893) p. 173.

CONFLICTING VERDICTS

WELL QUALIFIED JUDGES render conflicting verdicts on the question of California's susceptibility to secession. Rhodes[12] thinks that at the outbreak of war she was in danger of joining the South, but Joseph Ellison attacks his opinion as unwarranted by the facts. Ellison concedes, however, that in 1861 a strong sentiment did exist in favor of an independent Pacific Republic, but maintains that even this died down by the end of the year. His judgment comports with that of General Albert Sidney Johnston, who had written to his son in the spring of '61 that only a small minority favored secession. General Johnston should have been a good judge, by virtue of an excellent intelligence service. But General Sumner, who inherited the very same service, saw a rebel under every sagebush. Ellison, characterizing Sumner as an alarmist, deems General Wright, his successor, a wiser judge of the actual facts.

But the ultra loyalists accused him [Wright] of catering to the secessionists. They petitioned the War Department to remove General Wright, and they asked General McDowell, who succeeded General Wright, to institute a proper inquiry into the matter. In his letter to the adjutant general at Washington General Wright claimed that his policy was "fully endorsed by the sensible portion of the community. . . . Were I to be guided by the dictates of the radical press I should crowd my forts with men charged with disloyalty, keep this country in constant ferment. . . . These radicals seem to believe that it is my special

[12] James Ford Rhodes, *History of the United States from 1850* (1892) Vol. V, p. 255.

duty to arrest every man or woman whose sentiments do not coincide exactly with the Government."

Ellison further believes that the extent and strength of the secret societies themselves was highly exaggerated, "as was to be expected of an overheated war-mind at a time when even the most judicious people become credulous and ready to make a mountain out of a molehill." But how is it possible to disparage the gravity of the Hastings and Terry movements, especially the latter? Nevertheless, the most recent investigator, Benjamin F. Gilbert, says flatly that Confederate propaganda in California "was of small magnitude, the unorganized effort of a minority to express their sympathies and to win support for a cause they believed justified." [13]

The present writer feels incompetent to pass a clean-cut judgment on the question, although he has carefully considered all the available evidence. The trouble is that comparatively little evidence *is* available, due to the secrecy obscuring such forces as those of the two bands of "Knights" on the disunionist side, and "the Home Guard" on the Union side, which latter veiled itself just as carefully in its secret efforts to prevent secession. [14] Even the available evidence

[13] *California Historical Society Quarterly*, June, 1941.

[14] The great San Francisco meeting of May 11, 1861 appointed "a Union Committee of Thirty-four" to take such measures as might become necessary for the "detection and suppression of any treasonable combinations or conspiracies against the Union and the public peace." On Aug. 30 this Committee issued a secret call for a "Home Guard," appointing "an Executive Committee of Five" to organize it; appointing Lucius H. Allen, an ex-Army officer, as its Commander; and authorizing Horace Davis (later Starr King's son-in-law) to obtain members. These took the following pledge: "We, the undersigned, do hereby solemnly pledge ourselves to support the Government and Constitution of the United States, and promptly and faithfully to obey, within the City and County of San Francisco, during the existing war, any and all orders emanating from the military officers of this organization for the purpose of protecting the lives and property of the citizens and for

usually has to be discounted, because of the hot passions of the times.

One fact, however, seems obvious: that the surge of popular devotion to the Union which began forming in the spring of 1861 and rolled steadily onward into an irresistible wave was evoked to an extraordinary degree by the magnetic personality and the unsparing efforts of Thomas Starr King.

THE DRIFT TOWARD UNIONISM

IN SAN FRANCISCO two pulpits fulminated on opposite sides, Dr. William A. Scott of Calvary Presbyterian Church "interlarding his sermons with disunion politics," and Thomas Starr King of the Unitarian Church flaming with passion for the Union.

Dr. Scott, who served the foremost congregation in the city, was gifted both as pulpit orator and as a great-hearted lover of his fellows. But he came from New Orleans, was dyed through and through with Southern sentiment, and lacked the wisdom of discretion. In 1856 he had grown overbold not only in opposition to the Vigilantes, to whom nearly all the "chivalry" were opposed, but in support of the Southern view of national questions. His congregation divided pretty evenly on these questions, but all were horrified one

the suppression of treason and insurrection." Mr. Davis, who described the "Home Guard" in *The Pacific Ocean in History* (Macmillan, New York, 1917, p. 260), said that the only active service it ever performed was to keep the peace at the polls on the election day that made Leland Stanford first Republican governor of California with 46.8% of the total vote cast, and that "as soon as we knew that a governor was elected who was true to the Union, and loyal to the Lincoln administration, the Home Guard was dissolved and our Committee disbanded." Starr King was a member.

October Sunday morning, as they assembled for worship, to behold their pastor hanging in effigy in front of his church, which stood on Bush Street between Montgomery and Sansome. The disgraceful deed had been so thoroughly done that it was twilight before the effigy could be dislodged, and to this day the miscreants are unknown. The Doctor's courage, undiminished but rather augmented by the cowardly insult, continued working overtime, and on the actual outbreak of war he offered public prayers for the president of the Confederacy; whereupon he was hanged a second time in effigy, and relieved his people from further embarrassment by leaving the city.

Coleman's leadership of the Vigilantes, already mentioned, set such a strong undercurrent of Unionism flowing that San Francisco, regardless of what might be happening elsewhere in the State, grew steadily more and more national, until its sentiment finally crystallized in the celebration of Washington's Birthday in 1861, described by General Albert Sidney Johnston in a letter to his son:[15]

A huge Union meeting was held here on the 22d. The day was a perfect holiday for the whole population, who filled the streets, and in their best dresses seemed to enjoy the beautiful weather. The resolutions adopted testified to a devoted loyalty to the Union, declared against secession as a right, and repudiated the idea of a Pacific republic as impossible. They express fraternal feelings for all the States, and declare that their interest and honor demand every exertion on their part to bring about harmony again. I presume that the sentiment of these resolutions, which are those of the people of this city, may be set down as those of the State, with the exception of a small minority.

[15] *Life*, p. 269.

PART SIX

THE STARS AND STRIPES FOREVER

JESSIE MEETS THOMAS STARR
KING AND BRET HARTE

IN 1859, the year of the famous duel, Jessie was living at San Francisco in the house of her dreams. One day up in Mariposa County, when a solid week of dust storms had shut her indoors and the suffocating heat was so intense that the thud of the stamp-mills seemed to pound upon her brain, her gay husband asked in a suspiciously offhand way, "Would you like a trip to town?"

"Nothing better," she replied; so through the dust and heat they drove to Stockton, whence a nightly steamer churned the San Joaquin to San Francisco. Arrived there, she felt refreshed at once by ocean breezes, and audibly wished they might remain a week. "Madam, how would you like a lifetime of it?" Frémont asked, and then revealed his purchase of Black Point.

This marvelous spot, now appropriated by unromantic officers of the United States Army, was and is a promontory jutting out into the bay toward the island fort of Alcatraz, its name derived from a dense carpet of black mountain laurel. A cozy house nestled under its sheltering summit, commanding glorious views both east and west. "Here," said Frémont to wondering Jessie, "are the three things we have always held as requirements for a home: the sound of the sea, a view, and a gentle climate. I can get the twelve acres from Mark Brumagim, the banker, for $42,000. It shall be in your name, to have and to hold for your heirs forever."

"Even as he spoke," said Jessie afterward, "I saw myself

walking along the glassed-in corridor connecting the house,
Virginia fashion, with the outside kitchen and the servants'
quarters, and glancing out at the La Marque roses already
climbing its roof."

She had the fancy, while Frémont—for the moment—had
the ability to turn her fancy into fact. Within a month the
forsaken house was a home. There was even a "sunset bench"
looking out toward the Golden Gate, protected from the
wind by a vine-covered trellis. "The flapping of sails," Jessie
said, "the swearing of ship captains, came in our quiet parlor
as distinctly as the lapping of the waves, for the channel is
narrow and strong between our point and the Island of Alcatraz only a mile off. The revolving light made my night
light. I loved this sea home so much that I had joy even in
the tolling of the fogbell."

On the 29th of April, 1860, the Unitarian church of San
Francisco was thronged to hear the first sermon of a young
Universalist minister from Boston, who had sailed in through
the Gate only the day before. When somebody had remon-
strated with him in Boston for his easy change from one
church to another, he had gleefully replied that the difference was one of tweedledum and tweedledee; the Unitarians
think God is too good to damn all men forever, the Univer-
salists that they are too good to be damned.

But Jessie didn't know this when she went to hear his first
sermon. Despite the fame that had preceded him, she felt
distinctly disappointed when he walked into the pulpit, "a
frail beardless youth whose painful thinness was scarcely
disguised by his ministerial robe, and whose lank yellow hair
hung nearly to his shoulders. But when he turned and faced
her, and then began to speak, she fell under the spell of his
dark luminous eyes and his deep, strange, rich voice, so that
she forgot everything but his eloquence," says Mrs. Phillips.

When it was over and she had come to, and the congregation had heaved the deep sigh which is the best tribute a preacher can receive, and then had gone up to crowd round the chancel rail and welcome him, she waited to be among the last. She then went up to invite him and Mrs. King to dinner.

Before dinner on that first evening, Starr King christened Jessie's house. As he and Mrs. King stood with her at the sunset bench and he gazed out westward he said, "You must call your house the Porter's Lodge—the Porter's Lodge for the Gate your husband named"; and the Porter's Lodge it was. Later in the evening he confessed, whimsically, that he felt small and despised in this land of big trees, big water-falls, big vegetables. "Tell me," he asked, "do you think it sacrilegious for a man constitutionally hilarious to be a min-ister?"

Jessie and he disagreed on a number of things, but espe-cially on the city. "I love its every sand-dune!" Jessie ex-claimed, and he retorted that the streets were simply bilious with Chinamen. His distaste was genuine, for he wrote to an editor of the *Transcript,* "It is a noble place to preach in, and they need it. The city as a place to live in?—*O mein Gott!*"

His immediate and overpowering popularity drove him from his home to a sheltered spot amid the laurel bushes near the Porter's Lodge, where he found the needful morn-ing privacy to prepare his sermons and patriotic lectures, which he always wrote out with meticulous care. At noon, Jessie sent out a bowl of broth, and he often wrote on till tea-time, when he might read a lecture to her. One day she introduced to him a shy typesetter from the *Golden Era,* in whose writing she had become interested in a peculiar way. Her trusty Indian coachman Isaac, driving her and her three-year-old son down from Mariposas to Stockton in the hottest weather, had insisted, for their sakes as well as for his team's, that instead of pushing on through a suffocating fog that came on towards evening, they stop overnight at the unsavory Ten-Mile House. It was kept by an evil old man of elephantine proportions who was "hipped" with what he thought a bad case of dropsy, and who couldn't walk. Isaac always knew his own mind, so Jessie, dead tired but apprehensive, gave in to him. "Isaac leading," she writes, "I and the child followed him up the path to the porch, where sat an enormously large old man who roared at us. Recognizing Isaac, he moderated, but broke out afresh at my name. He wanted no —— —— black Republicans coming into *his* house!"

But Isaac coolly told his mistress to lead her frightened child over to the far side of the porch where the ogre couldn't follow, and went off to stable his team and look after the famous surrey.

"See here, you!" roared the old man at Jessie presently, for he had a vestigial heart, "Come out o' that fog! Why don't you go set in the parlor?"

Jessie, so tired that she was almost crying, but afraid to enter the house with its evil reputation, begged to be allowed to sit out under the young locust trees, which filled the air with a remembered fragrance. "They remind me of home and Father," she pleaded.

"Where *is* your home? Who *is* your father?" roared the ogre.

"St. Louis; Senator Benton," answered Jessie.

"WHAT? TOM BENTON?"

The old man's previous roaring seemed as but the murmuring of little waves compared with the surge of breakers as he bawled, "YOU, IKE!" and began shouting orders inside the house behind him.

Isaac came running, and Mine Host commanded him to go round to the kitchen and send that woman there to come and wait on Missy, "and there's young chickens and eggs; git the lady a supper! And wine, mind you, wine"—to Jessie's dismay, as she drank only water. "Tom Benton's daughter! Good Lord! How I useter fight fer him, them Bank times back in Mizoury!"

He had himself pushed along in his great chair to the end of the porch, where the locust blossoms reminded Jessie of a snowfall. "Them locuses! I planted 'em to remind me of old Mizoury!" Before long he was talking almost gently. Complaining of his dropsy, he found a sort of comfort when Jessie reminded him of Old Hickory's sufferings and death from the same disease. "That's so!" he said. "I know that's so! Well, well, what was good enough for Andy is good enough for me!"

He had not heard of Benton's death, and could hardly believe it; "so much will and strength and accumulated power, gone," as Jessie says. "What am I?" he kept repeating. "I'm nothin' to nobuddy. Nobuddy minds me now I cain't git round; they pertend they don't hear me call, an' I gits mad. Well, well, I shore am glad to have Tom Benton's daughter in my house before I die!"

He was in pain, though, and had to be carried off, begging Jessie to stay as long as she had a mind to. But very, very early the following morning she was off for Stockton, where the river boat for San Francisco was waiting. "On the boat," writes Jessie, "I found the *Golden Era*, the literary paper of the coast, and in it a bit of description I felt to be so faithful to the sort of man I had just seen, where the germ of good survived the wrong uses of a life, that it thoroughly interested me. I knew the editor, and, again seeing more such writing in his paper, asked who his contributor was. 'My compositor.' I had to insist this very shy young man should come to see me; but soon he settled into a regular visit on Sunday, his only time of leisure, and for more than a year dined with us that day, bringing his manuscripts; astonished by the effect of some, at times huffed by less flattering opinion on others, but growing rapidly into larger perceptions as he saw much of various people to whom I made him known. Chief of these was dear Starr King." And General Frémont wrote later that it was beautiful to hear the young man's voice and Jessie's together, low and well-modulated, and "when to them was added the deep and vibrant tone of King's voice, it was a trio as good as music."

Starr King took the deepest interest in young Bret Harte, still in his early twenties. Forwarding one of his articles to the *Boston Transcript,* he sponsored it with the comment, "Mr. Frank Bret Harte will yet be known more widely in our literature"; the first public prediction of its author's fame. "But," as Jessie said, "a man cannot live on praise as a humming-bird does on honey-dew," and it was through one of Mr. King's parishioners, the superintendent of the Mint, that Harte was appointed a clerk there, with an income that enabled him to devote most of his time to authorship.

Thus with natural kindness as well as magnetic eloquence, Starr King bound an ever widening circle of admirers to him. His church overflowed on Sundays, and on weekday evenings the public clamored for his lectures. His first was delivered before the Mercantile Library Association of San Francisco, and he humorously wrote to a friend back East: "Last evening I commenced the course with 'Substance and Show,' and drew a glorious picture at the close (colored with the lecturer's genius!) of San Francisco stretched out on its desolate hills rubbing the dust out of its eyes and washing the fleas off its feet in the great Pacific basin." Repeating "Substance and Show" in the First Congregational Church, he drew a capacity audience, and the box-office receipts were unprecedented. The mining regions clamored for him, and he came back exulting to Jessie: "I never knew the exhilaration of public speaking until I faced a front row of revolvers and bowie knives!" He told with delight of a pioneer woman who said to him, "I'm so glad you talkative fellows are comin' round ag'in; for myself, I've got such a thirst for intellectooal people that I could jes' set an' listen to lectures from now on till the Fourth o' July!" But his best story was of a diggin's in which he was billed to lecture at early candlelight on "Socrates and His Age"; and of how, as he strolled for exercise during the afternoon along its straggling street, he saw two red-shirted miners staring at his poster, and overheard one of them remark disgustedly to his pardner, "Say, Bill, who wuz Socrates, anyhow, an' who the hell keers how old he wuz?"

Only as he learned by actual experience the prevalence of disunion sentiments did the plan take shape to become an evangelist of nationalism, and presently it pressed upon him as a duty. Bred as he had been near the mound called Bunker Hill, and drilled as he was in the passionate patriotism of such men as Theodore Parker and Wendell Phillips, secessionist sentiment and the rumors of it assailed his soul like bloodcurdling blasphemy, and a holy zeal possessed him to be up and at it. His first tilt with Apollyon occurred at the next Washington's Birthday celebration, and in preparation for it he wrote to a friend: "I am in the agony of writing my long oration on Washington for the 22nd." That shows how seriously he conceived of his duty, and his reaction after the success of his initial onslaught on the "forces of evil" lifted him to the seventh heaven of joy. To an intimate Boston friend he wrote, in staccato phrases of pure exuberance:

In the evening the lecture was to come off at 7:30. Tickets a dollar each. The house would comfortably seat 1,000. No tickets given away even to the press, but there was a press I can tell you! They had to turn away people by the hundred. Dignitaries

on the stage. I laid my manuscript on a small stand covered with
the American flag. Aristocracy on hand, lots of them from the
South. Lecture two hours and a quarter long—and such a time!
Such stillness, and then such laughter! Such applause, and then
such ominous quiet when I gave them a "free soil" touch! Mrs.
Frémont was out and told me she hadn't been so stirred in years.
I pitched into Secession, Concession, and Calhoun, right and left,
and made Southerners applaud. I pledged California to a Northern Republic and to "a flag that should have no treacherous
threads of cotton in its warp," and the audience came down with
thunder. At the close it was announced that I would repeat it
the next night, and they gave three rounds of cheers.[1]

Then a sudden shadow falls across the page: "But alas,
yesterday I was very hoarse, and the repetition is postponed
till the 4th of March. I copyrighted the address, to save it
from the piracy of stenographers, and am urged to give it
all over the State, and help kill the Pacific Republic folly. It
was *the* occasion, thus far, of my existence."

His throat had eased sufficiently for him to repeat his
"Washington and the Union" lecture as billed, and his restless energy prompted him to prepare a new one, on "Webster and the Constitution," for the night of St. Patrick's Day,
which, in San Francisco, is a gala occasion. By that time he
had repeated his Washington lecture in both Marysville and
Stockton, said to be the twin headquarters of the secessionists
in northern California. In Stockton he drew a hiss or two,
and perhaps it was then that he invented his famous silencer,
"There are only two kinds of animals that express themselves
by a hiss, the goose and the snake."

In labors that almost tax belief he overrode his throat
trouble in his unsparing campaign, and on May 11 experienced the deep satisfaction of seeing in San Francisco a
Union demonstration actually surpassing that of February

---

[1] This was the same celebration described by Gen. Johnston on p. 289.

22, leading the city's historian, John S. Hittell, to attribute to it the determination of national policy for both California and Oregon. In consequence of it, on May 17 the legislature formally pledged the State to the Union, in this notable resolution:

RESOLVED by the Senate, the Assembly concurring, that the people of California are devoted to the Constitution and Union of the United States, and will not fail in fidelity and fealty to that Constitution and Union now in the hour of trial and peril. That California is ready to maintain the rights and honor of the national government at home and abroad, and at all times to respond to any requisition that may be made upon her to defend the republic against foreign or domestic foes.

Starr King's friend and biographer, Charles W. Wendte, persuaded him to give a lecture on "The New Nation to Issue from the War" before the Sumner Light Guard of San Francisco, exactly a month after the adoption of the vital resolution just cited, and as if to symbolize what had happened. The State authorities, predominantly Southern in their sympathies, "had forced the California militia" to wear Confederate gray, and the Sumner Guard sat on the platform in a half-circle around the speaker clad in the telltale color. But the box-office receipts of the evening enabled them and all the other State militia to change over to uniforms of "true Union blue." Naturally, this was "news," and nothing would do but the overtaxed orator should repeat "The New Nation" from Yreka to San Diego.

STARR KING AND THE SANITARY
COMMISSION

WHILE CALIFORNIA, although the draft was never applied there, furnished her quota of support to the Union in both men and means, it was her work for the Sanitary Commission that really distinguished her; and, as Fitz Hugh Ludlow said, "Starr King *was* the Sanitary Commission of California."

Rhodes devotes fifteen pages of his History to the United States Sanitary Commission (V, 244-259), of which Dr. Henry W. Bellows was president, and the famous architect Frederick Law Olmsted general secretary. The commission encountered rough sledding at first, not only the Surgeon General of the army opposing it, but President Lincoln, himself.

Influenced no doubt by this official, he dubbed it "a fifth wheel to the coach." The President was won over only after Dr. Bellows, who knew he liked a good joke, went to see him and told him what he thought of the "stupid seniority system" of the Medical Bureau, "in which one venerable non-compos succeeded another through successive ages." "It reminds me," said the head of the struggling Sanitary Commission, "of the man who, on receiving a barrel of apples, ate every day only those on the point of spoiling, and so at the end of his experiment found that he had devoured a whole barrel of rotten apples!"

"An act to reorganize and increase the efficiency of the Medical Department of the Army" was approved April 16, 1862, after which Mr. Olmsted, a brilliant administrator, made the Commission an efficient machine running beside the Medical Bureau wherever the Union armies went, and achieving marked results not only in the alleviation of suffering, but in the mental as well as physical condition of soldiers in the field.

At first the households of the North contributed out of their superfluity enough bedding and clothing to keep the work of the Commission up to a high standard, while the farmers, also out of their abundance, sent forward ample supplies of vegetables, so as to avert the scourge of scurvy; "it being as easy to get ten dollars' worth of materials made with women's hands or of produce raised on men's farms as it was to get one dollar in money." But after the first two years of the war, the superfluity in the households was exhausted, while the demand for potatoes, onions, curried cabbage, lemons, oranges, anti-scorbutics, and tonics, had far exceeded the available supply. Actual cash was required for the purchase of such life-saving materials, and cash was so scarce that up to October, 1862, total receipts amounted to less than $170,000. Precisely in this moment of emergency, the mayor of San Francisco telegraphed to President Lincoln that $100,000 had been raised in his city for sick and wounded soldiers. Within a month a second $100,000 was forwarded. Stillé, the historian of the Sanitary Commission, says that this saved it from ruin.

California's generosity excited emulation in other States; but in no other part of the country was the work of collecting money so systematically or successfully organized. Dr. Bellows wrote, on February 8, 1864, that of a million dollars in cash which in three years reached the central treasury of the Commission, nearly three-quarters came from the Pacific Coast, and by far the greater part from California. Rhodes says that "this faraway country contributing more than half as much as all the Northern States" during the first year of the Commission's existence spurred them to a marked increase in giving; so that the actual total cash credited to the State in the Commission's final report—$1,233,831.31—should be multiplied in computing its proper proportion of the entire sum—$4,800,000—received and expended.

Dr. Bellows had numbered himself among Starr King's friends and admirers in Boston. No sooner did the young preacher, now in San Francisco, hear of his older friend's undertaking "back East" than he rushed to its support with an impetuosity that no considerations of his health could deter. He not only went everywhere preaching this new gospel of charity, but racked his inventive brain to devise ways and means of enticing gold from unexpected sources; so that, as Rhodes says, a large amount of money was raised "in novel and grotesque ways." On October 20, 1862, King writes to Bellows:

Your letter to our Committee, in reply to the first remittance of a hundred thousand, is a glorious gush of eloquence, and touches California exactly in the right spot. The only mistake was in your allusion to the individuals that have helped the fund, etc. Who can they be? I shall speak this week in the interior to stir up the fund contributions. San Francisco is today *the most loyal city* of the nation.

STARR KING BURNS HIMSELF OUT

GOING AS FAR AFIELD as Oregon, it was on a Columbia River trip that King became "possessed by a wild impulse to seize a traitor by the throat and hurl him into the stream below," because the man argued with his fellow-passengers in behalf of secession and slavery. Making effective use of the incident in subsequent addresses, King said that he restrained himself only on remembering that the river was *clean!* Sometimes he indulged in invective, as when he called Jefferson Davis "a representative to my soul and conscience of a force of evil; his cause is a pollution and a horror; his banner is a black flag!" Three of his patriotic sermons bore the titles, "The Choice between Barabbas and Jesus," "The Treason of Judas Iscariot," and "Rebellion Pictures from Paradise Lost." His son-in-law, the Hon. Horace Davis, said in his old age: "I can distinctly remember the fire and passion of those terrible indictments of treason and rebellion." But King was gifted also "with an exquisite, a delicious sense of the ludicrous," and Dr. Bellows called him "the best story-teller of his time."

Before he died he saw the completion and dedication of his handsome church on Geary Street, to which he himself contributed $5,000 in cash, "raising the money," as his biographer says, "by lectures wrung from his overworked brain." "The new church completed and paid for," he himself had written, "I shall be ready to drop into my grave"; for he was inexpressibly tired, and knew that his strength was permanently broken. The church was dedicated January 10, 1864, John Greenleaf Whittier contributing a beautiful hymn of consecration. The last Sunday of February its doors were closed, the physicians having diagnosed its pastor's malady as diphtheria. This developed into pneumonia, from which King rallied only to relapse into a more severe attack. On the morning of March 4 he summoned all his strength to ask his physician, Dr. Eckel, "How long can I live?" It was hard to tell him the truth, but impossible to lie to him. "Not

half an hour," the physician answered. "Are you sure?"
"Yes!" Then, says an eye-witness, his sufferings left him, and
his voice, which had been a whisper, responded to his summons in full strength and power. Calmly dictating his will,
he had it read to him, one paragraph at a time, approving
at the close of each one, and saying at the close, "It is just
as I want it." With a steady hand he signed his name as
firmly as he had ever done in his life, punctuating it and not
forgetting a flourish at the end. As his friends and faithful
servants came one by one to the bedside he grasped their
hands with fervor, saying in his gentle voice, with a smile,
"Good-bye!" To the nursemaid, Sarah, he expressed especial
thanks for all her care of him, and commended to her his
little son. Considerate to the very end, he whispered to his
wife, "Be sure to tell Dr. Eckel I think he has done everything a human agent could do." To the congregation he sent
the message: "It is my earnest desire that they pay the remaining debt on the church; let the church, free from debt,
be my monument; I want no better." Then to his wife: "Do
not weep for me." In a clear, well modulated voice he repeated the Twenty-Third Psalm, emphasizing the "walk
through the valley of the shadow of death." Finally his infant
son was brought to his side. "Dear little fellow," he smiled;
"he's a beautiful boy." And as the child was borne away he
kissed his hand to him, the last act of his life; for he now
closed his eyes, and slept.

Bret Harte, moved by the loss of his benefactor, reached
the heights of his inspiration in the verses, "On a Pen of
Thomas Starr King":

> *This is the reed the dead musician dropped,*
> *With tuneful magic in its sheath still hidden;*
> *The prompt allegro of its music stopped,*
> *Its melodies unbidden.*

But who shall finish the unfinished strain?
  Or wake the instrument to awe and wonder?
And bid the slender barrel breathe again,
  An organ-pipe of thunder?

His pen! what humbler memories cling about
  Its golden curves! what shapes and laughing graces
Slipped from its point, when his full heart went out
  In smiles and courtly phrases!

The truth, half jesting, half in earnest flung;
  The word of cheer, with recognition in it;
The note of alms, whose golden speech outrung
  The golden gift within it.

But all in vain the enchanter's wand we wave:
  No stroke of ours recalls his magic vision:
The incantation that its power gave
  Sleeps with the dead magician.

Jessie, helping her husband, now a General, to make headway against almost overwhelming difficulties at the seat of war, sent the telegram, "Put violets for me on our dear friend who rests." Her violets lay on his breast as he rested before the altar of his church, his body shrouded by the flag to which he had given himself with no less zeal than to his gospel. All day long people poured through the doors in a final gesture of devotion, but the two of the thousands who moved onlookers to uncontrollable tears were the black women who paused by the bier while the throng flowed on, knelt down by the motionless form of this friend of their race, and with passionate sobs kissed the folds of the flag that had brought them freedom.

Twenty thousand people surged in and about the church, flags dropped to half-mast on all public buildings and on the

many ships in the harbor, cannon saluted the soldierly spirit
from the fortress at Alcatraz, the judges stepped down from
their benches and declared the courts closed in his honor,
the legislature suspended its sessions for three full days, and
memorial services were held in New York and Boston. But
what would have pleased Thomas Starr King most was the
fact that when Dr. Bellows arrived later in the spring to
spend four and a half months in a tour of the State in behalf
of the Sanitary Commission, this tour became a continuous
ovation as the people poured out their bounty because of
the frail young man who had served the cause of the Union
to the last full measure of devotion.

He lay buried in the yard of his new church, the city
council having suspended an ordinance forbidding burials
in the crowded business sections, so that the sight of his
tomb might constantly remind passers-by of a life that could
never die. And nearly a generation later, when Golden Gate
Park had grown into an almost unearthly beauty out beside
the ocean, the citizens of San Francisco, still remembering,
by popular subscription summoned the sculptor Daniel
Chester French to re-create their unforgotten friend in heroic
and imperishable bronze, to be a guide to their children forever. Two mountain peaks also commemorate him: Mount
Starr King in the White Mountains that he loved in New
Hampshire, and Mount Starr King in the Yosemite Valley,
which he loved with an equal fervor. He knew neither East
nor West, but only the Union.

This fact was appropriately symbolized in 1931, when the
whole people of California placed another statue, wrought
by Haig Patigian, also in heroic bronze, in the national capitol, side by side with one of Junípero Serra, who represents
the best of the old régime, as Thomas Starr King the new.
The senior senator said in his speech of presentation,
"Neither was either warrior or statesman, but they possessed

THOMAS STARR KING. *Courtesy of Mrs. C. C. Phillips*

STATUE OF STARR KING IN ROTUNDA OF THE NATIONAL
CAPITOL. *Courtesy of the Sculptor, Haig Patigian*

the highest qualities of both. . . . Junípero Serra [1713-1784] identified himself with California while California was yet foreign territory, in order to educate, train, and help the Indians dwelling in that region. . . . Thomas Starr King [1824-1864] at the beginning of the Civil War found the people of his adopted State . . . uncertain as to her future course. With dauntless purpose and high enthusiasm, he entered the momentous struggle there, and by his matchless eloquence and indefatigable labors he contributed in great measure to maintaining California as a member of the Federal Union, and earned for himself the immortal epitaph, 'He saved his State to the Union.' "

CONCLUSION

FIVE MORE diverse personalities could hardly be found than the chief protagonists of the California drama.

Frémont, slight in stature but of a massive brain and an o'ertopping ambition; not only brave, but impetuous, rushing headlong where sober judgment would have halted; loved by his men out on the trail as heartily as he was disliked by swivel-chair Washington; piling error on error in the course of his career, but, as James Buchanan said, "better entitled to be called the conqueror of California than any other man," because, with all his faults, he had the qualities of a conqueror: confidence and will-power to follow his own judgment in emergencies with utter disregard of personal consequences—such was the man under whose leadership the Mexican flag gave way, as it had given way in the case of Texas, to one with a single star upon it, which Frémont desired with all the passion of his soul should be added to the starry flag of the Union, and not snared into some foreign constellation.

Gwin, sharply contrasted with Frémont, not only in physique but in temperament and training; imposing on the platform, coolly calculating in legislative halls and lobbies; "a composite type with the democratic principles of a frontiersman, the aristocratic bearing of a Southern planter, and the diplomatic nature of a statesman"; "all things to all men" like Paul of the Bible, yet almost equally able to say with him, "This one thing I do" in the service of his cause, California; who, more than any other man except Frémont, made her a part of the Union.

Albert Sidney Johnston, whose career seemed predestined to tragedy by his birth and education, and grew in tragedy to the very end; whose influence, despite himself, strengthened the movement among California secessionists to transfer the Union's thirty-first star to his own adopted flag, the Stars and Bars—and yet, as his distinguished son says, responsible beyond all others for the exemption of the Pacific Coast from the calamities of civil war.

Last of the four heroic men stands that slender flaming candle, Thomas Starr King, burning himself up for his cause, which, in its triumph, fixed California's star where it is, forever.

With all their contrasts, their startling differences, these four men were alike in a dutiful answering to the call of service, each as he conceived his duty, and the result of their leadership of the myriads of pioneers appears in the California of today.

Frémont outlived the others, his career tempestuous almost to the end. As Commander of the Department of the West he impetuously freed all the slaves within that immense territory on August 31, 1861, anticipating Lincoln, a fact that caused him to be hailed in Lincoln's own native State as The Anti-Slavery Crusader, so that the sorely harassed but always patient President felt doubly shocked, both by his subordinate's precipitancy and by the danger of losing the critical State of Kentucky. He dispatched his boyish secretary John Hay to deliver personally into Frémont's hands a missive requesting a modification of the impulsive order freeing the slaves, closing with the gentle plea that the letter had been written "in a spirit of caution, not of censure," and adding, "I send it by special messenger, in order that it may certainly and speedily reach you."

Frémont's answer seems wholly reprehensible. He not only spurned Lincoln's concession that he might retain his important post by a mere modification of his order, but presumptuously demanded of the President that "if upon reflection your better judgment still decides that I am wrong, . . . I have to ask that you openly direct me to make the correction."

This Lincoln sternly did, despite Jessie's personal visit to the White House, with the result that Frémont ultimately exchanged his important command for a trivial one in Virginia, where, with Generals Banks and McDowell, he suffered ignominious defeat at the hands of General Stonewall Jackson. Carl Schurz, sent by Lincoln to make a confidential investigation into Frémont's responsibility for this defeat, completely exonerated him, but incidentally left a memorable little etching of the Pathfinder as he appeared in 1862 —of "elegant build, muscular, and elastic, dark hair and beard slightly streaked with gray, a broad forehead, a keen eye, fine regular features," unaffected manners and a gentle voice suggesting reticence; his whole personality "rather attractive—and yet, *one did not feel quite sure.*" [2]

[2] Author's italics.

Of Frémont's acceptance of a second presidential nomination from a composite political group headed by Horace Greeley, a group bent on defeating Lincoln, and of his subsequent withdrawal from the campaign, there is no need to write here, nor of his financial débâcle due to the Mariposas incubus, nor even of his death in New York City on July 13, 1890, aged seventy-seven. Jessie had unintentionally written his perfect epitaph, *"From the ashes of his campfires cities have sprung."*

It seems fitting to take leave of him on his return to San Francisco, after long absence, in 1878, when on his way with Jessie and their son to his installation in the governorship of Arizona Territory. A third of a century had passed since the Bear Flag Revolt, and sixteen years since Carl Schurz described him, but old acquaintances observed that he still retained the personal qualities "that had made him such a favorite when California had plenty of bears besides the one on his flag, and when the gold fever was at its height." Survivors of those pioneer days made much of his visit. A reunion was held, and Frémont swapped reminiscences with his old guide Alexis Godey. "Onlookers regarded the pair with awe. Here in the flesh were two men who had known California when it was a Mexican province, remote and backward, almost completely cut off from the ambitions of a hustling and acquisitive world." [3]

In this new world Jessie, whose richly endowed nature sustained her father, inspired her husband, stimulated Gwin, understood Johnston, and invigorated King, lived on twelve years longer than General Frémont, and indeed lives on forever as one of the West's greatest women, "a woman who made history."

Most of these dozen years she spent in a vine-embowered cottage given to her by the women of Los Angeles. To them

[3] Oscar Lewis and Carroll D. Hall in *Bonanza Inn:* New York, 1940.

she personified California as an American State. She also
embodied an ideal womanhood.

"Let us not burden our remembrances
With a heaviness that's gone,"

she had learned from Prospero. Instead of heaviness, she
delighted in remembering the lighter things of life. When
too weak to accept the special invitation from San Francisco
to attend the unveiling of the Golden Gate statue of Starr
King, she took out of a treasure chest the letters of her
"hilarious friend," as she called him, and read them over
again as she rejoiced in the tribute to him. His later assignment to the national capitol would have pleased her equally.
Unable to accept a literary commission from the Daughters
of the American Revolution, she wrote when declining it:
"I am in unusually good health for my age, but have to
practice what Carlyle calls 'enlightened selfishness' to protect and retain it. . . . I keep as much as any thinking crea-
ture can out of the rush of life, and find it wise, for its mere
echo as it reaches me in the day's news still deeply interests
me. But nature has her inflexible law of retirement and I
obey it."

Even the echo of "the rush of life" challenged her lively
mind to keep apace of the changing age. Mrs. Phillips says
that instead of feeling embittered by the exposure of the
fallacies of her early religious beliefs, she took joy in the
solidarity of human culture, foreseeing the time when music,
painting, and literature would construct a new world of the
spirit. As she commented on her father's portrait, her friends
thought of her that she showed the same "energy, will, and
directness, but all softened by time and the influence of a
mind constantly freeing itself from purely personal views."

Old friends were struck by this deepening likeness, one

of them writing that while "Mrs. Frémont's hair was white as snow, she showed few other indications of aging, and talked as brilliantly as ever. She greatly resembled her father even in gestures and manner, when animated by conversation, and, with lineaments somewhat softened, inherited his studious and logical mind and his commanding spirit. Her sons were both tall, black-haired, black-eyed, and 'bearded like the pard.' And both, like their sister, showed strains of Gallic blood, the influence of their grandfather, the poor scholarly French gentleman who came to Virginia at the beginning of the century and found their grandmother in her teens."

Another caller, a young woman, came with a copy of *Souvenirs of My Time,* so that its author might sign it. "We found Mrs. Frémont sitting in the garden watching the sun set behind the acacia trees," she wrote. "Though as fragile as a china figurine, she sat up very straight in her chair. Her white hair was covered with a lace cap, and about her shoulders was a fleecy white shawl. Her keen appraising glance was offset by her welcoming smile." A "slashing, sluicing California rain" coming on, "we went into the house and found tea already set for four. I found Miss Lily Frémont a dear, as my friend had described her. The animated conversation among the others gave me an opportunity to look about casually. My glance rose to the portraits on the wall. Directly above the desk was the life-size portrait of General Frémont [subsequently given to the Southwest Museum]. Facing this portrait was that of a girl whose soft brown hair was drawn with a Madonna sweep over the oval cheeks; her lips were full and red; her eyes, deep and serious. Her gown was of soft luminous white stuff with a twist of light blue ribbon at the neck-line [see the frontispiece]. Suddenly this vivid portrait of youth in contrast to that white-haired, ex-

quisite figurante of age gave me a sense of unreality that
remained until our visit ended. I forgot my errand completely and returned home with the unautographed book
under my arm!"

Between that portrait and the elderly woman lay the birth
and growth of a State.

Among her distinguished visitors, perhaps President Mc-
Kinley and his secretary of state, John Hay, pleased Mrs.
Frémont most. The President bowed low over her hand and
gave her the gardenia from his buttonhole. Jessie, mischie-
vously recalling a previous visit from John Hay as the boyish
messenger from President Lincoln, exclaimed, "My good-
ness, John, how you have grown!"

When, as the result of a serious fall, she had to take to her
bed, she became a gracious and patient invalid, only asking
that her favorite likeness of the General be placed within
reach, "for my eyes to rest upon last." Her eyes still saw him
"young, rested, and as handsome as that day in '41 when
I saw him swinging down the avenue in his new uniform"—
such is the transfiguring power of love. In this final year of
her life, 1902, she wrote the unpublished recollections now
kept in the Bancroft Library.

Her two liveliest reminiscences are concerned with father
and husband.

Her father had been ailing when her husband was summoned on a business trip to California, early in 1858. The
old Spartan knew well enough that his trouble was incurable
—cancer—but he imposed silence on his physicians, saying,
"My daughters are young mothers, and must not be subjected to anxiety and grief." Wrestling with his self-imposed
task, "A Digest of Congressional Debates," he kept at work
only by taking opiates at night. When the time approached
for Frémont to board the southbound *Moses Taylor,* he

feigned a "remarkable improvement" so as to let Jessie go with him. When she had left the house he went to bed, never to get up again. But Jessie knew nothing of this.

Besides Lily and their two young sons, the Frémonts took with them the Colonel's niece, Nina, an attractive young lady of nineteen, and the seventeen-year-old British youth Douglas Fox, nicknamed "Foxy," intrusted by his father to Colonel Frémont with the double hope that the California climate might improve his frail health and that he might learn something of mining. Although the *Golden Age*, which bore the party of seven northward from the Isthmus, proved unusually comfortable, Jessie suffered from "a deep depression amounting to mania," she said, and later, in view of what was happening back home, she became convinced of telepathic communication with her father.

The heat at Mariposas being intense, Frémont insisted on camping high up in the mountains, at a scenic point which afforded a panorama of the Yosemite with its far-off silver falls, and the verdant Merced Valley. Isaac, the devoted half-breed, so wooed the wild life that Jessie saw a hen partridge leading her chicks into his outdoor kitchen to pick up his scattered rice. And a woodpecker remained motionless as she sat near him, only turning his intelligent eyes to follow her motions. A spring of coldest water bubbled up into a little pool, keeping the milk and butter and claret as cool as any refrigerator. She had a dressing-room under the boughs of an oak, and the tent, with one side anchored down, made the best obtainable sleeping quarters, for the other sides were open to the breeze by night as by day. Here the Frémonts were visited by Horace Greeley and by "Two-Years-before-the-Mast" Dana, in Jessie's phrase; who delighted her by saying that there was "only one Colonel." Unexpectedly, the Colonel's lawyer, accompanied by his wife, came up by horseback one day. The two men went into the tent for a talk, the wife not dismounting. Although Jessie took an instinctive dislike to her, hospitality led her to approach the horsewoman, who greeted her with the cry:

"Oh, how well you look! And you're wearing colors again, too!"

Jessie protested that she was quite well, and liked colors, which elicited the reproachful exclamation,

"So soon after your father's death, too!"

Jessie went white as the two men rushed out, the lawyer so exasperated that he leaped the fence and seized his wife's bridle and galloped away with her "heedless of bushes and every obstacle," while the Colonel stood speechless. He had been trying to break the news ever since receiving it a few days before, but had lacked the courage.

"Is my father dead?"

For answer, her husband gathered her into his arms, and when she saw his tears she said, "You loved him too." A sudden turn had hastened the end, and at the time she was so strangely ill on the ship "the Soul was freed," she wrote.

They had been in camp some six weeks when Jessie, unable to sleep one night because of the deadly heat, heard from her chair near the opening the approach of a mounted man who muttered to her husband:

"The Hornitos crowd have come over and jumped the Black Drift," one of the Mariposas mines only three miles away.

Puzzled, she repeated the phrase, but Frémont exclaimed, "Never mind that! It's cooler now, go back to bed."

Next morning she found that after he had coaxed her to sleep he had loped away, so Isaac said, "to defend his people."

While the Supreme Court at Washington, after a long legal battle, had confirmed Frémont's title to the Mariposas estates Larkin had turned over to him, the redoubtable

Chief Justice Terry of the California Supreme Court had decided that the State law gave all persons the right to enter any "unoccupied" claim or mine. In this case the Merced Company, under guise of "the Hornitos League," "had bribed the night watchman of the Black Drift to leave his shaft open to them, and had at once entered and fortified it," according to Allan Nevins. "They are a dangerous crowd," said Isaac to Jessie, "but if they come," he added with one of those good intentions that hell is paved with, "they shan't do you or Miss Lily or Miss Nina any harm, for I have the Colonel's orders to shoot the women first!"

"Foxy," learning from this Job's comforter how very dangerous the Colonel knew the League to be, disobeyed the Colonel's orders never to leave camp, as Frémont regarded his guardianship as a sacred trust. Saddling Lily's pet mare Ayah, and muffling her feet, he led her cautiously up a dry creek bed to the mountain summit, mounted her there and dashed along the Merced River into Coulterville, from which a pony express was dispatched on the double-quick to Stockton, eighty miles away, in quest of help.

Six of Frémont's miners were barricaded in another shaft of the Black Drift, while the owner himself, although Jessie did not know it, held a narrow defile down the road with a score of picked men to prevent reinforcements reaching the besiegers, who already numbered a hundred or more, all heavily armed.

"Night came without Mr. Frémont," writes the widow of seventy-eight in the last year of her life. "I was wild, but it had to be borne, and in silence."

Toward sunset of the following day she saw Foxy riding along the Mill Road near camp with the white puggaree of "Victory" on his hat, while he whistled the tune agreed on to denote aid was coming, "The Girl I Left Behind Me." Jessie's sister Sarah was married to a British officer stationed in India, and her long descriptive letters about the Great Mutiny of 1857 had not been lost on Foxy.

Jessie goes on:

The day was ours! He came in cool and fresh and boyish in his triumph, to be welcomed as you can guess. A spirit of mad exultation possessed me. Perhaps I *was* off my head with the long uncertainty about Mr. Frémont. I had just read a note from the head of the League, signed "Dinis O'Briant, Prisident," telling me I "might have twenty-four hours to quit the place, taking my children and my clothes, or take the consequences." With the half-mad feeling of an officer who dresses in full uniform to go into battle, I told Isaac to put to the best open wagon the carriage horses, with their blue rosettes on their harness, and himself dress up. I put off my mourning, and taking out an unused French dress of white muslin with lilac ribbons in the puffings, and a little bonnet of violet velvet and white lace in place of my wide black straw hat, I opened my white parasol and told Isaac to drive to Bates Tavern in the village where the League had headquarters. There I drew up and called Mr. Bates, a timid sort of a publican. To him I returned the note of Mr. O'Briant and said there was *no answer*. That what they demanded was against the law. "You may come and kill us—we are but women and children and it will be easy—*but you cannot kill the law*." . . .

Then I said, "You can drive home, Isaac." But I felt cold quivers running down my back as we turned the long circle in front of those angry men. I fully expected to be shot in the back.

They came around the house after night—exploding powder flasks at it. Not very near, however, for Isaac was there and his fiercest dogs were let loose. And the friendly men were coming, hurrying in. And Mr. Frémont came in too, to be told of young Fox's loyal disobedience, and thank him for it. Things quieted down. A woman told me, "These hills would have run blood if you had not stayed up here with the Colonel."

Cannot you see the spirited old lady putting down her pen to wipe proud tears from her eyes? And here is the explanation of her exploits, every one of them, as she phrases it in an adaptation of Portia's well-known lines in "Julius Caesar":

> *Being so father'd*
> *And so husbanded,*
> *Should I not be stronger than my sex?*

She had told her husband a final goodby a dozen years ago, and forty-four years had elapsed since her father had died, but it is still her boast that she is "Cato's daughter," and "a woman that Lord Brutus took to wife."

END

APPENDIX

APPENDIX

ITEM 1

EARLY OVERLAND VISITORS

WHILE MOST of the early American immigrants came to California, like Larkin, by sea, a few rugged individualists hazarded the overland passage. The first was the greatest: the young New Hampshire "theolog," Jedediah Smith. In 1826, when 28 years old, "his Bible in one hand and his rifle in the other, trusting in the Lord" but keeping his powder-horn handy, he led 15 men across the grueling Salt Desert Trail and through the Cajon Pass down to the San Bernardino and San Gabriel missions—the very first Americans to make the transcontinental journey. Suffering indignities and actual hardships from Californian officialdom, and murdered at last by Indians, this "Pathfinder of the Sierras" is honored today by California's historians as unexcelled among pioneers for both piety and heroism.

In 1827 two fur traders from Kentucky, Sylvester Pattie and his son James Ohio Pattie, reached San Diego via the Grand Canyon, the old town of Santa Fé, and the Gila, Colorado, and San Quentin rivers, only to be jailed and subjected to such cruelty that the father died in his cell. The son, after a really notable career of exploration, published (in 1831) his *Personal Narrative*, which Frémont himself must have read. "One sees in his pages," Reuben Thwaites says, "the beginnings of the drama to be fought out in the Mexican War—the rich and beautiful country which excited the cupidity of the American pioneer; the indolence and effeminacy of the inhabitants which inspired the backwoodsman's contempt; and the vanguard of the American advance, already touching the Rockies and ready to push on to the Pacific." James Ohio Pattie's scathing indictment of the Californians that had killed his father and treated himself with cruelty incited nation-wide prejudice against them, but his praise of the climate of southern California attracted some settlers, nevertheless.

Such sporadic immigrants as Young, Jackson, Wolfskill, and Walker left no records, but in 1841 their example was followed by the first wagon train, which included John Bidwell, of Bear Flag fame.

Isaac Graham, a Tennesseean far inferior to the Patties, gained notoriety by leading border-ruffians to assist the unscrupulous politician Juan Alvarado in unseating the regular Governor of California appointed from Mexico City and seating himself in his stead. The consequent "revolution of 1836" seemed to suspicious Californians to be patterned so closely after what had happened in gringo-ridden Texas, even to the devising of a lone-star flag, that in 1840, when the gringos notably increased, they seized Graham, with several score other *Ingles,* and flung them into the Monterey jail. Graham, alarmed when Alvarado himself turned against him, besought Larkin, as the most prominent American resident, to save him and his fellow prisoners from actual starvation. Thomas Farnham, a traveling writer, tells the sequel in *Life and Adventures in California:* "Mr. Larkin made arrangements with the [local] government today to furnish the prisoners with food and drink. Their cells were examined and found destitute of floors. The ground was so wet that the poor fellows sunk into it several inches at every step. On this they stood, sat, and slept. From 50 to 60 were crowded into a room 18 to 20 feet square. They could not all sit at once, even in that vile pool, still less lie down. The cells were so low and tight that the only way of getting air enough to sustain life was to divide themselves into platoons, each of which, in turn, stood at the grate a while to breathe. When I arrived at the prison, some of them were frantic; others, in a stupor of exhaustion, appeared to be dying." One of them, "Doctor" John Marsh, was ever after haunted by the cries, "Breathe fast, for God's sake! I must come to the grate soon, or suffocate! Give me water, give me air!" But so tough was the pioneer fiber that these wretched Americans and Englishmen endured the black hole of Monterey for 13 days. On the fourteenth, they were herded aboard the *Joven Guipuzcoana* bound for San Blas, to the tune of a *Te Deum* chanted on the plaza, Governor Alvarado participating, as he gave thanks for the delivery of California from *Americanos*. Respectable Yankee merchants up and down the coast, while repudiating the likes of Isaac Graham, felt so indignant over this affair that they petitioned Washington for a special warship.

On December 4, 1841, the Secretary of the Navy announced that an increased naval force was needed on the Pacific, and he soon dispatched Commodore T. A. C. Jones in charge of a squadron. Jones overplayed his hand—or did he? Misinformed at Callao that we had opened war with Mexico, he hurried up to Monterey with a sloop and a frigate, and on October 19, 1842, ran up the Stars and Stripes on the plaza, displacing the Mexican flag, and forestalling the rumored plot of the British to accept California in payment of Mexican debts. Convinced next day of his error, he sheepishly hauled down his flag, only to question his own sanity when many Californians voiced their regret that he hadn't left it flying, so strong was their hatred of Mexico.

Such were the conditions immediately preceding Frémont's arrival, characterized by Josiah Royce as "a time of extremely complex political intrigue and conflict. The jealousy that Californians now more and more felt against all Mexican interference was henceforth joined with a rapidly growing jealousy between the northern and southern parts of the territory of California itself, to the disturbance of all political relations."

ITEM 2

BUCHANAN-POLK LETTER

Letter sent by special messenger, Lieut. Archd. Gillespie, from the Polk Administration to Larkin [and Frémont]:

Department of State,
Washington, October 17, 1845

Thomas O. Larkin, Esq.,
Consul of the United States at Monterey.

Sir:

I feel much indebted to you for the information which you have communicated to the Department from time to time in relation to California. The future of that country is a subject of anxious solicitude for the government and people of the United States. The interests of our commerce and our whale fisheries on the Pacific Ocean demand that you should exert the greatest vigilance in discovering and defeating any attempt which may be made by foreign governments to acquire a control over that country. In the contest between Mexico and California (which was at times acute) we can take no part, unless the former should commence hostilities against the United States; but *should California assert and maintain her independence*,[1] we shall render her all the kind offices in our power, as a sister republic. This government has no ambitious aspirations to gratify

[1] Author's italics.

and no desire to extend our Federal system over more territory than we already possess, unless by the free and spontaneous wish of the independent people of adjoining territories. The exercise of compulsion or improper influence to accomplish such a result would be repugnant both to the policy and principles of this Government. But whilst these are the sentiments of the President, he could not view with indifference the transfer of California to Great Britain or any other European power. The system of colonization by foreign monarchies on the North American continent must and will be resisted by the United States. It could result in nothing but evil to the colonists under their dominion, who would naturally desire to secure for themselves the blessings of liberty by means of republican institutions, whilst it must prove highly prejudicial to the best interests of the United States. Nor would it in the end benefit such foreign monarchies. On the contrary, even Great Britain, by the acquisition of California, would sow the seeds of future war and disaster for herself, because there is no political truth more certain than that this fine province could not long be held in vassalage by any European power. The emigration to it of people from the United States would soon render this impossible. I am induced to make these remarks in consequence of the information communicated to this Department in your despatch of the 10th July last. From this it appears that Mr. Rea, the agent of the British Hudson Bay Company, furnished the Californians with arms and money in October and November last, to enable them to expel the Mexicans from the country; and you state that this policy has been reversed, and now no doubt exists there, but that the Mexican troops about to invade the province have been sent for this purpose at the instigation of the British Government; and that "it is rumored that two English houses in Mexico have become bound to the new general to accept his drafts for funds to pay his troops for eighteen months." Connected with these circumstances, the appearance of a British vice-consul and a French consul in California at the present crisis, without any apparent commercial business, is well calculated to produce the impression, that their respective governments entertain designs on that country which must necessarily be hostile to its interests. On all proper occasions you should not fail prudently to warn the government and people of California of the danger of such an interference to their peace and prosperity; to inspire them with a jealousy of European dominion, and *to arouse in their bosoms that love of liberty and independence so natural to the American continent.*[1] Whilst I repeat that this Government does not, under existing circumstances, intend to interfere between Mexico and California, it would vigorously interpose to prevent the latter from becoming a British or French colony. In this they might surely expect the aid of the Californians themselves. Whilst the President will make no effort and use no influence to induce California *to become one of the free and independent States of this Union,*[1] yet if the people should desire to unite their destiny with ours *they would be received as brethren,*[1] whenever this can be done without affording Mexico just cause of complaint. Their true policy for the present with regard to this question is to let events take their course, unless an attempt should be made to transfer them without their consent either to Great Britain or France. This they ought to resist by all the means in their power, as ruinous to their best interests and destructive of their freedom and independence. I am rejoiced to learn that "our countrymen continue to receive every assurance of safety and protection from the present government" of California and that they manifest so much confidence in you as consul of the United States. You may assure them of the cordial sympathy and friendship of the President, and that their conduct is appreciated by him as it deserves.

In addition to your consular function, the President has thought proper to appoint you a confidential agent in California, and you may consider the present despatch as your authority for acting in this character. The confidence which he reposes in your patriotism and discretion is evinced by conferring upon you this delicate and important trust. You will take care not to awaken the jealousy of the French and English agents there by assuming any other than your consular character. Lieutenant Archibald H. Gillespie of the Marine Corps will immediately proceed to

[1] Author's italics.

Monterey, and will probably reach you before this despatch [which, as it turned out, he delivered to Larkin himself]. He is a gentleman in whom the President reposes entire confidence. He has seen these instructions and will co-operate as a confidential agent with you in carrying them into execution.

You will not fail by every safe opportunity to keep this Department advised of the progress of events in California and the disposition of the authorities and people towards the United States and other governments.

We should also be pleased to learn what is the aggregate population of that province and the force it can bring into the field. What is the proportion of Mexican, American, British, and French citizens, and the feelings of each class towards the United States; the names and character of the principal persons in the Executive, Legislative, and Judicial departments of the Government, and of other distinguished and influential citizens. Its financial system and resources; the amount and nature of its commerce with foreign nations; its productions which might with advantage be imported into the United States, and the productions of the United States which might with advantage be received in exchange.

It would also be interesting to the Department to learn in what part of California the principal American settlements exist; the rate at which the settlers have been and still are increasing in number; from what portions of the Union they come, and by what routes they arrive in the country. These specifications are not intended to limit your inquiries. On the contrary, it is expected that you will collect and communicate to the Department all the information respecting California which may be useful or important to the United States.

I am, sir, respectfully,
Your obedient servant,
James Buchanan.

ITEM 3

CONSTITUTION OF
1849

WE, the People of California, grateful to Almighty God for our freedom, in order to secure its blessings, do establish this Constitution.

ARTICLE I.

Declaration of Rights.

Sec. 1. All men are by nature free and independent, and have certain inalienable rights, among which are those of enjoying and defending life and liberty, acquiring, possessing, and protecting property: and pursuing and obtaining safety and happiness.

Sec. 2. All political power is inherent in the people. Government is instituted for the protection, security, and benefit of the people; and they have the right to alter or reform the same, whenever the public good may require it.

Sec. 3. The right of trial by jury shall be secured to all, and remain inviolate forever; but a jury trial may be waived by the parties, in all civil cases, in the manner to be prescribed by law.

Sec. 4. The free exercise and enjoyment of religious profession and worship, without discrimination or preference, shall forever be allowed in this State: and no person shall be rendered incompetent to be a witness on account of his opinion on matters of religious belief; but the liberty of conscience, hereby secured, shall not be so construed as to excuse acts of licentiousness, or justify practices inconsistent with the peace or safety of this State.

Sec. 5. The privilege of the writ of *habeas corpus* shall not be suspended, unless when, in cases of rebellion or invasion, the public safety may require its suspension.

Sec. 6. Excessive bail shall not be required, nor excessive fines imposed, nor shall cruel or unusual punishments be inflicted, nor shall witnesses be unreasonably detained.

Sec. 7. All persons shall be bailable, by sufficient sureties: unless for capital offences, when the proof is evident or the presumption great.

Sec. 8. No person shall be held to answer for a capital or otherwise infamous crime, (except in cases of impeachment, and in cases of militia when in actual service, and the land and naval forces in time of war, or which this State may keep with the consent of Congress in time of peace, and in cases of petit larceny under the regulation of the Legislature) unless on presentment or indictment of a grand jury; and in any trial in any court whatever, the party accused shall be allowed to appear and defend in person and with counsel, as in civil actions. No person shall be subject to be twice put in jeopardy for the same offence; nor shall he be compelled, in any criminal case, to be a witness against himself, nor be deprived of life, liberty, or property, without due process of law; nor shall private property be taken for public use without just compensation.

Sec. 9. Every citizen may freely speak, write, and publish his sentiments on all subjects, being responsible for the abuse of that right; and no law shall be passed to restrain or abridge the liberty of speech or of the press. In all criminal prosecutions on indictment for libels, the truth may be given in evidence to the jury; and if it shall appear to the jury that the matter charged as libellous is true, and was published with good motives and for justifiable ends, the party shall be acquitted; and the jury shall have the right to determine the law and the fact.

Sec. 10. The people shall have the right freely to assemble together, to consult for the common good, to instruct their representatives, and to petition the legislature for the redress of grievances.

Sec. 11. All laws of a general nature shall have a uniform operation.

Sec. 12. The military shall be subordinate to the civil power. No standing army shall be kept up by this State in time of peace;

and in time of war no appropriation for a standing army shall be for a longer time than two years.

Sec. 13. No soldier shall, in time of peace, be quartered in any house, without the consent of the owner; nor in time of war, except in the manner to be prescribed by law.

Sec. 14. Representation shall be apportioned according to population.

Sec. 15. No person shall be imprisoned for debt, in any civil action on *mesne* or final process, unless in cases of fraud; and no person shall be imprisoned for a militia fine in time of peace.

Sec. 16. No bill of attainder, *ex post facto* law, or law impairing the obligation of contracts, shall ever be passed.

Sec. 17. Foreigners who are, or who may hereafter become *bona fide* residents of this State, shall enjoy the same rights in respect to the possession, enjoyment, and inheritance of property, as native born citizens.

Sec. 18. Neither slavery, nor involuntary servitude, unless for the punishment of crimes, shall ever be tolerated in this State.

Sec. 19. The right of the people to be secure in their persons, houses, papers and effects, against unreasonable seizures and searches, shall not be violated; and no warrant shall issue but on probable cause, supported by oath or affirmation, particularly describing the place to be searched, and the persons and things to be seized.

Sec. 20. Treason against the State shall consist in levying war against it, adhering to its enemies, or giving them aid and comfort. No person shall be convicted of treason, unless on the evidence of two witnesses to the same overt act, or confession in open court.

Sec. 21. This enumeration of rights shall not be construed to impair or deny others retained by the people.

ARTICLE II.

Right of Suffrage.

Sec. 1. Every white male citizen of the United States, and every white male citizen of Mexico, who shall have elected to become a citizen of the United States, under the treaty of peace exchanged and ratified at Queretaro, on the 30th day of May, 1848, of the age, of twenty-one years, who shall have been a resident of the State six months next preceding the election, and the county or district in which he claims his vote thirty days, shall be entitled to vote at all elections which are now or hereafter may be authorized by law: Provided, that nothing herein contained, shall be construed to prevent the Legislature, by a two-thirds concurrent vote, from admitting to the right of suffrage, Indians or the descendants of Indians, in such special cases as such a proportion of the legislative body may deem just and proper.

Sec. 2. Electors shall, in all cases except treason, felony, or breach of the peace, be privileged from arrest on the days of the election, during their attendance at such election, going to and returning therefrom.

Sec. 3. No elector shall be obliged to perform militia duty on the day of election, except in time of war or public danger.

Sec. 4. For the purpose of voting, no person shall be deemed to have gained or lost a residence by reason of his presence or absence while employed in the service of the United States; nor while engaged in the navigation of the waters of this State, or of the United States, or of the high seas; nor while a student of any seminary of learning; nor while kept at any almshouse, or other asylum, at public expense; nor while confined in any public prison.

Sec. 5. No idiot or insane person, or person convicted of any infamous crime, shall be entitled to the privileges of an elector.

Sec. 6. All elections by the people shall be by ballot.

ARTICLE III.

Distribution of Powers.

The powers of the Government of the State of California shall be divided into three separate departments: the Legislative, the Executive, and Judicial; and no person charged with the exercise of powers properly belonging to one of these departments, shall exercise any functions appertaining to either of the others, except in the cases hereinafter expressly directed or permitted.

ARTICLE IV.

Legislative Department.

Sec. 1. The Legislative power of this State shall be vested in a Senate and Assembly, which shall be designated the Legislature of the State of California; and the enacting clause of every law shall be as follows: "The people of the State of California, represented in Senate and Assembly, do enact as follows."

Sec. 2. The sessions of the Legislature shall be annual, and shall commence on the first Monday of January, next ensuing the election of its members, unless the Governor of the State shall, in the interim, convene the Legislature by proclamation.

Sec. 3. The members of the Assembly shall be chosen annually, by the qualified electors of their respective districts, on the Tuesday next after the first Monday in November, unless otherwise ordered by the Legislature, and their term of office shall be one year.

Sec. 4. Senators and Members of Assembly shall be duly qualified electors in the respective counties and districts which they represent.

Sec. 5. Senators shall be chosen for the term of two years, at the same time and places as Members of Assembly; and no person shall be a member of the Senate or Assembly, who has not been a citizen and inhabitant of the State one year, and of the county or district for which he shall be chosen six months next before his election.

Sec. 6. The number of Senators shall not be less than one-third, nor more than one-half, of that of the Members of Assembly; and at the first session of the Legislature after this Constitution takes effect, the Senators shall be divided by lot as equally as may be, into two classes; the seats of the Senators of the first class shall be vacated at the expiration of the first year, so that one-half shall be chosen annually.

Sec. 7. When the number of Senators is increased, they shall be apportioned by lot, so as to keep the two classes as nearly equal in number as possible.

Sec. 8. Each house shall choose its own officers and judge of the qualifications, elections, and returns of its own members.

Sec. 9. A majority of each house shall constitute a quorum to do business; but a smaller number may adjourn from day to day, and may compel the attendance of absent members, in such manner, and under such penalties, as each house may provide.

Sec. 10. Each house shall determine the rules of its own proceedings, and may, with the concurrence of two-thirds of all the members elected, expel a member.

Sec. 11. Each house shall keep a journal of its own proceedings, and publish the same; and the yeas and nays of the members of either house, on any question, shall at the desire of any three members present be entered on the journal.

Sec. 12. Members of the Legislature shall, in all cases except treason, felony, and breach of the peace, be privileged from arrest, and they shall not be subject to any civil process during the session of the Legislature, nor for fifteen days next before the commencement and after the termination of each session.

Sec. 13. When vacancies occur in either house, the Governor, or the person exercising the functions of the Governor, shall issue writs of election to fill such vacancies.

Sec. 14. The doors of each house shall be open, except on such occasions as, in the opinion of the House, may require secrecy.

Sec. 15. Neither house shall, without the consent of the other, adjourn for more than three days, nor to any other place than that in which they may be sitting.

Sec. 16. Any bill may originate in either house of the Legislature, and all bills passed by one house may be amended in the other.

Sec. 17. Every bill which may have passed the Legislature, shall, before it becomes a law, be presented to the Governor. If he approve, he shall sign it; but if not, he shall return it, with his objections, to the house in which it originated, which shall enter the same upon the journal, and proceed to reconsider it. If, after such reconsideration, it again pass both houses, by yeas and nays, by a majority of two-thirds of the members of each house present, it shall become a law, notwithstanding the Governor's objections. If any bill shall not be returned within ten days after it shall have been presented to him, (Sunday excepted,) the same shall be a law, in like manner as if he had signed it, unless the Legislature, by adjournment, prevent such return.

Sec. 18. The Assembly shall have the sole power of impeachment; and all impeachments shall be tried by the Senate. When sitting for that purpose, the Senators shall be upon oath or affirmation; and no person shall be convicted, without the concurrence of two-thirds of the members present.

Sec. 19. The Governor, Lieutenant Governor, Secretary of State, Comptroller, Treasurer, Attorney General, Surveyor General, Justices of the Supreme Court and Judges of the District Courts, shall be liable to impeachment for any misdemeanor in office; but judgment in such cases shall extend only to removal from office, and disqualification to hold any office of honor, trust or profit, under the State; but the party convicted, or acquitted, shall nevertheless, be liable to indictment, trial, and punishment, according to law. All other civil officers shall be tried, for misdemeanors in office, in such manner as the Legislature may provide.

Sec. 20. No Senator, or member of Assembly, shall, during the term of office for which he may have been elected, be appointed to any civil office of profit, under this State, which shall have been created, or the emoluments of which shall have been increased, during such term, except such office as may be filled by elections by the people.

Sec. 21. No person holding any lucrative office under the United States, or any other power, shall be eligible to any office of profit, under this State: provided, that officers in the militia, to which there is attached no annual salary, or local officers and postmasters whose compensation does not exceed five hundred dollars per annum, shall not be deemed lucrative.

Sec. 22. No person who shall be convicted of the embezzlement, or defalcation of the public funds of this State, shall ever be eligible to any office of honor, trust, or profit under this State; and the Legislature shall, as soon as practicable, pass a law providing for the punishment of such embezzlement, or defalcation, as a felony.

Sec. 23. No money shall be drawn from the treasury but in consequence of appropriations made by law. An accurate statement of the receipts and expenditures of the public moneys shall be attached to and published with the laws at every regular session of the Legislature.

Sec. 24. The members of the Legislature shall receive for their services a compensation to be fixed by law, and paid out of the public treasury; but no increase of the compensation shall take effect during the term for which the members of either house shall have been elected.

Sec. 25. Every law enacted by the Legislature shall embrace but one object, and that shall be expressed in the title; and no law shall be revised, or amended, by reference to its title; but in such case, the act revised, or section amended shall be reenacted and published at length.

Sec. 26. No divorce shall be granted by the Legislature.

Sec. 27. No lottery shall be authorized by this State, nor shall the sale of lottery tickets be allowed.

Sec. 28. The enumeration of the inhabitants of this State shall be taken, under the direction of the Legislature, in the year one thousand eight hundred and fifty-two, and one thousand eight hundred and fifty-five, and at the end of every ten years thereafter; and these enumerations, together with the census that may be taken, under the direction of the Congress of the United States, in the year one thousand eight hundred and fifty, and every subsequent ten years, shall serve as the basis of representation in both houses of the Legislature.

Sec. 29. The number of Senators and members of Assembly shall, at the first session of the Legislature, holden after the enumerations herein provided for are made, be fixed by the Legislature, and apportioned among the several counties and districts to be established by law, according to the number of white inhabitants. The number of members of Assembly shall not be less than twenty-four, nor more than thirty-six, until the number of inhabitants within this State shall amount to one hundred thousand; and after that period, at such ratio that the whole number of members of Assembly shall never be less than thirty, nor more than eighty.

Sec. 30. When a congressional, senatorial, or assembly district shall be composed of two or more counties, it shall not be separated by any county belonging to another district; and no county shall be divided, in forming a congressional, senatorial, or assembly district.

Sec. 31. Corporations may be formed under general laws, but shall not be created by special act, except for municipal purposes. All general laws and special acts passed pursuant to this section may be altered from time to time, or repealed.

Sec. 32. Dues from corporations shall be secured by such individual liability of the corporators, and other means, as may be prescribed by law.

Sec. 33. The term corporations as used in this article shall be construed to include all associations and joint-stock companies, having any of the powers or privileges of corporations not possessed by individuals or partnerships. And all corporations shall have the right to sue, and shall be subject to be sued, in all courts, in like cases as natural persons.

Sec. 34. The Legislature shall have no power to pass any act granting any charter for banking purposes; but associations may be formed, under general laws, for the deposite of gold and silver, but no such association shall make, issue, or put in circulation, any bill, check, ticket, certificate, promissory note, or other paper, or the paper of any bank, to circulate as money.

Sec. 35. The Legislature of this State shall prohibit, by law, any person or persons, association, company, or corporation, from exercising the privileges of banking, or creating paper to circulate as money.

Sec. 36. Each stockholder of a corporation, or joint-stock association, shall be individually and personally liable for his proportion of all its debts and liabilities.

Sec. 37. It shall be the duty of the Legislature to provide for the organization of cities and incorporated villages, and to restrict their power of taxation, assessment, borrowing money, contracting debts, and loaning their credit, so as to prevent abuses in assessments and in contracting debts by such municipal corporations.

Sec. 38. In all elections by the Legislature, the members thereof shall vote *viva voce,* and the votes shall be entered on the journal.

ARTICLE V.

Executive Department.

Sec. 1. The supreme executive power of this State shall be vested in a Chief Magistrate, who shall be styled the Governor of the State of California.

Sec. 2. The Governor shall be elected by the qualified electors, at the time and places of voting for members of Assembly, and shall hold his office two years from the time of his installation, and until his successor shall be qualified.

Sec. 3. No person shall be eligible to the office of Governor, (except at the first election) who has not been a citizen of the United States and a resident of this State two years next preceding the election, and attained the age of twenty-five years at the time of said election.

Sec. 4. The returns of every election for Governor shall be sealed up and transmitted to the seat of government, directed to the speaker of the Assembly, who shall, during the first week of the session, open and publish them in the presence of both houses of the Legislature. The person having the highest number of votes shall be Governor; but in case any two or more have an equal and the highest number of votes, the Legislature shall, by joint vote of both houses, choose one of said persons, so having an equal and the highest number of votes, for Governor.

Sec. 5. The Governor shall be commander-in-chief of the militia, the army and navy of this State.

Sec. 6. He shall transact all executive business with the officers of Government, civil and military, and may require information in writing from the officers of the executive department, upon any subject relating to the duties of their respective offices.

Sec. 7. He shall see that the laws are faithfully executed.

Sec. 8. When any office shall from any cause become vacant, and no mode is provided by the Constitution and laws for filling such vacancy, the Governor shall have power to fill such vacancy by granting a commission, which shall expire at the end of the next session of the Legislature, or at the next election by the people.

Sec. 9. He may, on extraordinary occasions, convene the Legislature by proclamation, and shall state to both houses, when assembled, the purpose for which they shall have been convened.

Sec. 10. He shall communicate by message to the Legislature, at every session, the condition of the State, and recommend such matters as he may deem expedient.

Sec. 11. In case of a disagreement between the two houses, with respect to the time of adjournment, the Governor shall have power to adjourn the Legislature to such time as he may think proper; provided, it be not beyond the time fixed for the meeting of the next Legislature.

Sec. 12. No person shall, while holding any office under the United States, or this State, exercise the office of Governor, except as hereinafter expressly provided.

Sec. 13. The Governor shall have the power to grant reprieves and pardons after conviction, for all offences except treason and cases of impeachment, upon such conditions, and with such restrictions and limitations, as he may think proper, subject to such regulations as may be provided by law relative to the manner of applying for pardons. Upon conviction for treason he shall have the power to suspend the execution of the sentence until the case shall be reported to the Legislature at its next meeting, when the Legislature shall either pardon, direct the execution of the sentence, or grant a further reprieve. He shall communicate to the Legislature, at the beginning of every session, every case of reprieve or pardon granted, stating the name of the convict, the crime of which he was convicted, the sentence, and its date, and the date of the pardon or reprieve.

Sec. 14. There shall be a seal of this State, which shall be kept by the Governor, and used by him officially, and shall be called "The great seal of the State of California."

Sec. 15. All grants and commissions shall be in the name and by the authority of the people of the State of California, sealed with the great seal of the State, signed by the Governor and countersigned by the Secretary of State.

Sec. 16. A Lieutenant Governor shall be elected at the same time and places, and in the same manner as the Governor; and his term of office, and his qualifications of eligibility shall be the same. He shall be President of the Senate, but shall only have a casting vote therein. If, during a vacancy of the office of Governor, the Lieutenant Governor shall be impeached, displaced, resign, die or become incapable of performing the duties of his office, or be absent from the State, the President of the Senate shall act as Governor, until the vacancy be filled, or the disability shall cease.

Sec. 17. In case of the impeachment of the Governor, or his removal from office, death, inability to discharge the powers and duties of the said office, resignation, or absence from the State, the powers and duties of the office shall devolve upon the Lieutenant Governor for the residue of the term, or until the disability shall cease. But when the Governor shall, with the consent of the Legislature, be out of the State in time of war, at the head of any military force thereof, he shall continue commander-in-chief of the military force of the State.

Sec. 18. A Secretary of State, a Comptroller, a Treasurer, an Attorney General, and Surveyor General, shall be chosen in the manner provided in this Constitution; and the term of office, and eligibility of each shall be the same as are prescribed by the Governor and Lieutenant Governor.

Sec. 19. The Secretary of State shall be appointed by the Governor, by and with the advice and consent of the Senate. He shall keep a fair record of the official acts of the legislative and executive departments of the Government, and shall, when required, lay the same, and all matters relative thereto, before either branch of the Legislature; and shall perform such other duties as shall be assigned him by law.

Sec. 20. The Comptroller, Treasurer, Attorney General, and Surveyor General shall be chosen by joint vote of the two houses of the Legislature, at their first session under this Constitution, and thereafter shall be elected at the same time and places, and in the same manner as the Governor and Lieutenant Governor.

Sec. 21. The Governor, Lieutenant Governor, Secretary of State, Comptroller, Treasurer, Attorney General and Surveyor General shall each, at stated times during their continuance in office, receive for their services a compensation, which shall not be increased or diminished during the term for which they shall have been elected; but neither of these officers shall receive for his own use any fees for the performance of his official duties.

ARTICLE VI.

Judicial Department.

Sec. 1. The judicial power of this State shall be vested in a Supreme Court, in District Courts, in County Courts, in Probate Courts and in Justices of the Peace. The Legislature may also establish such municipal and other inferior courts as may be deemed necessary.

Sec. 2. The Supreme Court shall consist of a Chief Justice and two Associate Justices, any two of whom shall constitute a quorum.

Sec. 3. The Justices of the Supreme Court shall be elected at the general election, by the qualified electors of the State, and shall hold their office for the term of six years from the first day of January next after the election; provided that the Legislature shall, at its first meeting, elect a Chief Justice and two Associate Justices of the Supreme Court, by joint vote of both houses, and so classify them that one shall go out of office every two years. After the first election the senior justice in commission shall be the Chief Justice.

Sec. 4. The Supreme Court shall have appellate jurisdiction in all cases when the matter in dispute exceeds two hundred dollars, when the legality of any tax, toll, or impost, or municipal fine is in question, and in all criminal cases amounting to felony, on questions of law alone. And the said court, and each of the justices thereof, as well as all district and county judges, shall have power to issue writs of *habeas corpus* at the instance of any person held in actual custody. They shall also have power to issue all other writs and process necessary to the exercise of their appellate jurisdiction, and shall be conservators of the peace throughout the State.

Sec. 5. The State shall be divided by the first Legislature into a convenient number of districts, subject to such alteration from time to time as the public good may require, for each of which a district judge shall be appointed by the joint vote of the Legislature, at its first meeting, who shall hold his office for two years from the first day of January next after his election; after which, said judges shall be elected by the qualified electors of their respective districts, at the general election, and shall hold their office for the term of six years.

Sec. 6. The district courts shall have original jurisdiction, in law and equity, in all civil cases where the amount in dispute exceeds two hundred dollars, exclusive of interest. In all criminal cases not otherwise provided for, and in all issues of fact joined in the probate courts, their jurisdiction shall be unlimited.

Sec. 7. The Legislature shall provide for the election, by the people, of a clerk of the Supreme Court, and county clerks, district attorneys, sheriffs, coroners and other necessary officers; and shall fix by law their duties and compensation. County clerks shall be ex officio clerks of the district courts in and for their respective counties.

Sec. 8. There shall be elected in each of the organized counties of this State one county judge, who shall hold his office for four years. He shall hold the county court and perform the duties of surrogate or probate judge. The county judge, with two justices of the peace, to be designated according to law, shall hold courts of sessions, with such criminal jurisdiction as the Legislature shall prescribe, and he shall perform such other duties as shall be required by law.

Sec. 9. The county courts shall have such jurisdiction, in cases arising in justices' courts, and in special cases, as the Legislature may prescribe, but shall have no original civil jurisdiction, except in such special cases.

Sec. 10. The times and places of holding the terms of the Supreme Court, and the general and special terms of the district courts within the several districts, shall be provided for by law.

Sec. 11. No judicial officer, except a justice of the peace, shall receive to his own use, any fees or perquisites of office.

Sec. 12. The Legislature shall provide for the speedy publication of all statute laws, and of such judicial decisions as it may deem expedient; and all laws and judicial decisions shall be free for publication by any person.

Sec. 13. Tribunals for conciliation may be established with such powers and duties as may be prescribed by law; but such tribunals shall have no power to render judgment to be obligatory on the parties, except they voluntarily submit their matters in difference, and agree to abide the judgment, or assent thereto in the presence of such tribunal, in such cases as shall be prescribed by law.

Sec. 14. The Legislature shall determine the number of justices of the peace to be elected in each county, city, town, and incorporated village of the State, and fix by law their powers, duties and responsibilities. It shall also determine in what cases appeals may be made from justices' courts to the county court.

Sec. 15. The Justices of the Supreme Court and judges of the district courts shall severally, at stated times during their continuance in office, receive for their services a compensation to be paid out of the treasury.

Sec. 16. The Justices of the Supreme Court and district judges shall be ineligible to any other office during the term for which they shall have been elected.

Sec. 17. Judges shall not charge juries with respect to matters of fact, but may state the testimony and declare the law.

Sec. 18. The style of all process shall be "The people of the State of California"; all the prosecutions shall be conducted in the name and by the authority of the same.

ARTICLE VII.

Militia.

Sec. 1. The Legislature shall provide by law for organizing and disciplining the militia, in such manner as they shall deem expedient, not incompatible with the Constitution and laws of the United States.

Sec. 2. Officers of the militia shall be elected, or appointed, in such manner as the Legislature shall from time to time direct, and shall be commissioned by the Governor.

Sec. 3. The Governor shall have power to call forth the militia, to execute the laws of the State, to suppress insurrections, and repel invasions.

ARTICLE VIII.

State Debts.

Sec. 1. The Legislature shall not in any manner create any debt or debts, liability or liabilities, which shall singly, or in the aggregate, with any previous debts or liabilities, exceed the sum of three hundred thousand dollars, except in case of war, to repel invasion or suppress insurrection, unless the same shall be authorized by some law for some single object or work, to be distinctly specified therein, which law shall provide ways and means, exclusive of loans, for the payment of the interest of such debt or liability, as it falls due, and also pay and discharge the principal of such debt or liability within twenty years from the time of the contracting thereof, and shall be irrepealable until the principal and interest thereon shall be paid and discharged; but no such law shall take effect until, at a general election, it shall have been submitted to the people, and have received a majority of all the votes cast for and against it at such election; and all money raised by authority of such law, shall be applied only to the specific object therein stated, or to the payment of the debt thereby created; and such law shall be published in at least one newspaper in each judicial district, if one be published therein, throughout the State, for three months next preceding the election at which it is submitted to the people.

ARTICLE IX.

Education.

Sec. 1. The Legislature shall provide for the election, by the people, of a superintendent of public instruction, who shall hold his office for three years, and whose duties shall be prescribed by law, and who shall receive such compensation as the Legislature may direct.

Sec. 2. The Legislature shall encourage, by all suitable means, the promotion of intellectual, scientific, moral and agricultural improvement. The proceeds of all lands that may be granted by the United States to this State for the support of schools, which may be sold or disposed of, and the five hundred thousand acres of land granted to the new states, under an act of Congress distributing the proceeds of the public lands among the several states of the Union, approved A. D. one thousand eight hundred and forty-one, and all estates of deceased persons who may have died without leaving a will or heir, and also such per cent as may be granted by Congress on the sale of lands in this State, shall be and remain a perpetual fund, the interest of which, together with all the rents of the unsold lands, and such other means as the Legislature may provide, shall be inviolably appropriated to the support of common schools throughout the State.

Sec. 3. The Legislature shall provide for a system of common schools, by which a school shall be kept up and supported in each district at least three months in every year; and any school district neglecting to keep up and support such a school may be deprived of its proportion of the interest of the public fund during such neglect.

Sec. 4. The Legislature shall take measures for the protection, improvement, or other disposition of such lands as have been or may hereafter be reserved or granted by the United States, or any person or persons, to this State, for the use of a University; and the funds accruing from the rents or sale of such lands, or from any other source, for the purpose aforesaid, shall be and remain a permanent fund, the interest of which shall be applied to the support of said University, with such branches as the public convenience may demand for the promotion of literature, the arts and sciences, as may be authorized by the terms of such grant. And it shall be the duty of the Legislature, as soon as may be, to provide effectual means for the improvement and permanent security of the funds of said University.

ARTICLE X.

Mode of Amending and Revising the Constitution.

Sec. 1. Any amendment, or amendments to this Constitution, may be proposed in the Senate or Assembly; and if the same shall be agreed to by a majority of the members elected to each of the two houses, such proposed amendment or amendments shall be entered on their journals with the yeas and nays taken thereon, and referred to the Legislature then next to be chosen, and shall be published for three months next preceding the time of making such choice. And if, in the Legislature next chosen as aforesaid, such proposed amendment or amendments shall be agreed to by a majority of all the members elected to each house, then it shall be the duty of the Legislature to submit such proposed amendment or amendments to the people in such manner and at such time as the Legislature shall prescribe; and if the people shall approve and ratify such amendment or amendments by a majority of the electors qualified to vote for members of the Legislature voting thereon, such amendment or amendments shall become part of the Constitution.

Sec. 2. And if, at any time two thirds of the Senate and Assembly shall think it necessary to revise and change this entire Constitution, they shall recommend to the electors at the next election for members of the Legislature to vote for or against a convention; and if it shall appear that a majority of the electors voting at such election have voted in favor of calling a convention, the Legislature shall, at its next session, provide by law for calling a convention, to be holden within six months after the passage of such law; and such convention shall consist of a number of members not less than that of both branches of the Legislature.

ARTICLE XI.

Miscellaneous Provisions.

Sec. 1. The first session of the Legislature shall be held at the Pueblo de San Jose; which place shall be the permanent seat of government, until removed by law; *provided, however,* that two thirds of all the members elected to each house of the Legislature shall concur in the passage of such law.

Sec. 2. Any citizen of this State who shall, after the adoption of this Constitution, fight a duel with deadly weapons, or send or accept a challenge to fight a duel with deadly weapons, either within this State or out of it; or who shall act as second, or knowingly aid or assist in any manner those thus offending, shall not be allowed to hold any office of profit, or to enjoy the right of suffrage under this Constitution.

Sec. 3. Members of the Legislature, and all officers, executive and judicial, except such inferior officers as may be by law exempted, shall, before they enter on the duties of their respective offices, take and subscribe the following oath or affirmation:

"I do solemnly swear (or affirm, as the case may be,) that I will support the Constitution of the United States, and the Constitution of the State of California, and that I will faithfully discharge the duties of the office of ———— ————, according to the best of my ability."

And no other oath, declaration, or test, shall be required as a qualification for any office or public trust.

Sec. 4. The Legislature shall establish a system of county and town governments, which shall be as nearly uniform as practicable throughout the State.

Sec. 5. The Legislature shall have power to provide for the election of a board of supervisors in each county, and these supervisors shall jointly and individually perform such duties as may be prescribed by law.

Sec. 6. All officers whose election or appointment is not provided for by this Constitution, and all officers whose offices may hereafter be created by law, shall be elected by the people, or appointed, as the Legislature may direct.

Sec. 7. When the duration of any office is not provided for by this Constitution, it may be declared by law; and if not so declared, such office shall be held during the pleasure of the authority making the appointment; nor shall the duration of any office not fixed by this Constitution ever exceed four years.

Sec. 8. The fiscal year shall commence on the 1st day of July.

Sec. 9. Each county, town, city, and incorporated village, shall make provision for the support of its own officers, subject to such restrictions and regulations as the Legislature may prescribe.

Sec. 10. The credit of the State shall not in any manner be given or loaned to or in aid of any individual, association, or corporation; nor shall the State, directly or indirectly, become a stockholder in any association or corporation.

Sec. 11. Suits may be brought against the State in such manner and in such courts as shall be directed by law.

Sec. 12. No contract of marriage, if otherwise duly made, shall be invalidated for want of conformity to the requirements of any religious sect.

Sec. 13. Taxation shall be equal and uniform throughout the State. All property in the State shall be taxed in proportion to its value, to be ascertained as directed by law, but assessors and collectors of town, county and State taxes shall be elected by the qualified electors of the district, county, or town in which the property taxed for State, county, or town purposes is situated.

Sec. 14. All property, both real and personal, of the wife, owned or claimed by her before marriage, and that acquired afterward by gift, devise or descent, shall be her separate property, and laws shall be passed more clearly defining the rights of the wife in relation as well to her separate property as to that held in common with her husband. Laws shall also be passed providing for the registration of the wife's separate property.

Sec. 15. The Legislature shall protect by law, from forced sale, a certain portion of the homestead and other property of all heads of families.

Sec. 16. No perpetuities shall be allowed, except for eleemosynary purposes.

Sec. 17. Every person shall be disqualified from holding any office of profit in this State, who shall have been convicted of having given, or offered a bribe, to procure his election or appointment.

Sec. 18. Laws shall be made to exclude from office, serving on juries, and from the right of suffrage, those who shall hereafter be convicted of bribery, perjury, forgery, or other high crimes. The privilege of free suffrage shall be supported by laws regulating elections, and prohibiting, under adequate penalties, all undue influence thereon from power, bribery, tumult, or other improper practice.

Sec. 19. Absence from this State on business of the State, or of the United States, shall not affect the question of residence of any person.

Sec. 20. A plurality of the votes given at any election shall constitute a choice, where not otherwise directed in this Constitution.

Sec. 21. All laws, decrees, regulations, and provisions, which from their nature require publication, shall be published in English and Spanish.

ARTICLE XII.

Boundary.

The boundary of the State of California shall be as follows: Commencing at the point of intersection of 42d degree of north latitude with the 120th degree of longitude west from Greenwich, and running south on the line of said 120th degree of west longitude until it intersects the 39th degree of north latitude; thence running in a straight line in a southeasterly direction to the River Colorado, at a point where it intersects the 35th degree of north latitude; thence down the middle of the channel of said river, to the boundary line between the United States and Mexico, as established by the Treaty of May 30th, 1848; thence running west and along said boundary line to the Pacific Ocean, and extending therein three English miles; thence running in a northwesterly direction, and following the direction of the Pacific Coast to the 42d degree of north latitude, thence on the line of said 42d degree of north latitude to the place of beginning. Also all the islands, harbors, and bays, along and adjacent to the Pacific Coast.

Schedule.

Sec. 1. All rights, prosecutions, claims and contracts, as well of individuals as of bodies corporate, and all laws in force at the time of the adoption of this Constitution, and not inconsistent therewith, until altered or repealed by the Legislature, shall continue as if the same had not been adopted.

Sec. 2. The Legislature shall provide for the removal of all causes which may be pending when this Constitution goes into effect to courts created by the same.

Sec. 3. In order that no inconvenience may result to the public service from the taking effect of this Constitution, no office shall be superseded thereby, nor the laws relative to the duties of the several officers be changed until the entering into office of the new officers to be appointed under this Constitution.

Sec. 4. The provisions of this Constitution concerning the term of residence necessary to enable persons to hold certain offices therein mentioned, shall not be held to apply to officers chosen by the people at the first election, or by the Legislature at its first session.

Sec. 5. Every citizen of California declared a legal voter by this Constitution, and every citizen of the United States a resident of this State on the day of election, shall be entitled to vote at the first general election under this Constitution, and on the question of the adoption thereof.

Sec. 6. This Constitution shall be submitted to the people for their ratification or rejection at the general election to be held on Tuesday, the thirteenth day of November, next. The Executive of the existing government of California is hereby requested to issue a proclamation to the people, directing the prefects of the several districts, or, in case of vacancy, the sub-prefects or senior judge of first instance, to cause such election to be held on the day aforesaid in their respective districts. The election shall be conducted in the manner which was prescribed for the election of delegates to this convention, except that the prefects, sub-prefects, or senior judge of first instance ordering such election in each district shall have power to designate any additional number of places for opening the polls, and that in every place of holding the election a regular poll list shall be kept by the judges and inspectors of election. It shall also be the duty of these judges and inspectors of election, on the day aforesaid, to receive the vote of the electors qualified to vote at such election. Each voter shall express his opinion by depositing in the ballot box a ticket whereon shall be written or printed "For the Constitution," or "Against the Constitution," or some such words as will distinctly convey the intention of the voter. These judges and inspectors shall also receive the votes for the several officers to be voted for at the said election, as herein provided. At the close of the election the judges and inspectors shall carefully count each ballot, and forthwith make duplicate returns thereof to the prefect, sub-prefect, or senior judge of first instance, as the case may be, of their respective districts; and said prefect, sub-prefect, or senior judge of first instance shall transmit one of the same, by the most safe and rapid conveyance, to the Secretary of State. Upon the receipt of said returns, or on the tenth day of December next, if the returns be not sooner received, it shall be the duty of a board of canvassers, to consist of the Secretary of State, one of the judges of the Superior Court, the prefect, judge of first instance, and an alcalde of the District of Monterey, or any three of the aforementioned officers, in the presence of all who shall choose to attend, to compare the votes given at said election, and to immediately publish an abstract of the same in one or more of the newspapers of California. And the Executive will also, immediately after ascertaining that the Constitution has been ratified by the people, make proclamation of the fact; and thenceforth this Constitution shall be ordained and established as the Constitution of California.

Sec. 7. If this Constitution shall be ratified by the people of California, the Executive of the existing government is hereby requested, immediately after the same shall be ascertained, in the manner herein directed, to cause a fair copy thereof to be forwarded to the President of the United States, in order that he may lay it before the Congress of the United States.

Sec. 8. At the general election aforesaid, viz.: the thirteenth day of November next, there shall be elected a Governor, Lieutenant-Governor, members of the Legislature, and also two members of Congress.

Sec. 9. If this Constitution shall be ratified by the people of California, the Legislature shall assemble at the seat of government on the fifteenth day of December next; and in order to complete the organization of that body, the Senate shall elect a president *pro tempore* until the Lieutenant-Governor shall be installed into office.

Sec. 10. On the organization of the Legislature, it shall be the duty of the Secretary of State to lay before each house a copy of the abstract made by the board of canvassers, and, if called for, the original returns of election, in order that each house may judge of the correctness of the report of said board of canvassers.

Sec. 11. The Legislature, at its first session, shall elect such officers as may be ordered by this Constitution, to be elected by that body, and within four days after its organization, proceed to elect two Senators to the Congress of the United States. But no law passed by this Legislature shall take effect until signed by the Governor after his installation into office.

Sec. 12. The Senators and Representatives of the Congress of the United States, elected by the Legislature and people of California, as herein directed, shall be furnished with certified copies of this Constitution, when ratified, which they shall lay before the Congress of the United States, requesting, in the name of the People of California, the admission of the State of California into the American Union.

Sec. 13. All officers of this State, other than members of the Legislature, shall be installed into office on the fifteenth day of December next, or as soon thereafter as practicable.

Sec. 14. Until the Legislature shall divide the State into counties and senatorial and assembly districts, as directed by this Constitution, the following shall be the apportionment of the two houses of the Legislature, viz.: The districts of San Diego and Los Angeles shall jointly elect two Senators; the districts of Santa Barbara and San Luis Obispo shall jointly elect one Senator; the district of Monterey, one Senator; the district of San Jose, one Senator; the district of San Francisco, two Senators; the district of Sonoma, one Senator; the district of Sacramento, four Senators; and the district of San Joaquin, four Senators. And the district of San Diego shall elect one member of the Assembly; the district of Los Angeles, two members of Assembly; the district of Santa Barbara, two members of Assembly; the district of San Luis Obispo, one member of Assembly; the district of Monterey, two members of Assembly; the district of San Jose, three members of Assembly; the district of San Francisco, five members of Assembly; the district of Sonoma, two members of Assembly; the district of Sacramento, nine members of Assembly; and the district of San Joaquin nine members of Assembly.

Sec. 15. Until the Legislature shall otherwise direct, in accordance with the provisions of this Constitution, the salary of the Governor shall be ten thousand dollars per annum; and the salary of the Lieutenant-Governor shall be double the pay of a State Senator; and the pay of members of the Legislature shall be sixteen dollars per diem, while in attendance, and sixteen dollars for every twenty miles' travel by the usual route from their residences, to the place of holding the session of the Legislature, and in returning therefrom. And the Legislature shall fix the salaries of all officers, other than those elected by the people, at the first election.

Sec. 16. The limitation of the powers of the Legislature, contained in Article VIII of this Constitution, shall not extend to the first Legislature elected under the same, which is hereby authorized to negotiate for such amount as may be necessary to pay the expenses of the State government.

R. SEMPLE, *President of the Convention and Delegate from Benicia.*

WM. G. MARCY, *Secretary.*

ACKNOWLEDGMENTS

FIRST I wish to acknowledge with deep appreciation Dr. Frederic L. Paxson's kindness in reading my manuscript in its early stages and improving it with valuable suggestions. I am also indebted to his *History of the American Frontier,* which has been my vade-mecum since its appearance in 1924, and never more so than in the preparation of *Thirty-First Star.*

Part I, "From Drake to the Bentons," is a highly condensed summary which owes much to *Drake's Plate of Brass,* published by the California Historical Society in 1937, Henry R. Wagner's *Sir Francis Drake's Voyage Around the World,* published by John Howell in 1926, and the classic histories of Irving B. Richman and Robert G. Cleland. Dean Cleland further assisted with the loan of his rare pamphlet entitled, "The Early Sentiment for the Annexation of California." Besides such old standbys as Senator Thomas Hart Benton's *Thirty Years' View* and Richard Henry Dana's *Two Years Before the Mast,* Mr. Reuben Lukens Underhill's *From Cowhides to Golden Fleece* (Stanford University Press, 1939) placed at my disposal the fruits of recent research. I have also found most useful, not only in Part I but throughout the book, such studies as William R. Manning's *British Influence in Mexico,* made accessible in *The Pacific Ocean in History,* edited by H. Morse Stephens and Herbert E. Bolton, and published in 1917 in consequence of the Panama-Pacific Historical Congress held in "the Bay region" during the Panama-Pacific Fair.

Part II, "Frémont and the Bear Flag," relies chiefly on the

356

celebrated *Memoirs,* of which only the first volume was published (in 1887). But I have also canvassed most of the many books written about "the Pathfinder," of which the first and the last seem best: John Bigelow's *Memoir* of 1856, in which Mrs. Frémont assisted, and Allan Nevins's *Frémont, Pathmarker of the West* (1939), whose publishers, the D. Appleton-Century Company, kindly permit me to use it freely. I have taken equal advantage of a similar permission from Mrs. Catherine Coffin Phillips to use her delightful volume, *Jessie Benton Frémont, A Woman Who Made History* (1935). Mrs. Frémont's own best-known book, *Souvenirs of My Time* (1887), yielded treasure, but even more valuable was her unpublished manuscript in the Bancroft Library at the University of California; written in the last year of her life, but throbbing with vitality as she recalled exciting episodes ranging from her childhood to the deaths of her father and husband. Articles contributed by General Frémont and herself to The Century Magazine in 1891 also proved remunerative.

Other helpful writers on the period include, notably, John S. McGroarty (*California,* Grafton Publishing Co., 1911), George D. Lyman (*John Marsh, Pioneer,* Scribners, 1930), Erwin G. Gudde (*Sutter's Own Story,* Putnams, 1936), James P. Zollinger (*Sutter, the Man and His Empire,* Oxford University Press, 1939), and Joseph Henry Jackson (*Anybody's Gold,* D. Appleton-Century Co., 1941).

Part III, "Gwin at Monterey and Washington," covers the State Constitutional Convention of 1849 and the great Washington Debate of 1850,—occasioned by California's unprecedented demand for admission to the Union as a State, but involving the slavery controversy under such giant dialectic leaders as Webster and Calhoun, Clay and Benton. For the Monterey convention J. Ross Browne's official record (Washington, 1850) is the pre-eminent source book, but as interpretations and analyses Cardinal Goodwin's *Establishment of State Government in California* (1914) and the Rev. Samuel H. Willey's *Transitional Period of California* (1901) are beyond praise. Important side-lights are afforded by Bayard Taylor's *Eldorado* (1860), James Ford Rhodes's *History of the United States from 1850* (1892), *The Life of Thomas Hart Benton* by Theodore Roosevelt (1886), and *Memoirs of Cornelius Cole* (1908). Rich beyond all these sources, however, are Senator Gwin's own manuscripts in the Bancroft Library, and the unpublished dissertation entitled "William M. Gwin, Expansionist," by Miss Hallie McPherson, a copy of which was graciously lent by the Senator's grandson, Stanford Gwin, Esq., of San Francisco. My own former study of this critical period in our national history, *Cotton as a World Power,* also came in handy, as it was helped along by the personal aid of Senator James H. Hammond's son, Major Harry Hammond.

Part IV, "Storm Signals," derives material from H. H. Bancroft's *Popular Tribunals* (1887), James O'Meara's *Broderick and Gwin* (1881), John S. Hittell's *History of the City of San Francisco* (1878), Winfield Davis's *History of Political Conventions in California* (1893), and George H. Tinkham's *Men and Events in California* (1915). Once again a book of my own, *The Lion of the Vigilantes,* proved somewhat useful.

Parts V and VI, which deal with the crisis of the flags, are indebted to so many sources that individual credit becomes difficult. I have even ventured to use the picaresque but veracious *Great Diamond Hoax and Other Stirring Episodes in the Life of Asbury Harpending* (1913), which deserves rescue from the oblivion to which its peculiar character consigned it. At the other extreme, William Preston Johnston's *Life of General Albert Sidney Johnston* (1878) amply justifies the Encyclopædia Britannica's characterization as "a most valuable and exhaustive biography," which silences forever such reckless slanderers as Elijah R. Kennedy, whose pernicious *Contest for California in 1861* survives him. Mr. Henry Duque of Los Angeles generously allowed me to use his original study of General Johnston. On Thomas Starr King the biographical material is abundant, ranging from such slight but eloquent tributes as Ernest Carroll Moore's in *Socrates* to the definitive studies of Richard Frothingham (1865), William Day Simonds (1917), and Charles W. Wendte (1921).

Collateral material bearing on the battle of the flags was gathered from Kelly's *Salt Desert Trails* (1930), Davis and Rhodes and Tinkham as cited, and several monographs on the Confederate plots: one each by Rockwell D. Hunt and Percival J. Cooney in *Annual Publications of the Historical Society of Southern California for 1924,* one by Joseph Ellison in *University of California Publications in History for 1927,* and a fourth by Benjamin Franklin Gilbert in the *California Historical Society Quarterly* for June, 1941.

To all these writers and their publishers I feel profoundly grateful. And no less so to the patient but always courteous friends that led me to the sources: Director Herbert Ingram Priestley of the Bancroft Library, Miss Mabel Gillis and Miss Caroline Wenzel of Sacramento, Miss Dorothy Huggins of the California Historical Society, Mrs. Mary O. Carmody of the Mechanics' Institute, John and Warren Howell and Haig Patigian of San Francisco. In Los Angeles, Phil Townsend Hanna, Marshall Stimson, and Homer P. Earle assisted, besides Henry Duque.

For special services I thank Bessie and Paul Scherer, the officers of the Placerville Chamber of Commerce, the custodian of the old Larkin House in Monterey, John Adam Hussey of the University of California, Paul Elder, Mrs. Isabel

Morris, and the distinguished authors Reuben Lukens Underhill, Oscar Lewis, and Mrs. Catherine Coffin Phillips. Other acknowledgments are made in text and notes.

James A. B. Scherer.

May 22, 1942.

INDEX